MY
EIGHTY-ONE
YEARS OF
ANARCHY

A MEMOIR

MY
EIGHTY-ONE YEARS OF ANARCHY

A MEMOIR

by

May Picqueray

Translated by Paul Sharkey

PUBLISHED BY
AK PRESS AND THE KATE SHARPLEY LIBRARY

My Eighty One Years of Anarchy: A Memoir

Translation © 2019 Paul Sharkey
Introduction, editor's notes, chronology, and biographical
   appendices © The Kate Sharpley Library
This edition © 2019 AK Press (Chico, Edinburgh)
ISBN: 9781849353229
E-ISBN: 9781849353236
Library of Congress Control Number: 2018932234

AK Press   AK Press
370 Ryan Ave. #100   33 Tower St.
Chico, CA 95973   Edinburgh EH6 7BN
USA   Scotland
www.akpress.org   www.akuk.com
akpress@akpress.org   ak@akedin.demon.co.uk

Kate Sharpley Library
BM Hurricane
London WC1N 3XX
UK
www.katesharpleylibrary.net

The above addresses would be delighted to provide you with the latest AK Press
distribution catalog, which features books, pamphlets, zines, and stylish apparel
published and/or distributed by AK Press. Alternatively, visit our websites for the
complete catalog, latest news, and secure ordering.

Cover design by Margaret Killjoy | birdsbeforethestorm.net
Printed in the USA on acid-free, recycled paper

To my children, grandchildren, and great-grandchildren

Goddess of eyes so blue, may your day dawn,
Over a rosy morning in Salamis!
Strike our shredded hearts.
Anarchy! O torch-bearer,
Drive out the night, trample the vermin
And build in the heavens, atop our tombs, if need be
The shining Tower that looms over the waves!

Ballade Solness, by Laurent Tailhade

INTRODUCTION

"But it is not my intention to pen a history of anarchism.
Besides, I do not see how I could. Every time I read such
a history, I discover things I never knew before, and I
sometimes discover certain errors of detail. Just one of the
reasons that have prompted me to write this book."
—*MAY PICQUERAY*

May Picqueray spent most of her life as an anarchist and experienced directly or indirectly some of the most momentous events of the twentieth century. She was one of the numerous anarchists who visited Soviet Russia in the early days of its existence and was bitterly disillusioned by what she saw there. She took part in numerous international causes including the struggle to prevent the state murder of Sacco and Vanzetti and she provided material support to Spanish comrades in the aftermath of the defeat of the Spanish Revolution. Her work with those imprisoned in the brutal Le Vernet camp in support of exiled and imprisoned comrades alone deserves the highest praise we can give. Her country suffered fascist occupation and she worked from within this occupation to help people escape the country and avoid being sent to forced labor camps in Germany. She was also a courier for the French Resistance. After the Second World War she joined the Anarchist Federation (FA), holding various positions in the organization and fighting for the rights of French conscientious objectors during the Algerian War of Independence against French colonial rule. Like other anarchists she welcomed the injection of militancy that 1968 provided and during the nineteen seventies took an active role in the anti-nuclear struggle and edited the newspaper *Le Réfractaire* from 1974–1983.

May knew comrades such as Alexander Berkman, Emma Goldman, Louis Lecoin, Nestor Makhno, and Voline, and her autobiography presents her memories of them. Alongside these portraits she offers snatches of the history of anarchism that, to the uninitiated, offer a way into understanding some of our history. Of course these memories and vignettes are interesting but we have to be careful that we don't reduce the book to them alone. We don't want to lose May in her memories of others. She's important in her own right, and reading her autobiography, it doesn't take long for us to realize that we are in the company of a committed rebel. May walked to the beat of her own drum and in doing so she forces us to consider our own ideas as to what being a rebel—indeed being an anarchist—means to us. There is joy and passion in these pages, but above all there is a dignity and an acceptance that, given the circumstances that made up her life, she has done everything she could to make the beautiful ideal of anarchy a reality.

May's autobiography reflects an exuberance and passion that drove her life and drives our reading. When we put the book down we feel breathless; so much life lived in these pages and at such a pace. May's search for Mollie Steimer and Senya Fleshin set inside the Kafkaesque world of Bolshevik prisons in 1922 is especially haunting as she moves across the wintry Russian landscape that is mirrored by the attitude of the prison authorities to her and their prisoners. We sense the stark isolation of this nightmare and the casually vicious brutality of the Bolshevik system. Similarly, her pages describing working under the Nazi occupation of France stay with us as she details a claustrophobic world where one mistake could lead to summary execution. Even after these nightmarish experiences, or perhaps because of them, her belief in the creation of a better world remained undimmed. Indeed the flame appears to have burnt brighter in response.

The anarchist movement May encountered and joined was essentially an oral one and by the time May wrote her autobiography had all but disappeared. As she suggests in her quote above she was attempting to fill in a few gaps in anarchist history. Consequently, she is keen to at least name all the people she knew who influenced her in some way. It's all the more poignant that some of them are just names but it makes us realize that the history of anarchism is far more than newspapers and pamphlets. For May anarchism was the cabaret singers and the clubs where anarchists gathered. It was her friends, some anarchist, some not. They enriched her life and drew her into anarchism and she wants to let us know that. If that oral culture has died she has left us paths to resurrect it if we are lucky.

We have to be careful that other aspects of the anarchist movement that May knew are not lost to us. May was a pacifist and anti-militarist but that did not prevent her offering solidarity and support to those comrades who were not. There could always be disagreements but when needed solidarity was there, offered almost instinctively. That instinctive response was often all that some anarchists had time for as circumstances around them changed quickly and urgently. We might want to consider the implications of solidarity coming first and not the assertion of one type of anarchism over another. May was very clear about who the enemy was!

It's hard to know how to measure a life. We can read the thanks of those people May helped escape from Nazi Germany in the Appendices in this volume. We can also read the moving testimonials of those who knew and admired her. May Picqueray was a remarkable comrade and woman. Her autobiography will remain as a passionate affirmation of anarchism delivered with the exuberance and sense of possibility that sustained May over the years. It's more than that, though. It's a passing of the anarchist baton to us so we carry on the struggle. Only if we refuse to take it up can May's life be seen as a failure.

Kate Sharpley Library,
Summer 2018.

EDITORIAL NOTES

We have tried not to detract too much from the exhilarating pace of May Picqueray's memoirs. We didn't want to create more footnotes than text—something that is all too easy considering May's penchant for throwing out lists of names. Consequently, we have tried to put in a minimum of footnotes while, at the same time, trying to provide both a little background to some of the people and events she mentions and offer the reader suggestions for further reading about them. If May's memory forgets the odd salient fact readers can discover that for themselves. We have kept May's own footnotes as she intended, which are indicated as "note by M. Piqueray." All additional notes have been added by the KSL.

At the back of the book we have added a few appendices, including a primarily biographical appendix that covers many of the people May refers to in her text. A superscript asterisk in the text (*) denotes a name you'll find in the biographical appendix. We hope that her memoir and our notes encourage you to explore more about May's life as well as the beautiful ideal she dedicated her life to.

CHRONOLOGY

Marie-Jeanne—known as May—Picqueray (1898–1983)

1898   Born in Brittany, to a post office delivery man father and a seamstress mother. In her teens Picqueray moved to Canada with a school-teacher whose epileptic son she was engaged to look after. She returned from Canada after the death of one of her employers' children, followed by the death of her employer in action in the Great War, and then of the mother. On her return to France she found work as an interpreter and bilingual typist. She then met, married, and divorced her husband, a Dutch drug addict.

1918   Moved to Paris where she met and fell in love with Serbian medical student Dragui Popovitch. He introduced her to anarchist circles and she became active in the Anarchist Youth and Syndicalist Youth organizations.

1921   As part of her campaign on behalf of Sacco and Vanzetti, Picqueray sent a parcel bomb to the US Embassy.

1922   Became administrative secretary with the Metalworkers' Federation and was present at the founding congress of the CGTU. She was chosen to accompany Metalworkers' Federation secretary Lucien Chevalier to the second Profintern congress in Moscow that November. While in Moscow she helped secure the release of Mollie Steimer and Senya Fleshin. Chevalier was the father of May's daughter, Sonia.

1923   Arrested in Belgium after traveling from Russia on soviet-issued false papers. Her name was added to the Carnet B.

1924   Harbored Nestor Makhno when he and his family arrived in France. She quit the Metalworkers' Federation after the communists gained control of it. She found work writing copy and proofreading for a regional paper.

1926   Acted as Emma Goldman's private secretary and lived in Saint-Tropez with fisherman François Niel, father of Picqueray's son, Lucien.

1938   Returned to Paris, working for a number of charities such as the French Office for Children, the Spanish Children's Aid Committee, and the US Quakers.

1940   After the German invasion she relocated to Toulouse to oversee the provision of food, medicine, and clothing to refugees and those interned in the Noë concentration camp as "undesirables." Also made weekly deliveries to the Le Vernet camp, from which she helped smuggle out some escapees. She then spent the winter of 1940–1941 laying low in Andorra.

1941   On returning to Toulouse, she secured the release of Nicolas Lazarévitch and rescued Mollie Steimer from the camp in Gurs, before returning to Paris to help whomever she could.

1943   Joined French Mutual Aid and helped secure or fabricate papers for use by the resistance and people on the run. She also worked with an escape-line assisting French POWs escape from Germany. At that point she was in touch with Laureano Cerrada's Spanish group.

1944   Picqueray helped resister Suzanne Charisse by hiding her from the Gestapo and smuggling her over the demarcation line between the Occupied and the "Free" Zones.

1945   Traveled to Genoa in search of Fernando Gualdi, whom she had earlier tried unsuccessfully to break out of the Le Vernet camp. She also became a proofreader, accepted into the CGT's Proofreaders' Union on October 1, 1945 (at which point she was one of its only four or five female members).

When the paper for which she was working, *Libre Soir Express*, was closed down, she sued for and obtained compensation before moving on to work as a proofreader for *Le Canard enchaîné*.

1957   Joined the "Louise Michel" Group affiliated to the FA. Also active in the "Friends of Sébastien Faure" and "Friends of Han Ryner" societies.

1963   Now in retirement, she served as secretary to the FA's trade union commission and later as its foreign relations secretary.

'60s–'70s Worked with Louis Lecoin on his paper, *Liberté*, and in his work on behalf of conscientious objectors. She set up the "Friends of Louis Lecoin" society.

1974 Picqueray launched her own paper, *Le Réfractaire*, which survived until she died in 1983.

1970–80 Took part in the activities of the Pré-Saint-Gervais anarchist group. She was also involved in the Le Larzac campaign, the Plogoff women's resistance, and in 1978 was a contact for the draft resisters around the *Avis de Recherche* bulletin (Paris 1978–1981).

PREFACE

For the past half century, by word of mouth, written word, and action, a whole range of thinkers, writers, and libertarian propagandists have spread the anarchist teaching, its principles, and its methodology in every language and in every country, so that everybody ought to be in a position to embrace or reject anarchism, as there should not be anyone left today who is ignorant of it.

It is the lot of all torchbearers to be abominably slandered and persecuted, the fate of all social teachings that target the official lies and institutions in the process of being adulterated, held up to ridicule and fought against with the help of the most odious weapons.

But it is the duty of the heralds of the new truth to confound the slanderers and to oppose the incessant blows of the unrelenting response to truth.

For a start, who are we?

There has been the grossest misrepresentation of anarchists as individuals.

Some look upon us as harmless utopians, sweet dreamers; they treat us like day-dreamers with distorted imaginations, as half-fools, so to speak. Such folk deign to see us as sick people who can be rendered dangerous by circumstances but not systematic and conscious villains.

Others pass very different judgment upon us. They think that anarchists are ignorant brutes, filled with hate, inclined to violence, and fanatics against whom one could not be overly protected nor exercise too relentless a repression.

Both are wrong.

We are the heirs to the people who, living in an age of ignorance, wretchedness, ugliness, hypocrisy, iniquity, and hatred, caught a glimpse of a city of learning, well-being, liberty, beauty, candor, justice, fraternity and who, with all their might, worked to build that magnificent city.

Utopians, because we want evolution, following its course, to ferry us farther and farther away from modern slavery—wage slavery—and turn the producer of all wealth into a free, dignified, happy, and brotherly creature? Dreamers, because we foresee and herald the disappearance of the State, whose purpose is to exploit labor, enslave the mind, snuff out the spirit of revolt, stymie progress, thwart initiative, and act as a bulwark against the striving for improvement, persecute the honest, fatten the schemers, rob the tax-payer, feed the parasites, sponsor falsehood and intrigue, encourage murderous rivalry, and, when it senses that its power is in jeopardy, to scatter the fields of slaughter with everything the people has to boast that is most wholesome, most vigorous, and most beautiful?

We defy the informed and attentive minds of today to seriously accuse of being unbalanced the folk who plan and work toward such social transformations.

Rather, the madmen are those who imagine that they can bar the way to contemporary generations bound for social revolution the way a river makes its way to the ocean; and it may be that with the help of mighty dams and skillful diversion they slow, more or less, the river's flow, but it is inevitable that sooner or later it will flow to the sea.

No, anarchists are neither utopians nor dreamers, nor fools, and the proof of that is that, everywhere, governments track them and toss them into prison lest the gospel of truth that they spread be free to reach the ears of the disinherited, whereas, if libertarian education were so replete with fantasy or foolish notions, it would be so easy to burst the unreasonable and obscurity.

Anarchists have hatreds; their hatreds are long-lasting and many, but their hatreds are merely the consequence of their loves. They hate servitude because they love independence; they detest exploited labor because they love free labor; they violently combat lies because they ardently defend the truth; they despise iniquity, because they worship the just; they hate war because they fight passionately for peace.

We are not by nature hateful; rather, our hearts are affectionate and sensitive, our temperaments open to friendship, love, solidarity, and all that brings individuals closer together.

As to the charge of violence that they would hang upon us, it suffices to open one's eyes and notice how, in the modern world as well as in bygone centuries, violence rules, dominates, grinds down, and murders. It is the rule. It is hypocritically organized and systematized. It asserts itself, day in and day out, under the guise and appearances of the tax collector, property-owner, boss, gendarme, prison guard, executioner, and officer, all of them professionals, under multiple forms, in force, violence, and brutality.

Anarchists want to orchestrate free agreement, fraternal assistance, harmonious coexistence. But they know—from reason, from history, from experience—that they are not going to be able to pursue their craving for well-being and freedom for all other than on the ruins of the established institutions. They are conscious that only a violent revolution can overcome the resistance put up by the masters and their mercenaries.

Thus, for them, violence becomes an inevitability: they endure it but deem it merely a backlash made necessary by the ongoing state of self-defense in which the disinherited find themselves at all times.

We have an unshakable certainty that when the State, which feeds all sorts of ambitions and rivalries, when Property, which fosters greed and hatred, when Religion, which encourages ignorance and invites hypocrisy, have been struck down dead, the vices that those three wedded Authorities plant in men's hearts will vanish in turn. "Dead the beast, dead the venom!"

No one then will look to command, since, for one thing, no one will consent to obey and, for another, every weapon of oppression will have been smashed; no one will be able to enrich himself at the expense of another, since private fortunes will have been abolished; priests, liars, and hypocritical moralists will lose their ascendancy, since nature and truth will have recovered their rights.

That, in broad outline, is the libertarian doctrine. That is what the anarchists want.[1]

That quotation is not mine; it is lifted from Sébastien Faure.* I had to quote the whole thing before putting pen to paper, as it has guided me all my life. Even should I finish this book (when one is eighty years old, there are no guarantees), I do not yet know if I will let it be published. As far as I am concerned, it can only be a militant act. I do not tell my life story out of vanity nor with an eye to gain sympathy for myself. But I am keen to know, not whether my life has been a "success," but if I have been faithful to my ideas and served my cause well.

I was eighteen when I first read Faure's words. It was an accident that I had stumbled upon them. It was the man I loved who read them to me. For two years, we had been trying, together, to follow them in our everyday lives. It is on love that anarchy is based. And then the task struck him as more than he could manage. His family had cut off his income. He returned to his own country to carry on with his medical studies.

I carried on without him. It is more than sixty years ago now since we parted. I never set eyes on him again. I do not know if he is still alive. I do not know if he still remembers me. But when I think of him, it is with tenderness and gratitude.

---

1 The quotation is from Sébastien Faure, "Les Anarchistes, ce qu'ils sont, ce qu'ils ne sont pas" / *Anarchists, What They Are, What They Are Not* (1920).

I

A BRETON CHILDHOOD

When I summon up my most distant memories, before me appears a little girl with blue eyes, lively, even petulant, dressed in a white-collared red pinafore, tramping in galoshes along the Martigné-to-Châteaubriant road, holding her little brother Ernest by the hand and, in her other hand, a small basket containing savory tartlets.

We had a long road to travel to get to the nursery school where Sister Ludivine greeted us with her wide grin. Coquettishly wearing the severe sky-blue robes of the St. Vincent de Paul Sisters, her very pure oval face and laughing eyes stood out against the wide white wings of her wimple. From the big pockets of her apron, she produced treasures—cakes, angelica, pictures, etc.—that she slipped into our little hands, sometimes blue from the cold.

Dear Sister Ludivine, the memory of whom remains so vivid in my atheistic heart even after all these years!

I had no greater pleasure in life than following her into the little chapel adjoining the school, which she lovingly maintained. It was covered in flowers in every season and joyously resonated with the tunes she produced from its ancient organ "just for you," as she used to say. But I'm sure she took great delight in it too.

She was our singing teacher. I was more than a little proud of myself when prize day rolled around. Together with another young girl, Blanche Auvinet, I performed a musical scene, *The Queen and the Shepherdess*, in front of an audience of local civil and religious authorities and students' parents. We had been selected on account of our "beautiful voices," she used to say. In shepherdess costume, I answered my queen with all the aplomb and innocence of my four years. To this day, I can remember a few lines of my song. From time to time, my own children and grand-children hum them:

Once there was a shepherdess
By the name of Isabeau,
Who danced upon the ferns
While watching over her flock.
A queen happened by
On her white palfrey
And said to her, "I am taking you,
Isabeau, with me . . ."
The queen made all sorts of promises: Little Isabeau told her,
Greatly embarrassed,
"No, my lady," she said,
"Mama wouldn't like that!"

From the wings, the children sang the refrain:

Do-re-mi-fa-fa-fa
Do-re-mi-fa-fa-fa
Do-re-mi-fa-so-la-ti-do

Close to the school, there was a bridge with a little brook flowing underneath. Ernest and I were very often to be found leaning over the parapet, yearning to splash around in it, despite Sister Ludivine's formal prohibition of any such thing. But even then, obedience was not my strong suit . . .

Leaving school one evening, we set about sliding down the bank on our backsides and, with the water within reach, we hastened to remove our galoshes and socks. What joy it was to wade up to our calves into the cold water, which felt so wonderful! After a few moments, we felt something unusual and unpleasant on our legs, and the sight of it had us screaming so much that Sister Ludivine heard our cries and arrived to pull us out of there, giving us a strong scolding. She took us into the kitchen and brushed off the ghastly creatures, leeches, rubbing our legs down with coarse salt.

We set off for home, still reeling from our shock but nevertheless happy to have satisfied our desire. We promised not to do it again and our parents never got wind of the incident.

My mother was a plump woman, easy on the eye. She was a domestic dressmaker and could often be found singing as she worked the treadle of her Singer.

She had married very young, barely eighteen years of age, leaving her parents' farm for the town. At the time I am speaking of, she already had three children: Francis, four years older than me, Ernest, who was three years my junior, and myself.

My father, a post office deliveryman, spent much of his life on the railroad. He returned home at a very late hour. We saw very little of him. He was kindly but could not bear children talking around the dinner table. He used to threaten us (albeit without much conviction) with all manner of punishments as soon as we raised our voices. But he was neither mean nor brutal. In his free time, he would sometimes join in our games and take us out for strolls.

My parents lived in a big house, complete with a garden, on the road out of town. It was practically countryside. On Sundays, after my mother had finished her "work," we would go strolling together through the woods and fields. We would gather up whatever was ripe and in season, out of which she made splendid jams. I was often deprived of these outings, but I used to make up for it by setting off with a few urchins the same age as me to rob birds' nests or to fish for frogs in the pond near our home, which was, of course, forbidden to us. We used to attach a twisted pin concealed within a red rag at the end of a branch. We hooted with delight when one of those hapless creatures allowed itself to be caught and danced on the end of the line.

On such days, we would come home with feet drenched and our pinafores muddied, but we were oh so happy to have been able to unwind far from reproachful parental eyes. They made us pay dearly for our joy: some smacks always, and sometimes a proper beating. But that is another story . . .

One spring day, my mother took my brothers and me to a farmer's place, where she had been invited to come and pick some cherries. It was a very fine day, and we were playing in the farmyard. All of a sudden, I spotted three human figures, ageless, each restrained by straps in an armchair. I ventured over. The poor things were frothing at the mouth and writhing around at the very sight of us and groaning. We watched them without comprehending. The sight was at once odd and terrifying.

Their mother came over to stroke one of them tenderly, filled up our little baskets with cherries, chatted with my mother about this and that, and stepped back inside the farmhouse as if this was nothing out of the ordinary.

As we left the farm, I turned around, intrigued, my heart pounding, without quite knowing why. I have never forgotten the faces of those unfortunate children. Of what hereditary affliction were they victims?

At the foot of the fortified chateau overlooking the town, there was a pond, the waters of which mirrored the laundresses who went there to do their washing and use their washboards between gossiping and singing.

One evening whilst on our way home from a walk, the night had already fallen when something extraordinary presented itself to our marveling eyes: some boats glided slowly across the pond. It looked as if the men on board were dredging the bottom with long poles, whilst others used their torches to light their way. All those lights dancing across the dark waters conjured up a real fairy land. How beautiful it was! And we clapped our hands . . .

The following day we found out that a man had drowned in the pond and they had been searching for his body. That news made hardly impression on me. Only the beauty of the spectacle remained in my memory.

My father received a new posting, and we left Châteaubriant for Saint-Nazaire.

We had never set eyes on the sea. Nor had our mother.

After we had settled in, the talk turned to the sea. One Sunday, she brought us there. We were mad with delight! The moment we reached the beach, it was off with our boots, our pinafores were rolled up, and there was a mad scramble for the open sea. Which bore no resemblance to the frog pond or to the little brook with its leeches.

In those days, swimsuits were rare. In the company of family members, at any rate.

The moment a big wave crashed against us, we scuttled out of its path. Due to our not being used to it? One wave faster than my little legs knocked me over, swept me up into its arms, rolled me over and, as it retreated, left me disappointed, dumbfounded, and . . . drenched.

I made my way back towards my mother who angrily ordered me to stretch out on the sand "until my clothes dry out." By the time we were to leave, I was still drenched, as sea water is not that easily dried. So, she left me on my own on the beach. And I waited . . . Night fell, I was shivering and none too sure of myself. I started to cry. From the road leading to the sea, some youngsters spotted me and asked what I was doing at that hour. I recounted my adventure; taking pity on me, they brought me to my parents' house, with great difficulty since I did not know our exact address. My mother put me to bed after doling out one of her usual spankings.

So much for my first contact with the sea!

Then my sister was born. My rare moments of freedom grew rarer. It was up to me to watch over and put the baby to bed and, also, on many occasions, to prepare the meals and sweep the floor. At a very early age, I learned how to do chores and darn my socks. It may not have been a bad thing . . .

I hesitate somewhat to speak of the treatment my mother inflicted upon me; I never knew any softness or caresses . . . but a daily spanking with a highly flexible bulrush has left me with painful memories. It is true, I was a "devil," willful and rebellious, and I could not endure punishment without raising a fuss, wailing at the injustice of it, and hiding my tears, which led my mother to say that I had no heart.

Toys were an unknown to me, and on Christmas Day, the belt always figured prominently in my stocking. I reckon I endured all manner of vexation. . . Bah! Not that it ever stopped me from living, of course, but it was a life of rebellion, and that had a great impact on my future. At least I had the satisfaction of seeing my brothers and sister happy.

Yet it was to my home that my mother came to spend her final days at the age of almost eighty, in an atmosphere of kindness and happiness.

I bore my mother no grudge. But I could not quite comprehend why she had been so hard on me. With my brothers and my sister, she had asserted authority, but she had reserved for me a "special treatment." It was my impression—and this is horrible for any child—that she did not love me and that she was taking revenge on me for something of which I was unaware.

This question I have asked myself all my life. Although, I never dared pose it to my mother until a few days prior to her death. She answered me bluntly:

"I disliked you instantly," she told me. "I nearly died bringing you into the world . . ."

"This is scarcely my fault."

"No, but I was angry with you . . ."

Evidently, there are some things that mark you for life. For it was indeed my mother's behavior that inspired in me a rebellion against injustice that has never left me. At eighty-one years, she is still as alive as in my childhood.

When I was able to slip out of the house unseen, I rushed toward the docks: the departure or arrival of ships was a real party as far as I was concerned.

Back then, Saint-Nazaire was a very important commercial port. Ships would arrive from Scandinavia with their cargo of timber or from England laden with coal. From the West Indies, they imported all manner of exotic fruits unfamiliar to us: bananas, coconuts, oranges, pineapples.

The seamen or the dockers returning from the unloading of the ships would often offer me a piece of fruit or fill my apron. I would then ferry this unexpected harvest back home.

During one such escapade, I saw a cortège of men shackled in pairs, bound hand and foot, with a small bundle over their shoulders and dressed in homespun or, in some cases, striped cotton clothing.

They were shepherded by gendarmes brandishing rifles. They were convicts, and the word was that they were about to board the 'Loire' for the crossing from Saint-Nazaire to Cayenne.

Every age was represented: some were barely adults, others had graying hair, and several were bent over with age and shuffling along with difficulty.

They were downcast and wretched. A few managed to call out, "See you soon, my lovely!" or "'Til we meet again, friends!"

What had they done that they had wound up there?

Later, over the course of my activist career, I discovered that it did not take much to get one transported to the islands and that many of them were comrades of ours, shipped out because of strike activity or for having challenged some authority.

One of these men gestured hello to me and wore a sad smile. Maybe he was leaving behind a family and children? The sad leave-taking was witnessed by a few relatives, and lots of rubberneckers. I was too young to really understand, but I was on the verge of tears.

I used to attend the "community" school where I worked hard and well, as I was issued my elementary certificate of studies at the age of ten and a half with a grade of distinction.

I read everything that came within reach, and reading was my passion. I believe I had been through every single book in the school library. My mother did not want me to become a subscriber to the town library; she reckoned that to read was a waste of time. I had to use all my ingenuity to hide the books lent to me . . . and to read them, as my Pigeon lamp was taken from me once I went to bed. I got my hands on some candle ends and would hide them under my bed-clothes lest the light be seen. Come morning, I had to scrape off any drops of melted candle wax.

I would have liked to carry on with my studies, but at eleven years old, my mother took me out of school to work. I really resented that; however, I carried on, self-educating as and when I was able.

One school mistress who had befriended me did her best to help me. My mother took umbrage at this, and one day, in order to punish me for some "offense" or another, she ripped up the books and jotters, plus a magnificent and very well illustrated book that I had just been given. I cannot quite remember if it was *Le Petit Chose*[1] or Alphonse Daudet's *Jack*. But it was definitely one or the other.

Desperate, I resolved to hang myself. In the "cellar" where my father stored his gardening tools, I climbed onto a small bench, slipped a rope around a beam (whether it could have supported my weight I cannot say), and wrapped the rope around my neck; at that moment, my brother Ernest, my playmate who consoled me when my mother came on a bit strong, frightened to see me in that position took off

---

1 *Le Petit Chose* is a novel published in 1868 by Alphonse Daudet based on his experiences as a teacher. His novel *Jack*, published in 1876, is the story of an illegitimate child.

screaming to warn my mother, who arrived in the nick of time to cut me down.

I was treated to a masterly spanking designed "to rid me any notion of repeating such nonsense." My mother failed to appreciate just how deep was my despair.

I looked forward to the holidays with impatience, as it was a real joy to once again see my maternal grandmother—so sweet, so kind— in the small village of Angeleray. Angeleray was located on a hilltop affording a view of the Loire, its long, silvery ribbon snaking its way to the sea at Saint-Nazaire.

The farm there was happy, welcoming; along the front wall ran a trellis, and through the attic window, I could easily pick the lovely bunches of grapes.

There was a single living room with a dirt floor. A huge chimney around which were positioned two old armchairs. Overhead, a shelf on which were arranged a few books, magazines, and newspapers. Dangling from the end of a hook was the stew pot where Grandmother used to have some very fine soups simmering and in which she also cooked the potatoes that made up the evening meal, accompanied by some milk, butter, or curds. There was also a griddle, together with some tongs and bellows.

Attached to the chimney were some pewter brackets in which some candles flickered. The tallow gave off a nice smell, but they provided only a very dim light.

On each side of the hearth there was a huge bed with a feather duvet topped by a vast red eiderdown into which I sunk with joy. There was a flour bin used for the kneading of dough, which Grandmother cooked week after week and transformed into beautiful golden loaves in the oven (today unused and covered in ivy), and whose gorgeous smell tickles my nostrils even after all these years. With me in mind, she used to toss in a little milk roll or potato farl on whose golden crust I would munch.

That flour bin was the object of special care; it was "the furniture." It shone and smelled of wax. The household's linens were stored in two tall wardrobes. Grandmother had sewn them with her own hands over many a winter evening by the fireside. There were piles of fine cloth as well as rough sheets that grated against my little behind, and below them were her long-sleeved blouses, objects of my curiosity. She had grown the flax herself.

At the center of the room, there was a long table with a drawer at each end, where the cooking fat and the butter were stored. And on both sides of it, benches. Everything was polished and gleaming. A large oil lamp, lit only on grand occasions, illuminated the room. Shelves ran around the walls, supporting breadbaskets and jam jars.

Nearby, there was the cellar, where barrels of wine or cider were lined.

Upstairs was the hayloft where the wheat and buckwheat were stored along with the potato harvest. Occasionally, we could hear the scampering of a mouse. From the beam, onions and garlic dangled in trailing strings.

A large barn for the cows and a horse that I sometimes led out into the meadow sat adjacent to the pigpen, henhouse, and rabbit hutch.

A little path led to the mill, perched on top of a knoll. Its great wings turned with the wind. I clambered up the spiral staircase leading to the huge millstone. The ground wheat and flour smelled good. I descended covered in powder like *Pierrot*.[2]

My uncle, the eldest of four children my grandmother raised all but single-handedly, my grandfather having died very young, operated the mill and was in charge of the farm. My grandmother was a very hard worker. She died, worn out, at the age of sixty.

The mill was a casualty of the war in 1940 after a bomb opened up a big hole in its side that was never repaired, and it collapsed gently to the ground. From the train connecting Nantes to Saint-Nazaire, a few kilometers before it arrives at Savenay, one could long ago glimpse its proud silhouette. Last time I passed that way, the sight of the ruins tore at my heart.

So many memories of that mill, and the little village, almost all its inhabitants now gone. The hay making, the harvests, the grape-picking, all those festivals that gave free reign to the delights of youth. Everything was done in common, and the villagers got along well together. Around fifteen families, each with three or four children, lived in work, mutual aid, and pleasure.

Weddings were held in the barn draped in white sheets, covered in flowers, the great tables lined up and laden with roasts, stews, and cakes; the kindly faces of the peasants; and the Briands, the Gattepailles, the Lerays, and others did not need to be asked to

---

2 A mute figure from the Italian theater tradition. Pedrolino was adopted by the French pantomime theater as "Pierrot" from the 18th century onwards.

burst into song over dessert. Or dance to the sound of fiddles. Lavish servings of ice-cold cider drawn straight from the barrel, the bottles of aged wine brought out on grand occasions. The *joie de vivre*, the tough, simple, peaceful life . . . memories . . .

2

I START OUT IN LIFE

When I turned eleven, my moth-
er "placed" me with a big butter dealer in Penhoët, the home of the
shipyards that have produced such marvels as the *France* and many
other vessels.

My job was to make home deliveries of butter. I set out very early
in the morning with a basket over each arm and a sack tied around
my waist. Those baskets were heavy. Then I trudged for kilometers
through the surrounding suburbs. I was well-fed and slept on a fold-
down bed that I shared with two older female employees.

I received a few tips, which I would put carefully aside to buy
books. My wages were paid directly to my parents. But come the evening, I was so worn out that I often nodded off over dinner. I had one
Sunday afternoon a month off, "to go see my family."

The schoolteacher who had befriended me, upon learning of my
new circumstances, asked my mother if she could hire me to look after one of her children who was prone to epileptic seizures. He must
have been five or six years old. The first time I saw him have a seizure,
I remained frozen and had no idea what to do. It was a dreadful sight:
the poor boy would go rigid and shake back and forth, spittle running down his chin, his eyes rolling. It was my job to ensure that he

did not crash into the furniture and to stretch him out on the floor with a cushion under his head ... and to wait for the seizure to pass. Between seizures, we would play together.

His mother made me do my homework at the same time as her eldest son, who was the same age as me. I also did a few run-of-the-mill tasks, did the shopping, and tidied the house. I did not pine for my job in Penhoët.

The teacher's home was very good for me. There were no more smacks, no more punishments, and I was happy.

For a long time, they had been planning to move to Canada where they had family. And they had set the wheels in motion. I was sad at the thought of being separated from them. They felt the same. They asked my parents for permission to take me with them.

This idea displeased my father, and it took some insistence on the part of my new masters and myself before he eventually agreed to let me go. My mother had agreed straight off. The idea of being rid of me was by no means displeasing to her.

When the day of departure came, I wept buckets as I said good-bye to my father, brothers, and sister, but once the train set off, I dried my tears. The countryside claimed all my attention; this was my very first big journey. There was our arrival in Le Havre, the embarkation, and the hubbub as we set sail. I had never set foot on a ship that size before. I saw little, however, of our venture into the high seas, as I had to watch over my little patient; the sea was quite calm, but he was seasick, and I was somewhat queasy myself.

Coming into port, I was surprised to see the skyscrapers that were beginning to adorn the city. Canada had taken the United States as its example; it was Americanizing itself. The port, which looked out not at the sea but at the Saint Lawrence, was very busy. There were lots of boats coming and going.

Little by little, I got to know the city. We had outings every Sunday. The summers were as hot as the winters were severe. Canadians gird themselves against intemperate weather; the doors and windows are doubly thick and the homes well-heated. Clothing and footwear were suited to the climate. There were some very old and beautiful houses that neighbored those ghastly concrete cubes that are proliferating around the world these days and making it ugly.

The Canadian landscape is one of the world's most beautiful: pine, birch, and maple forests surrounded by enormous, glistening, limpid lakes. The little peasant girl in me was enthralled.

A brand-new life was starting for me. My time was divided between caring for my little patient, play, and study. And beautiful country walks. Discovering just how tough winter could be in that country. The snow and the ice. But the house was roomy and pleasant and well heated, with every comfort.

From time to time, we used to go to Trois Rivières, a picturesque little town, where a nephew of my employers ran one of the many paper mills feeding the newspapers in the area.

Later, I visited Québec and its old château, the old town boasting a wealth of historical museums on the origins of Canada, her fight for independence, the arrival of the French fleeing from various provinces around France with their rough, sing-song *patois*, arriving in the country to begin a new life.

The French-Canadian tongue is hard to understand and absorb, studded as it is with charming expressions that have died out back in France, other than in a few villages where the old folks have clung to the old terms, old expressions full of flavor. Likewise, older French customs and songs.

At parties in the village, they dance the polka, the bourrée, and the quadrille, to a violin accompaniment.

Behind my father's house there is a pond,
Where handsome ducks go to swim

Or

On my way to the clear fountain
To stretch my legs

. . . old tunes from the marshlands of Poitou or Charente, Breton and Norman airs. I even heard a Basque tune in which the shepherds called out to one another from one mountain to another . . .

I felt at home in Québec.

I was happy . . .

Two years after we arrived there, my little patient died, carried off by pneumonia, and I was devastated. I had grown attached to him, and, aside from those horrible seizures, he was so cuddly. What was going to become of me? His parents kept me on, and I was enrolled in a Montréal high school to continue my education. I was treated like part of the family. I worked hard by way of thanking them for the trouble they were taking to further my education. I passed my baccalaureate. As did their son.

Then along came the war. It erupted there like a bombshell. Lots of French Canadians signed up and left. Being French, my employer was called up and set off for France. I was aware that my older brother who had come back from Australia a fortnight before the war was declared, had, following a short period of training in La Rochelle, been dispatched to the Dardanelles. That my father had been called up as a territorial. Socialist in his leanings, he despised the war and grieved for the death of Jaurès.

I was eager to get home. But could I leave my benefactress just like that? One day, she received a notice of death; her husband had perished on the Somme. She worshiped the man, who was a good father and a fine husband. A few months after that, her grief was aggravated by ill health. Congestion finished her off. Misfortune had overwhelmed the family, leaving me out to sea.

I was left alone with the older son. An uncle claimed him and saw to my repatriation. A ship escorted by two torpedo boats brought me to Le Havre.

My brothers and sister were all grown up. They had a hard time recognizing me. My brother Ernest squeezed me tight, and our tears were of joy.

The war, the horrific war, was sewing devastation. This was my first brush with it. And I knew in an instant that no explanation could ever make me countenance it.

Every night, trains left, packed with French or British soldiers. We could tell them from their marching songs, gloomy in the night.

And then the trains would return laden with the injured and dying. The hospitals were inadequate. Certain schools and high schools were converted for use as ambulance stations.

Food was in short supply for the population, and the queues outside the shops were endless.

I had to earn my keep and help my mother and the youngsters in the absence of the head of the family. In Canada, I had learned English. I was taken on by a ship's chandler as an interpreter. I used to board the ships in order to take the orders, making deliveries with a staff member and banking the takings.

I had applied to serve as a nurse in the hospitals, but I had no medical training. My request was rejected.

Then the American army landed its men in Saint-Nazaire. Life was turned completely upside down. The ship's chandler hired several male staff to handle the greatly swollen workload, and I found myself out of a job. But not for long. The Americans were looking for office staff. The pay was attractive. I found myself hired as a bilingual typist. The downside was that I had to live in the Montoir camp outside of town. One corner of the camp had been set aside for the American and French female staff. Our shacks were, if not quite comfortable, at least tolerable. We had our own mess, a library, a cinema, and, prized above all else, a canteen where we enjoyed access to goods sorely missed by the general population: flour, sugar, chocolate, jam, soap, and cigarettes. I kept my mother supplied and used to send cigarettes off to my father and brother at the front.

The American female staff had organized a dance and sent out invitations to civilians and military. It was there that I met Fred, an engineering officer in the merchant marine. He was of Dutch origin. One evening, he invited me to the movies in town. During the newsreel, the *Marseillaise* was playing. Everybody stood up, except Fred. Since he did not get up, I did not get up either.

After the show, I asked him why he had stayed seated:

"Because I'm Jewish," he said.

"That's no excuse."

"Yes, it is," he answered. "I'll never forgive France for having convicted and deported Dreyfus."[1]

His ship left a few days later. He wrote to me several times, and his return was a real delight for me. He asked me to marry him. I accepted right away, but it took me some time to secure the blessing of my father, who believed I was too young.

Fred sorted out all the red tape with his consul so that we could get married quickly, as his ship would only be in port for a short while. The French authorities raised no problems. The marriage was quite quickly "signed and sealed."

---

1 The Jewish French army captain Alfred Dreyfus was arrested on October 15, 1894 for espionage and sentenced to life imprisonment on the penal colony of Devil's Island. Many felt that the sentence was proof of the prevalence of anti-Semitism in all levels of the French state apparatus. Dreyfus was eventually pardoned in 1899 and exonerated in 1906.

I was eighteen and was about to become a free woman at last. Or so I thought, at any rate.

I was quickly disillusioned. Fred was charming and gallant and affectionate. But lo and behold, he was a drug user. He had acquired this annoying habit over the course of his voyages. I have never known which drug he was using. But it was definitely a hard drug. Under its influence, he became crazy, he bit me, he struck me. Once he was back to his normal self, he regretted it, cried, showered me with gifts. Three weeks of living like that and I had had enough. I had had my fill of beatings.

His ship set sail again.

I returned to the camp with my mind made up never to set eyes on him again. And I never did.

For one's first love, it was not much of a success story.

The "Spanish" flu was raging among the civilian and military populations alike. Sometime after I returned to the camp, I was struck down and directed to the Saint-Nazaire high school, now in use as a hospital. There were just two of us women among hundreds of soldiers. But neither they nor we were of a mind to play footsie. I had a ferocious fever. I was still lucid enough, though, to see the nurses walking along the lines of beds and pulling the sheets over one face after another. Within a short time after death, brown stains appeared on the soldiers' faces. Within hours, their bodies turned black. Rumor had it that an epidemic of the plague had just broken out.

Every evening, the bodies were removed and transported by truck to the cemeteries outside of town. Every precaution was taken so as not to panic the locals.

It was harrowing to see the deaths of those tall, handsome lads in their prime, and I was expecting myself to be carted off the same way . . . However, I was lucky enough to pull through and was discharged from the hospital in a state of frightful thinness.

Besides, I was suffering from total amnesia.

I took a full month off to convalesce before returning to work. Nevertheless, I felt nauseous when I woke up each morning. I put that down to the flu and to the medicine I was still taking. But a visit to the major brought the news that I was with child. I was stunned. What? A child that would tie me to Fred, whom I had lived with for only three weeks and had decided to leave for good? It was impossible! I filled the doctor in on my circumstances.

"Rest assured," he said to me, "You won't be keeping it!" He was as good as his word. I returned to the hospital. The Spanish flu had done the trick for me . . .

Utterly determined not to hang around for Fred to reappear, I packed my bag and, with a small sum of money, "went up" to Paris. At our lodgings, I had left a letter intended for him, thanking him for his "tender care." He had his chance! I had not told my mother my plans and was careful not to let her have my address. Two years later, I secured my divorce.

In Paris, I wound up in a little hotel in the Rue Xavier-Privas, in the heart of the Latin Quarter, run by a couple from the Auvergne region. It was Spartan, but it was very clean. The clientele was made up of a few office workers and, above all, students.

That part of the Latin Quarter, these days overrun by Asian and African restaurants, amounted to a little village where Bougnats[2] or Bretons, bistrots or bouchons offered a fatherly welcome to their student clientele who would dine "*à l'ardoise*" and where the term "mutual aid" had retained some of its meaning.[3] Lack of money was the general rule, but gloominess was unknown.

I became acquainted with Paris. I wanted to see everything, but my funds were running out. Work, I needed to find work . . . I had no real trade. I could get by in English and as a typist, but this wasn't enough. I signed up for a shorthand course. Meanwhile, I found a job with an architect in the Boulevard Malesherbes, copying drawings.

It was a fairly long trip. With my room paid for in advance, I had barely enough left over to cover my Metro ticket there and back plus a bit of bread that I gnawed as I went strolling during my lunch hour. On Sundays, without the Metro, I treated myself to a coffee with cream. And so it carried on throughout the month, up until payday.

As soon as I could get by in shorthand, I found a job at the Institute of History and Geography. What a treat it was to spend one's days in the great book-lined rooms at the Institute, the former home of Madame de Sévigné! My boss was a lecturer at the Sorbonne; undemanding and a little withdrawn, we got along together very well.

---

2 Bougnats were immigrants to Paris from the Massif Central area of France.

3 *Bouchons*: family restaurants serving typically meat-heavy dishes native to the Lyon region of France. *A l'ardoise* is the equivalent of "table d'hôte," or chef's choice.

With his leave, I was allowed to browse in the library during my free time. The librarians were very good company.

In the evenings, I often dined at a little restaurant in the Place Saint-Michel, *Le Bouillon Bourdeau*. It was there that I met Dragui.

3

IN AMONG THE ANARCHISTS

Without Dragui, I wonder what would have become of my life.

I don't think I'd have turned into a meek *petite bourgeoise*. There was too much rebel in me. But, if not for him, I might never have discovered what I ought to make of that . . .

I had noticed him straightaway. He was a tall, good-looking boy, with an open, intelligent face. For a time, we watched each other from a distance. And then, one day, he settled himself in front of me . . .

That same evening, he settled himself in my life.

He brought me to Clarté* talks and then to the Sociétés Savantes in the Rue Danton. It was there that I first heard Sébastien Faure. It was a true revelation and an enchantment. What a speaker and what truth!

Dragui had enrolled at the college of science. He was preparing to study medicine. On his advice, I wasted no time in doing the same. Unfortunately, I could not sit in on all the lessons, despite an obliging boss who allowed me a great deal of freedom. Dragui passed the lessons on to me, and I would soak it all in. We worked together. I had just about passed my certificate of studies in physics, chemistry, and natural sciences, but, for want of the time and money, I could not see how I was going to be able to enroll in medical school. Yet was medicine not the finest profession in the world?

Dragui, an anarchist, was a wonderful creature with a very broad education and a highly developed social conscience. He came from a family of Serbian officers and received an allowance from his older brother, a military attaché in Germany. Me, I had to earn my own living . . .

My boss retired, and his replacement was a stickler for a full eight hours of attendance. I left the Institute and joined a print-works that specialized in producing labels in all sorts of languages.

I used to correct the English-language labels, and my colleagues referred to me as "*la Miss.*" It was nothing to get excited about, but I was relatively well-paid.

Without a doubt, that was the happiest and most exhilarating period of my life. Dragui and I lived life to the fullest, and we were madly in love. We met up every evening, dined together, and often spent our evenings at the Café de la Rotonde on the Boulevard du Montparnasse, meeting up with friends of every nationality, but mostly Bulgarians and Serbs. Over a slice of bread and a café crème, we would remake the world.

Our discussions were lively and impassioned. This was when I was becoming acquainted with the theorists of anarchy whom Sébastien Faure would sometimes quote during his talks: Proudhon, Bakunin, Kropotkin, Elisée Reclus, and so on . . . Everything we read was analyzed and debated, and it was fascinating.

I regularly attended Sébastien Faure's talks. I used to see him frequently: he helped me with his advice and guided me in my readings. He was my spiritual father, and I held him in the highest esteem.

He embarked upon a series of twelve talks, each one dealing with a different topic. The first one took place at the Sociétés Savantes Hall, which was packed. It very quickly came to our attention that some troublemakers had wormed their way into our ranks and that it would not take them long to make their presence known. Near to me, a sturdy fellow was packing his hat with paper, which was a sure omen of a brawl. I kept an eye on him. I had slipped up the sleeve of my jacket and held near my right wrist a little rubber club that a comrade had given me to defend myself if need be.

All of a sudden, a hail of nuts and bolts rattled the glass decorations around the hall and raucous shouting erupted pretty much everywhere. My neighbor was busy emptying his pockets. I climbed onto my chair so as to be able to reach him (he was tall, and I stand a measure of 1.55 meters) and managed somehow to deliver a blow of the club to his nose to calm him down.

I must have hurt him badly, for he packed in what he had been doing and tried to make for the exit. His pals did likewise, their "mission" accomplished. But the *anars* are no slouches: a few stout fellows picked them up at the exit and gave them a thrashing that reflected the damages we had to pay for out of our own pockets, in solidarity with the organizer.

That was my baptism by fire. And I had yet to be accepted into the *anar* ranks.

But that brawl made up my mind.

The anarchist group from the XIII and V *arrondissements* had just been launched in the basement of a building near the Place d'Italie. Some comrades introduced us to it. Dragui and I were very warmly welcomed and became active members of the group. In terms of numbers, it was one of the strongest, with about one hundred members, made up of workers and students. There was no shortage of work to do. As we were not wealthy, we made our own posters, stuck them up, and often had to contend with the "*sergots*" (our nickname for the cops in those days). We often concluded our evenings down at the police station.

Every week, we discussed a different topic, and while we did not always see eye to eye, a sound camaraderie prevailed within the group.

At election times, we would venture to disprove the "future leaders of the people." There was sometimes a fracas; when we were denied the right to speak, we took it by force, and that did not always turn out very well.

One of our great pranks, along with Thérèse,[1] was at noon, when the cops stepped out of the prefecture to board the packed Metro, to stick close to these cops and decorate their belts with anarchist flyers. It's great to be young!

When the weather was nice, we used to organize outings into the Parisian countryside to Saint-Cloud, Saint Cucuffa, Clelles, and Herblay. We set off on Saturday evening in joyous, rowdy gangs, knapsacks on our backs. We spent the night under the stars, with straw for bedding. Personally, I always carried with me a hammock that I would string between two trees. On Sundays, after a picnic,

---

1 Thérèse, Mado, Margo, and Marie were my best friends. (Note by M. Piqueray.)

35

there was a round of male and female singers and musicians. The splendid songs of Charles d'Avray,* Gaston Couté,* Loréal,* and others lured Parisian picnickers to us to whom we would offer our newspapers and hand out our leaflets. Sébastien Faure often joined us on his way back from some speaking engagement and needed no coaxing to break into song.

On the field of fair revolt
The old could only plough the furrow
Now you prepare the harvest
The harvest may be splendid and rich
Youngsters, do not wait for old age
Stick to the task in hand
Life's short and time passes and presses
Don't forget that you are the future.

In the evening, returning on the train, some of us had no hesitation in launching into the most explosive songs in the anarchist repertoire in order to throw a kindly scare into the good old Sunday buskers.

Are you, the sovereign people
About to cover the cost of their feasts?
When you labor
And yet have barely a crust to show for it?
So, don't be so foolish
Instead of voting
Give them a punch up the bracket
Then you'll have something to sing about.
If you would be truly happy
Let's have no more government!

Yes, we did a lot of singing in the anarchist ranks. We even had our own "concert café." A long, dimly lit hall above a café on the Rue de Bretagne, in the heart of the Marais quarter. At the far end of the hall, a stage draped in crimson velvet: such was the setting for the *Muse Rouge* jamboree.

The *Muse Rouge* was founded in 1900 by Victor Méric and Maurice Doublier. Its facilities were accessible free of charge to any avant-garde organization that was deemed appealing. For the most part, its singers were drawn from among fellow workers, poets, and composers. Some already had made names for themselves, while others were learning the ropes. One day, a shy young man turned up, apologizing for the fact that his "pipes were rusty"; this was André Isaac, known as Pierre Dac, who, under the latter, built himself a lengthy career.

All of the revolutionary factions were represented, but primarily one found there the long-haired anarchist in lavalière cravat, broad-brimmed hat and the likable, short-haired, sensible young man who read lots of books about social and economic doctrines and was feeling his way through anarchism's various tendencies.

The writers, poets, and singers included Gaston Couté, Charles-Auguste Bontemps,* Maurice Hallé, Xavier Privas and his wife Lorée-Privas, Jehan Rictus, Eugène Bizeau, Charles d'Avray, René Groffe, Louis Loréal, Roger Toziny, Noël-Noël, and Henri Jolivet. The actors included Claudine Boria, Aimée Morin, Odette Mouret, Yvonne George, Jeanne Monteil, Marguerite Greyval, and Cloarec Maupas. The musicians included Droccos, André Thumerelle. The stage designers included Georges Delatousche, Pierre Larivière, and Robert Lingat. And I almost forgot to mention our composer friend Monteil and the players Coladent, Mouret, Goublier, Henri Jacques, and the hilarious Clovys.

Naturally, the repertoire was revolutionary and anti-militarist, but love was not forgotten. The players and composers were warmly applauded.

The atmosphere was warm and brotherly, and the comrades were happy in one another's company.

Out of them all, I was most impressed by Charles d'Avray, whose real name was Charles-Henri Jean. Born in 1878, he died in Paris on November 7, 1960.

His father was an architect. Charles did not follow in his footsteps and made his debut very young in a number of Parisian cabarets. And was an instant success. A real bohemian, his pockets were always empty, but always finding someone worse off than himself to help him spend what little he earned during these "soirées." During the 1920s, I made his acquaintance at the Muse Rouge and was instantly carried away by his warm, captivating voice and his songs.

I reckon it was at about the same time that I became acquainted with Sébastien Faure, the fellow who won him over to his social and anarchist ideas. To mark Sébastien Faure's eightieth birthday, Charles dedicated this magnificent song to him[2]:

You were a great fighter and you were a great sage
You sowed the good seed in good times and bad
Permit me to pay you homage
Spiritual father of my long-gone twenties
You turn up, a veil is lifted
I am twenty years old, you open my eyes
And I espouse as my own your splendid dream
Of pure love, with neither laws nor gods.
Ah! My old anarchist friend
The only thing that has weakened us is the burden of our years
Old friend, great idealist
By your side, my hair has turned white.

Charles had a very wide-ranging repertoire: songs of old Montmartre (like *"Les Maisons"* or *"Les Pavés"*), quirky love songs (*"Amour et Volonté," "Jalousie," "Procréation consciente"*), songs by the dozens and dozens, which we learned by heart and used to sing on our outings and at our soirées.

He sang *"L'Idée," "Loin du rêve," "Le people est vieux,"* and so on. He glorified the outrages committed during the heroic era with *"Les Fous."* His songs come flooding back into memory! I cannot help but to hum them. I performed one of them at the Kremlin back in 1922 with all the fire of a twenty-five-year-old.

But I'll recount more of that to you when the time comes.

Charles was forever on triumphant tours across France. Through song, he had turned into a tireless propagandist of our ideas. And he never renounced his ideals. Something rare enough in his profession to be noteworthy: so many opportunities present themselves to talented folks to make a lot of money, provided they disregard their beliefs.

To afford even greater projection for the good word, Charles set up a singing school in Puteaux and his pupils carried his repertoire into the fashionable cabaret clubs.

So successful was he that he had to open up an offshoot of the Muse Rouge on the Butte. He dubbed it *Le Grenier du Gringoire.*

2 In 1938.

There I saw and heard lots of songwriters and lots of singers. I can still see Jehan Rictus, tall, thin and always dressed in black, wearing a black beard that made him look like Gaston Couté's *Christ en bois*. Among his poems, published in *Les Soliloques du pauvre* and in *Le Coeur populaire*, a few like "*Les petites barques*," "*Le Piège*," "*La jasante à la vieille*" are authentic masterpieces . . . which he would perform for us in his monotone voice on evenings when he was in a good mood. And Xavier Privas, who pounded away on the old piano as he sang "*Les Heures*" or "*Le Testament de Pierrot*."

Among the women, there was Claudine Boria, who enjoyed a measure of success thanks to support from our friend Jeanson who took her under his wing. We heard her perform at the Olympia. She was really tiny. Tuberculosis took her very quickly! Then there was Yvonne George, who sang every bit as well at the Grenier as she did at the Muse Rouge: what an extraordinary face that curious and endearing woman had! She drank and used drugs, but her voice grabbed you by the guts when she sang "*Hardi les gars, vire au guindeau*" or "*Petit bossu tordu*." Her private life was no concern of ours; the essential thing for us was hearing her and communing with her in the same love of beauty, the novel, and the "never before seen." She too passed away very young, and her death was a real loss to the arts scene. What a lovable friend she had been!

There was also Line Marsa, a performer awash with talent and sincerity. I can see her still, with her jet-black hair, her big nose, and laughing mouth. She would occasionally drop in on Louis Lecoin* at the premises of his paper, *Liberté* [*Freedom*]. She was a true Parisian sparrow. She could have made it, but the attractions of life and bohemia were too much for her. Her daughter, the Little Sparrow, has gone down in history.[3]

Towards the end of her life, Fréhel too would turn up at our gala events. She had once been very beautiful and had enjoyed a successful career, but she had taken to drinking, and it was at first a slow and then a steep decline into the blackest wretchedness. Despite her ravaged physique and her shambolic appearance, she would turn up on stage from time to time. Louis asked me to track her down and get her to perform at one of the *Liberté* fundraiser events. She performed several of her old hits, such as "*La java bleue*" or "*Où sont mes amis,*

---

3 "Little Sparrow" was the nickname of the internationally famous chanteuse, Giovanna Gassion, stage name: Édith Piaf (1915-1963).

mes copains?" The public insisted upon more. When she stepped off the stage, I saw her in the wings, tears streaming down her face. Her memory lives on in the minds of those who knew and loved her.

Another great songstress sang on behalf of *Liberté*: Damia, the tragedian who appeared in *Les Goélands*, *La Veuve*, and *Les deux ménétriers*. Jeanne Monteil, Aimée Morin, Nine Pinson, and so many other forgotten faces cast a spell over our youth. We owe them this affectionate remembrance.

It was in the Grenier du Gringoire one night that Philippe, the son of Léon Daudet,* sought refuge, having run away from home. This caused Charles lots of problems with Léon Daudet, Action Française, and the police.

Did he not, faithful to his habit, slip some money to and host this lad who happened to be penniless momentarily?

But I will speak of that in greater detail later in this book.

Charles died a pauper, just as he had lived as one. He is utterly unknown to today's youth. This is a great pity. His "*Le Triomphe de l'Anarchie*," though, has been recorded to disc by the "Quatres Barbus" group and by Marc Ogeret. In the United States, his pupil, Sonia Malkine [May's daughter], sings his songs with great talent.

Be that as it may, we should not be mistaken for harmless youngsters getting together to nibble at cherries in brandy, or downing glasses of beer and having sing-songs. For one thing, the songs themselves are weapons. Take "*Les Fous*" for example:

We are, we are the crazy whom your laws exterminate
When our arguments prevail over yours
While we live, you fear us, and when dead, you fear us even more
Cultivated soil can bring forth a treasure
If plenty of good seed is sown there
Under nature's gaze, it grows in silence
And it is that, as much as us, that you should be afraid of
For there are others, crazy, coming to blow you up

Neither are we boy scouts captivated by the open air and wide-open spaces, out to pick flowers from the meadows and to stroll along the rivers. Too many people imagine that anarchy is populated by sad faces. In anarchy, I have always found *joie de vivre* and friendship.

But we were not always "off duty." Every time some cause seemed just to us, off we would go to lend a hand to its champions, even if they had never heard tell of anarchy.

Following the clashes with the police at the Sociétés Savantes Hall, I did not have occasion to practice direct action against the cops. The seamstresses' strike allowed me to resume training.

The junior staff, the *midinettes*, those little worker-bees of the major fashion houses producing the masterpieces worn by performers and the ladies of the Parisian and international bourgeoisie, those girls one meets in the squares or in the Tuileries Gardens at noon, sharing their meager lunches with the sparrows, their friends, who are very poorly paid, surviving on little, and clothed in next to nothing, but tastefully so. *Midinettes* are known to every Parisian for their laughter, their songs, their fashion flair, and their tiny artists' hands.

But there is the other side of the coin too. Today, it is time to strike. No longer can they make ends meet. The bosses who shamelessly exploit them do not want to hear a word about awarding pay raises. So, the *midinettes* take to the streets.

That afternoon, a rally was held at the Bourse du Travail near the Place de la République. Our friends Margot, Marie, and Mado Ferré are out on strike. Out of solidarity, Thérèse and I made up our minds to join them and offer our support. The hall is packed. Young girls and women mount the rostrum one after the other to spell out the situation inside the fashion industry; whether in workshop or bedroom, they are equally exploited. They do not concede, and a delegation is appointed to enter into talks with the employers' union.

They depart like a flock of sparrows taking flight. Laughter, and coarse banter. We are taken aback to see several hundred construction and road workers show up, having quit work to bring the *midinettes* their moral and material support. Smashing! They are applauded and hugged. The decision is made to demonstrate outside the big fashion houses and then on to the Champs-Élysées. The lads link arms with the young girls and the light-hearted and picturesque procession makes ready to head for the Grands Boulevards. All of a sudden, a squadron of the Garde Républicaine arrives in the Place de la République, escorting some open-top calèches. The lead vehicle carries Poincaré.* The remainder, government figures.

"That's Poincaré, you know . . . the man who laughs in cemeteries."

He turned up quite simply to introduce a very curious exposition in the Place de la République. In some huts, equipment had been installed screening photographs of life in the trenches, the transportation of the wounded, and of dead bodies strewn across the battlefield and all the horrors of the war. And, to cap it all, the people of Paris were supposed to cough up money in order to view this.

We were standing on the edge of the pavement, getting ready to join the march. Poincaré alighted and gestured to the crowd, which had rushed over to greet him. Out of the blue, Mado broke away from us and strode in his direction, raising her hand and shouting into his face: "You bastard, you come to view your dead?" She was promptly punched by his escort and handed over to the cops who had rushed over (as had we, not wishing to be separated from her) and lo and behold, we were all on our way to the police station, man-handled and tossed into a cell like thieves, then interrogated by the superintendent who tore into us!

We were placed in a cell and held overnight. We were not proud! What were they going to do to us? Luckily, the "assault" was not taken too seriously. Of course, the order went out that we were to say nothing to the press; to put it another way, the whole business was hushed up.

We had come out of it unscathed, but we were fuming at having missed out on the march to the Champs-Élysées.

My enthusiasm for anarchism radiated in every direction. I was in danger of becoming ineffective due to lack of focus. Then fortune brought me into contact with Louis Lecoin. It was in 1921 that I made his acquaintance. From that point on, I dedicated the bulk of my time waging war on war.

Louis Lecoin was recently released from Albertville prison and had just been sentenced to eight years for his anti-militarism. The first thing that struck me about him was his pale blue eyes with their flicker of intelligence, with no hint of malice, but also kindness, energy, and courage. He even flirted with me a little. But, now twenty years old, I found this great fellow too short. Not that that stopped us from remaining life-long friends.

I was not disappointed; the legend that had grown up around him appeared justified. I knew him well enough from what I had been told by Sébastien Faure, Pierre Le Meillour, and others, with such warmth and fondness! I knew all about the incidents that had led to his being jailed: his refusal, as a young soldier, to be deployed against striking railroad employees and to open fire on them, in defiance of the military machine of which he was part. His anti-war campaign back in 1914, the handbill that he had distributed in the thousands, his long years of incarceration, punctuated by hunger strikes for the restoration of political prisoner status and for it to be awarded to fellow anarchist Jeanne Morand,* unjustly under suspicion of passing intelligence to the enemy.

As far we young libertarians and young syndicalists were concerned, Louis Lecoin was an example to be imitated. He had shown us that one could be a syndicalist, a libertarian, and anti-militarist at the same time.

Upon his release, he took over as administrator with *Le Libertaire* [*The Libertarian*], the newspaper of the Union Anarchiste,[4] not that this prevented him from being active inside his trade union (Construction) and speaking out forcefully and effectively at the Lille Congress in 1921 and again in Saint-Etienne in 1922.

Like most of us, he was enthusiastic about the Russian revolution, of which we had expected much but delivered nothing but disappointments, but he declined to let himself be subsumed into the Communist Party like certain other comrades.

In 1921, he mounted a campaign to prevent the extradition of three Spaniards—Ascaso, Durruti, and Jover[5]—who had been convicted in Argentina for a so-called hold-up. In reality, for being anarchists. Their extradition was imminent: a cruiser was on its way to collect them. Louis lobbied the most highly placed political and court authorities in the land and eventually pulled it off.

He also lobbied against the expulsions of Camillo Berneri[6] and Nestor Makhno[7] and managed to save them both.

4 In November 1920, at its 1st Congress, the FA (Anarchist Federation) re-named itself Union Anarchiste and adopted a profoundly anti-Bolshevik position. In 1926 the UA became the UAC (Anarchist-Communist Union) before, as a result of a merger with the AFA (Association of Anarchist Federalist) in 1934, it again became the UA. The newspaper *Le Libertaire*, was founded in 1895 by Sébastien Faure. A newspaper with the same title had existed in the United States between 1858-1861 and had been edited by Joseph Déjacque.

5 The campaign to prevent Francisco Ascaso, Buenaventura Durruti, and Gregorio Jover from being extradited from France to Argentina to answer charges of robbery and murder there took place between December 1926 and July 1927.

6 In 1934 Lecoin lobbied the French authorities to allow Camillo Berneri, Italian militant anarchist who was in exile from the Italian fascist regime, to stay in France.

7 In 1926 Lecoin had launched the Right of Asylum Committee and in May 1927 helped prevent Makhno's expulsion from France.

But his major campaign was the one on behalf of Sacco and Vanzetti. But perhaps we should rehearse the affair that shook the entire world more than sixty years ago:

On April 15, 1920, at three in the afternoon, cashier Parmenter and his guard, Berardelli, employees of a shoe factory, walked across the main street in South Braintree, in the state of Massachusetts in the USA. In two boxes, they were carrying the employees' weekly payroll: 15,776 dollars. Two individuals rushed them, cut them down with revolver shots, and made off with the boxes. A car pulled up, they climbed inside and fled from the scene.

At that time in America, lots of Italian immigrants arrived, most of them syndicalists and anarchists. They disseminated their ideas, which the government considered poisonous. So they say . . . a blast of xenophobia swept the country.

As for the South Braintree outrage, witnesses, five in all, turned up to claim that they could identify the culprits as Sacco and Vanzetti. Thirty-two witnesses came forward to contradict this, but the five were deemed credible and the pair were arrested.

Now, at three in the afternoon on April 15, Sacco was in Boston. He had just received news that his mother had died and was keen to get back to Italy. On that date and at that precise time, he was with the Italian consul, who came forward to confirm that.

As for Vanzetti, a street merchant in Plymouth, he had been seen throughout the day, from morning to night. There were thirteen witnesses to confirm that; one had sold him some cloth, another had taken him out fishing in his boat, and some others had bought fish from him.

They were both tried and sentenced to death.

And the witness statements? Worthless. These were Italians, foreigners, "*macaronis.*" That was the sort of language used to undermine some forty odd truthful testimonies, including that of the Italian consul.

The others might be mistaken, contradict themselves, or rack up unlikelihoods or lies, one might have been bribed and another insane . . . No matter, the witnesses for the prosecution were Americans and, therefore, above suspicion. Stupid nationalism, how many crimes have been committed in your name!

Judge Thayer, when posed the question "What was the basis for your conviction of these men?" replied: "In my view, these convictions were not determined by the witness statements since the defense witnesses outnumber the prosecution witnesses. The evidence that prompted the conviction of the accused results from the circumstances of the affair. The sort of evidence that is known in law as consciousness of guilt!"

There is something shameful about debating such infantile arguments. But on the basis of such childishness two men, two innocents, were going to be executed.

Who were these men?[8]

Nicola Sacco, born in 1891, came to the USA in 1908. He was seventeen years old. He had been living in Massachusetts for the past twelve years. A conscientious and modest worker, he had been in regular employment at a shoe factory for the past seven. He lived with his wife and child in a little house (complete with small garden) adjacent to the factory. He had no known vices. He did not drink and was very parsimonious.

Bartolomeo Vanzetti arrived in America in 1908 and was thirty-two years old when his life took this dramatic turn. He had been sacked by the Cordage Company in the wake of a strike in 1916. In order to hold onto his independence, he had become a street merchant. He sold fish in Plymouth.

Sacco was a man of the soil and Vanzetti virtually an intellectual. While Sacco gardened, Vanzetti read the poets and philosophers. He had fashioned a philosophy inspired by their dreams. He spread this in newspaper articles and in chats with local workers. The fact is that he wrote very well and, the word was, spoke even better. Neither of them had any previous convictions. One of them was the sentimental type, the other an enlightened, rational mind that believed in selfless ideas and in the exemplary power of living simply and lovingly. Could it really be argued that that was any overture to the crime?

There is every reason to think that the murderers were professionals. And were the attitudes of Sacco and Vanzetti, whose ways of life had not changed, typical of persons whose consciences were burdened by criminality?

On May 5, a police officer accosted them on the Bridgewater tram and arrested them. Now, how likely would it be that people who had

---

8 For more information about the Sacco-Vanzetti case see Paul Avrich, *Sacco and Vanzetti: The Anarchist Background* (Princeton: Princeton University Press, 1996).

gunned two men down with their revolvers in broad daylight would let themselves be taken and handcuffed by a single officer without resisting? It is unbelievable!

Besides, the culprits were known: their names were reported. They were the Morelli gang and one of them, by the name of Madeiros, made a written confession to the crime. It was ignored.

Why, then, were Sacco and Vanzetti convicted? For one thing, political passion. The trial was not judged as a trial of common law but a trial of opinion. They were not convicted for having murdered but because they were anarchists and foreigners, for having been draft-dodgers and strikers. Anarchists have never had a warm welcome in the USA and, in that time, things were even worse.

US Attorney-General Mitchell Palmer had pushed a $2.6 million allocation through Congress in 1919 for a drive against the "moral rats," which is how he referred to anarchists. And he successfully drew down on those funds. "In the mission to protect society against attacks by moral rats," Palmer admitted, "nothing is out of bounds: searches, seizures, arrests and torture used on anyone for any reason." To extract confessions, torture was used: in short, there was more concern over the efficacy of the trap than with the legality of how it was put together. Now, Sacco and Vanzetti were deemed moral rats. They were interrogated, not about the hold-up, but about the books they read, the handbills they distributed, in short, about their opinions. Judge Thayer pronounced this statement:

"If they did not carry out this crime, they could have committed it; crime is part and parcel of their social principles!"

That was the rationale underpinning their conviction.

Sacco and Vanzetti were not judged but executed. The death sentence passed on them was a lynching rather than a sentencing. The newspapers, however, were quite slow to realize this and to choose a side.

Driven by Louis Lecoin and Nicolas Faucier, the Sacco-Vanzetti Committee led all the demonstrations held in the Salle Wagram, where the chief of police unleashed his baton-wielding goons against us youngsters who were milling around on the pavement outside, due to lack of space inside the hall. But a grenade hurled from the entrance landed in the middle of their charge and curbed their enthusiasm.

Another mass rally at the Winter Circus drew thousands of people. There was an overflow of twenty thousand. Loudspeakers were set up. The orators were Blum, Turati, Séverine,* Frossard, Urbain Gohier, Vaillant-Couturier, Marc Sangnier, the attorney Henri Torrès, Jouhaux, and Sébastien Faure.

America remained unmoved.

I was following this campaign enthusiastically. In 1921, the major newspapers were silent about this legal crime that in the offing. *Le Libertaire* was alone in campaigning against it. From time to time, the left wing press would spare it a few lines. How was this affair to be afforded its proper magnitude? What could we do to save them?

It was at that point that I made up my mind to seize the initiative. I was seething at the systematic silence maintained by the bourgeois newspapers about this injustice. So I broke ranks. That was easy enough for me to do back then, but these days, I have difficulty making up my mind to lift the lid on my initiative. Not from cowardice; I would not like anybody to think it was on the part of braggadocio... Be that as it may, it is historically the fact that I played a small part in this affair. I posted a parcel of perfume to the USA ambassador in Paris. A very pretty parcel of perfumes.

I had ventured to enclose within it a stun grenade primed to go off once the package was opened. And it went off. But the ambassador's butler was the person who unwrapped the package. He had seen service during the war, realized what was afoot, and had just enough time to hurl the grenade to the far end of the room before it went off.

He emerged from the incident unscathed. Luckily for him! The room, on the other hand, sustained serious damage. In my eyes, what mattered was that, from that moment on, the Sacco-Vanzetti affair was catapulted into the "news" section and the "major newspapers" reckoned it now merited further mention. And it was covered abundantly.

Bravo, grenade! . . . It made no more noise than any ordinary grenade, but it had hit its mark.

Little by little, honest research, scrutiny of the facts, and conscientious examination of the circumstances were to open the eyes of every "impartial observer" to the innocence of the two men.

I returned to my place in the ranks and reverted to being just another little pawn of anarchy among others. But the struggle pressed on. For seven long years, without failure, Sacco and Vanzetti unceasingly affirmed that they had had no hand, act, or part in the crimes charged against them. All to no avail.

They were to be sent to the electric chair in 1927 and redeemed in 1978, after their innocence was proven.

How many other anarchists have been lawfully murdered in most countries around the world! In France, there was Auguste Vaillant* in 1893, Émile Henry* in 1894, Ravachol* in 1892, Liabeuf* in 1910. In Germany, Erich Mühsam* perished under torture. In Italy, there were Sante Caserio* in 1894, Gaetano Bresci* in 1900, Michele Schirru* in 1932. In Argentina, Paulino Scarfò in 1931. The Swede Joe Hill,* in 1915. In Spain, Francisco Ferrer* and many an anarchist have been executed by means of the garrote. In Japan, there was Sakae Ōsugi* in 1923. And all those that I forget, without speaking of those who died in prison or in penal colonies for their beliefs.

Let me quote Sébastien Faure again:

A queer fate. Anarchists campaign relentlessly in writing, by word of mouth, and by means of action to ensure that well-being and freedom are no longer the preserve of the privileged few, but effectively become the inheritance of all. In so doing, they consent to the daily sacrifice of their own lives, since well-being and freedom are, in their eyes, the only blessings that make life worth living!

But it is not my intention to pen a history of anarchism. Besides, I do not see how I could. Every time I read such a history, I discover things I never knew before, and I sometimes discover certain errors of detail. Just one of the reasons that have prompted me to write this book.

4

MY APPRENTICESHIP

We come now to two affairs in which I played virtually no part but about which I want to testify, in that I experienced them from within the libertarian movement.

For a start, there was the Germaine Berton* affair.

Germaine was dark-haired. She was younger than me (having been born in Puteaux on June 7, 1902). I had very little to do with her. However, we did bump into each other at a rally organized in the Salle Wagram by Action Française.[1]

You might be taken aback that I attended a far-right meeting. But I was really keen to get a good look at someone like Léon Daudet. What I read about him in *L'Action francaise* [*French Action*] seemed to me to be so scary that I wondered if he really existed.

War was his hobbyhorse topic. He spoke of it with a violence that was truly hysterical. At one point he shrieked:

"Never forget that, towering over love, there is hate . . ."

Even before the applause started, a young boy had leapt to his feet:

"No, sir," he called out. "Looming larger than hate, there is love. Or at the very least, that's what I was always taught . . ."

---

1 A far-right movement with a newspaper of the same name. L'Action francaise was founded in 1908 and led by Charles Maurras and Léon Daudet. Essentially it was ultra-Catholic and pro-monarchist with a commitment to the authoritarian state. Quasi-fascist, it supported the Vichy government during the Second World War.

Not only was he silenced by the *"camelots du roi"* in attendance in the hall, but they expelled him in a rain of baton blows.

Léon Daudet returned to his speech. He employed bellicose language, dispatching his troops to war and to restoration of the monarchy. I was utterly dumbfounded.

L'Action francaise, the royalist newspaper of which he was the manager, carried the refrain:

Tomorrow, over their graves
The wheat will sprout more beautiful.

What baffled me was that the youngsters who drank in his every word appeared to be eager to serve as fertilizer.

Leaving the meeting, I was frankly depressed. Germaine Berton was even more outraged than I was. She said to me:

"That bastard does not deserve to live!"

She had only recently taken to frequenting anarchist circles but already had a good grounding in anti-militarism and pacifism. She spoke up often in discussions inside her group and always in an intelligent way.

She lived with a young book delivery boy, Armand Gohary.* I spotted him a few times, and he seemed a likable sort. They say he held certain documents concerning the "Bonnet Rouge"* affair.[2]

He was discovered dead in his room, most likely murdered.

An anarchist comrade by the name of Taupin,* a friend of his, "committed suicide." At least, that was the official version.

I hadn't seen Germaine since and hadn't taken what she had said in her indignation seriously.

I was mistaken.

On January 23, 1923, a while after that rally, carrying a revolver in her handbag, she turned up at the Action Française headquarters asking to speak to Léon Daudet. He sent word that he was not there and sent Marius Plateau* out to receive her. She was ushered into a large room with splendid blue armchairs adorned with *fleur de lys*.

Monarchist he may have been, but Marius Plateau was one coarse fellow. His treatment of Germaine was unspeakably vulgar, sordid, and arrogant. He accused her of being in the pay of the police "like

2 A satirical left-wing paper that was openly pacifist during the First World War. For more details of the incident see appendix.

all anarchists, I might add." He made her the offer of money "for the information she assuredly had to offer him," etc.

Outraged by his remarks, she drew her weapon and gunned him down without a word. Then she fired a shot in her own direction, missed, and fainted. The *camelots* on duty rushed in at the sound of gunshots and thought that she was dead; otherwise, they would assuredly have lynched her.

Standing up to attacks and slanders coming from *L'Action française*, *Le Libertaire* threw itself behind the defense of Germaine Berton and swapped from weekly to daily publication, something it had been planning to do for quite some time. It asked Maître Henri Torrès to represent Germaine Berton. He was just starting out in his career as an attorney, which did not prevent him from defending her brilliantly. Séverine, Louis Lecoin, and other personalities rallied around Germaine Berton, and she was acquitted.

The aggressive attitude adopted by Léon Daudet and Maurras* and their bellicosity did not appeal to the sympathy of the jury. Instead, it proved a significant factor in the acquittal of Germaine Berton.

After the trial, little more was ever seen of Germaine Berton in the anarchist movement. She was catapulted back into prominence for a while at the time of the Philippe Daudet* affair. She declared that once upon a time she had been his mistress, following a random encounter with him in the Latin Quarter some months earlier.

"Pure imagination" said all of the comrades better acquainted with her than I was. She tried to take her own life in the Belleville church before vanishing from our milieu.

The affair surrounding the death of Léon Daudet's son was very murky. One that occupied the front pages of the newspapers throughout late 1923, and *L'Action française* cranked it out like a daily serial.

Just to sum up the facts:

A young man of around fifteen, although he looked older, had shown up at the *Le Libertaire* premises at No. 9, rue Louis Blanc, insisting that somebody should provide him with a revolver. He was planning to "strike out and kill some important personage." He claimed that his name was Philippe, that he was on the run, and penniless. His parents were bourgeois, and he had no wish to return home.

The young anarchist poet Georges Vidal,* who dealt with him, talked with him at some length, explaining that an anarchist did not kill people just for the pleasure of killing and that if he was going to sacrifice his life his deed would need to have some meaning to it. He then treated him to dinner and, in order to distract him and change his mind, brought him to the 'Grenier Gringoire' on La Butte, a cabaret club belonging to our friend Charles d'Avray. And he spent the evening in the company of a squad of comrades who welcomed him like a brother. Charles slipped him some money for lodgings, but one of the comrades there (and his partner) took him back to their place for the night. That comrade's name was Jean Gruffy.

How did it come to pass that the son of somebody like Léon Daudet felt an attraction to anarchy?

After his death, certain journalists reckoned that he had been trying to infiltrate anarchist circles so as to avenge the death of Marius Plateau, as he had been one of his warmest admirers . . .

Now let us try to stick to the facts:

Even though he had failed to procure the gun that he had asked for, Philippe revisited *Le Libertaire*. This time Georges Vidal was not around, and he met up with a certain F who brought him to Le Flaouter,* the bookseller, who might just sell him a weapon. In fact, Le Flaouter promised he would have one for him the following day.

As arranged, the bookseller admitted him to the basement of his bookstore. At which point an impenetrable blackout curtain falls.

The official version was that Le Flaouter sold him a gun, that Philippe caught a taxi on the boulevard near the Bastille and asked the driver to take him to the Medrano circus. As they neared the Gare de l'Est, the driver is supposed to have heard a gunshot within his vehicle and, turning around, saw his passenger sprawled across the back seat in a pool of blood. According to witnesses arriving at the scene, the carpet and floor of the taxi were already drenched in blood. The driver absorbed the scene and then ferried the "injured party" to Lariboisière. There, he was recorded as dead on arrival and his body was removed to the morgue.

The other version, the anarchist version, was that Philippe had supposedly been mistaken for a dangerous anarchist and shot, down in the basement, by a police officer who had been tipped off by Le Flaouter, and then loaded into a police-hired taxi, the other details being mere stage-play. Philippe was already dead when the driver "found" him.

Bear in mind that Le Flaouter had very close ties to one police office and was in all likelihood his informer. They played cards with each other every evening.

Fretting about Philippe's absence, the Daudet family scanned the newspapers daily; its eyes were drawn to a report of a suicide by a young man, whose description fitted Philippe's. With a friend in tow, Léon Daudet visited the hospital where he could not help but identify the corpse.

He held the anarchists responsible for Philippe's death and, from the pages of L'Action française, launched an extremely violent campaign, answered blow for blow by Le Libertaire. Léon Daudet was particularly scathing about Georges Vidal, who had first greeted Philippe. Philippe had handed him a farewell letter for his mother in the event that anything might happen to him. That letter, the contents of which Georges Vidal was not aware, was addressed to Madame Daudet. There was no mention made of Philippe's father's name.

Irked by the disclosures in Le Libertaire, the whole of L'Action française resorted to rococo invention, attempting to peddle huge lies on the back of a glimmer of truth.

I have always been a good learner. Where anarchy was concerned, there was no reason I would show less application. I continued to read frantically. I took notes. I came across a little notebook in which I used to jot down the sentences that had most struck a chord with me:

> The people should not look beyond themselves for their emancipation. Human progress will only become possible once labor violence has demolished the economic, political, and religious oppress that are a feature of the current society.
> —Malatesta, 1907, the Amsterdam International Congress.

> Under the influence of our ideas, the working class is increasingly tending, in the West especially, to desert the old workaday, conservative trade unionism for the byways of revolutionary syndicalism. This the great Western Miners' Federation, in its memorable struggles against the bourgeoisie and the government in Colorado, has vigorously resorted to direct action.
> —Emma Goldman

Labor organization, strike, general strike, direct action, boycott, sabotage and armed insurrection per se, these are merely the means. Anarchism is the end. The anarchist revolution we want look far beyond the interests of one class and aims at the comprehensive liberation of today's thrice-enslaved humanity, enslaved economically, politically and morally. So, let us steer clear of any unilateral, simplistic course of action. Trade unionism, an excellent means of action in terms of the labor resources it places at our disposal, cannot be our sole means. And we should not lose sight of the only goal worth the effort: anarchy!
—Malatesta, 1907 Amsterdam International Congress.

I had "embraced anarchy" instinctively. My hatred of injustice and my rebelliousness blossomed there. But I did not yet have a completely coherent view of the doctrine. My ideas now fit into place. Through discussions and my reading, I was being "cultivated." But my "culture" did not consist merely of adding to my bookish knowledge. It was to drive me to action, and I found anarcho-syndicalism to be an ideal setting for this.

Practically and historically, anarcho-syndicalism is the organic form assumed by anarchy in its struggle against capitalism. It stands in fundamental opposition to political and reformist trade unionism.

The anarcho-syndicalist movement allows for the harnessing together of action directed at the struggle for day to day demands and the workers' loftiest aspirations.

Anarcho-syndicalism is the revolutionary school where the worker learns to become conscious; it is the organization of the fight in the here and now, the organization of production, distribution and administration in the future.

Anarcho-syndicalism is the human thinking that trains the truth on the lying dogmas that bar the proletariat's way, it is the science that shines its bright torch on all harmful institutions: God, Fatherland, State, Capital. It is rebellion that rushes forth and turns a merciless lash upon every authority and every iniquity; it is humanity seeking to live free and triumph and which intends to stand proud and magnificent upon the ruins of dying tyrannies.

Anarcho-syndicalism is the unrelenting action of the workers in revolt on behalf of the expropriating general strike and establishment of the society of tomorrow. It marches straight at its goal: anarchism.[3]

All that I needed to do now was put my ideas into action.

It was a massive undertaking, you might say. But I was far from daunted by the arduous, tough endeavor; indeed, it just made me all the keener.

I had left my label-making factory and hired on as an administrative clerk with the Fédération des Métaux [Metalworkers' Federation] in the Rue de la Grange-aux-Belles and campaigned actively within the unions.

That time was rich in social movements: strikes, demonstrations in the street. Returning from the front, soldiers found it hard to come by work; their households had been destroyed; and discontent prevailed among the working class.

My apprenticeship as a militant was not all hearts and flowers; I took to the streets alongside the metalworkers and with the boys from the Construction Union (the SUB), as well as the road workers for whom I had a special soft spot. They were rough-and-ready lads, tough at work and tough in brawls. They looked good in their corduroy suits and baggy trousers tied in at the ankles and their red or blue, or sometimes black woolen "*tayole*" (belt) wrapped around their waists. "Petite May" was pretty much their mascot. I was always well supported.

Contacts with the cops were not the friendliest. Baton blows, and above all blows from rolled-up shoulder-capes (*pèlerines roulées*), fell fast and thick.

May Day of 1920 and 1921 were particularly brutal. As we set off from the Bourse du Travail, Place de la République and Boulevard Magenta, the mounted police saber-charged us, and one of them caught me with the flat of his saber in such a manner that I believed he had beheaded me. For a long time, I carried the mark of his saber on my face, and I had a swollen and splendidly blackened eye.

I do not speak about those May Days with nostalgia for bygone days. Because that is what the May Days of my youth were like.

---

3 These lines are taken from Pierre Besnard's 1937 IWA/AIT secretary's report to the International Anarchist Congress of that year.

But what I will say, categorically, is that those May Days were "authentic."

The communists had not yet hijacked that day of struggle and turned it into a labor "holiday."

Allow me here to re-establish the historical facts:[4]

In 1886, Chicago was just a town full of emigrants coming from every corner of Europe. It boasted a variety of factories, canneries, and slaughterhouses. Lack of hygiene and physical protection, inhuman fast work-rates, low pay, lack of secure employment, prompted the workers to band together for protection against the exploitation of which they were the object. Not just in Chicago but across the entire continent of America, the class struggle existed in a pure state. Trade unionism was making inroads in the United States. But not without difficulty. The American workers expressed an instinctive suspicion in regard to socialist ideas emanating from Europe. Newspapers printed in German and English and French declared: "fighting against private ownership is a right and indeed a duty."

Several Chicago industrialists and bankers asked the mayor to ban these newspapers and arrest their editors. To which the mayor replied:

"We have policing well in hand. Nothing is going to happen and we do not fear them."

A few days later, though, a grumbling sea of humanity packed the streets and red and black banners floated over the crowd.

"We are fighting for the eight-hour workday, for better pay, for betterment of our working conditions, for the abolition of the black lists," was the word heard at the factory gates every evening.

There was no right to strike, in the respect that once a strike had ended, the bosses would re-hire whomever they liked, sowing discord between workers. There was brawling between workers and the police intervened with great brutality.

On May 4, a big rally was to be held in the Haymarket and labor leaders were scheduled to speak. Six thousand strikers from the McCormick plant were already in position when the factory whistle sounded and the scabs working there ventured out. The strikers left the rally and fighting erupted between the workers.

The police stepped in and opened fire on them; the toll on the

---

4 For a detailed account of the Haymarket affair see Paul Avrich, *The Haymarket Tragedy* (Princeton: Princeton University Press, 1986).

workers' side was one dead and six with serious gunshot injuries, an indeterminate number of sundry wounded, and a few injuries on the police side. Haymarket was a great square with a capacity for 20,000 people. August Spies, a typesetter with the *Arbeiter Zeitung* [*Workers' Times*], Fischer, who had left Germany at the age of fifteen and become an anarchist-socialist, Parsons, the American editor of *The Alarm*, a man who had served in the army during the Civil War at the age of thirteen, and Fielden, an Englishman who moved to the USA in 1868, were scheduled to speak, but the rain started and they made for a near-by hall to conclude the gathering. When they arrived there, Fielden was on the rostrum when, all of a sudden, a troop of police invaded the hall, officers leading the way, and they issued the order to disperse. The speakers had started climbing down from the platform when a "bright, round object" flew through the air, followed by a loud explosion.

At first there was silence . . . then the police opened fire on the screaming, fleeing crowd of workers. Within minutes it was all over. The square was emptied, and the only sound was the groans from the wounded. Seventy people had been wounded and one policeman killed.

"Last night, the anarchists ushered in the reign of disorder. They laid an ambush for the policemen and hurled a bomb . . ." declared the reactionary press. Now, workers had not thrown that bomb, and the bomb had flown from the police ranks.

The labor leaders—Spies, Fielden, Schwab, Waller, G. Engel, Oscar Neebe, W. Singer, and L. Lingg—were rounded up. Parsons was nowhere to be found. Two hundred arrests were made in the space of one week. A climate of inquisition and xenophobia prevailed. Four attorneys offered their services to the accused, despite the threats made against them. A jury was selected from a panel of 981 individuals. In fact, all twelve of those eventually selected had their minds made up in advance.

From the outset of the proceedings, the judge announced that it did not matter who had thrown the device, that all of the accused were answerable for it.

Fifty-year-old George Engel stated:

"I wasn't at the rally but was at home with my wife and friends."

Adolph Fischer acknowledged his part in the rally; Samuel Fielden was accused of having shouted: "Behold the ferocious brutes, comrades, and do your duty."

Although, some of the policemen agreed that all he had said was: "We are peaceful . . . "

Parsons, who showed up at the trial after having been on the run since the day of the rally, declared:

"My name has been on the blacklist for ten years and for two I have been publishing *The Alarm*. I fight against the wretchedness of the workers . . . "

Addressing the lawyers representing the civil litigants, Spies stated:

"My defense is your very accusation itself."

Michael Schwab and Oscar Neebe, who had not been in the Haymarket, were also charged with murder. Neebe uttered these words:

"The police response is unacceptable."

Louis Lingg was charged with having assembled the bomb. A number of witnesses testified that he had not been at the rally.

"That I have assembled bombs is true," he stated, "but not that one."

The lawyers representing the civil litigants told the jury on twenty occasions:

"Your choice is between law and anarchy, between good and evil. Your decision will be a watershed in history. The responsibility upon you is beyond measure. Do not let yourselves err on the side of mercy."

The defense contended that the accused were on trial for their views, in the absence of all evidence. The summations ended on August 19.

On the morning of the August 20, a police cordon sealed off the entrance to the court and patrols roamed the city. The jurymen were first into the courtroom, followed by the lawyers for the two sides. Then the Court. The judge rose to his feet and everyone else followed suit.

The sentence was death for all of them, except for Neebe, who got fifteen years of imprisonment. There was some murmuring in the courtroom. The eight men left the room without a word, in great dignity.

Two minutes later, there was a great roar from the crowd, followed by applause. The crowd was afraid . . .

The general view was articulated by the press: "The verdict has killed anarchy off in our city. It represents a caution to the snakes from Europe, these socialists, communists, and anarchists. Chicago's verdict will at least curtail the immigration into this country of organized killers."

Many letters were sent to Governor Oglesby by well-known figures in the United States and Europe: Walter Besant, Walter Crane, Stafford Brooke, Ford Madox Brown. A huge rally was organized in London, attended by William Morris, Bernard Shaw, Annie Besant, Kropotkin, Stepniak, etc.[5]

The governor suggested:

"The convicted men might have to abjure their doctrine."

"Make a gesture," the lawyers told their clients.

The convicted men greeted that proposal with high disdain. Liberty or death, they demanded.

Extraordinarily, five of the most important bankers who held supreme power in Chicago gathered to determine whether the condemned men should be spared or not. Mercy was not a consideration: "The executions may spark disturbances; no point in breathing fresh life into the agitation . . ." Should the men be spared? Some were supportive of clemency. Others opposed it.

On the morning of November 10, warders heard a detonation coming from Lingg's cell. They could see blood all over the place. Lingg's face had been ripped off. There was talk of a bomb. He had used a tablet of fulminate of mercury. Some doctors wanted to save Lingg by passing him off as mad. He had opted for death rather than the asylum. On his cell wall there was this inscription, scrawled in his own blood: "Long live anarchy!"

That same day, Fielden and Schwab were reprieved, their sentences commuted to life terms. The others were executed.

The gallows were erected quite close to the prison on the night of November 10–11, 1887. On the morning of November 11, the condemned men had a quiet breakfast and wrote letters.

At 8:40 a.m., an attorney arrived: the person responsible for the bomb had been picked up in New York, and he was demanding that the execution be set aside. At 10:15 a.m., the governor replied: "No!"

At 11:30 a.m., the sheriff arrived to read out the sentence to each of the prisoners. They were handcuffed and dressed in white muslin shrouds. Fischer helped to arrange his. The four men were fitted with hoods. They were then allowed a few last words:

5 This meeting took place at the South Place Institute on October 14, 1887.

Spies: "A day will come when our silence will speak louder than the voices you seek to strangle this day!"

Fischer: "Long live anarchy! This is the most beautiful moment of my life!"

Engel: "Long live anarchy!"

Parsons: "Will you allow me to speak, oh Americans? Let me speak, Sheriff Matson, so that the people's voice can make itself heard! Let . . ."

That was all.

The funerals took place on Sunday, November 13. "No placards, no flags, no speeches," Chicago's mayor had ordered. Upwards of 250,000 people lined the funeral procession; about 15,000 people entered the cemetery. The procession advanced in utter silence. Four orators then spoke, including Black, the convicted men's attorney.

Five years after that, a monument was erected on the graves of the executed men, and Waldheim cemetery became a place of pilgrimage.

The novelist Henry James, the American equivalent of Marcel Proust, wrote at that time: "We have become sensible of a sinister world, inferior and anarchic, seething in its pain, its power, and its hatred . . ."

That sinister world was the working class, which was at that point exploited and downtrodden. The grumblings of revolt that the Americans were starting to sense were about to build until shaking the world.

Ever since then, May 1 has been the day of rebellion across the world, marked in France (as it was in Cléry and in Fourmies[6]) and elsewhere, by violence and bloodshed.

Petain tried to turn May 1 into a "celebration" of patronage.

And, deliberately or otherwise, communists have embraced that notion of his and brought it back into fashion.

But as far as the "old hands" are concerned, May 1 will always be synonymous with demands, struggle, and REVOLT.

Luckily, there was more going on than brawling! The syndicalist youth were active and studious, old hands would deliver well-attended lectures on trade unionism, and the festivals we organized in various

---

6 On May 1, 1891, workers demonstrating in Fourmies (Nord department) were fired upon by French army troops who killed nine workers and wounded a further sixty.

arrondissements where we staged avant-garde and anti-militarist plays, as well as plays by Courteline and even the classics, were very well attended and topped up our solidarity funds.

We produced handbills and posters, for which some youngsters were arrested and prosecuted. During the 1920s, the political wing of La Santé prison welcomed a range of visitors. Alongside the syndical-ists, communists, and anarchists, there were even some royalists!

Coming back one evening from La Bellevilleoise where I had listened to a number of speakers and making my way home to my room in the Latin Quarter, I caught the metro at République. In one corner of the carriage, I noticed some long-haired youngsters in crumpled cloth-ing, looking weary, and, near them, some bundles. A pretty young girl and a little girl of about ten accompanied them. They spoke in a for-eign language that seemed oddly akin to Russian. Their appearance, albeit a bit rough, was not off-putting. I was bombarded by questions: who were they? Where were they from? I felt drawn to them.

All of a sudden, one of them opened up a newspaper: *Le Libertaire*. So, they were friends. I went up to them and said as much. They had a pretty good command of French. They came from Bulgaria: in Lyon they had been put up by Claude J., a sound comrade of whom I had heard tell. They were students who had come to study at l'Université de Paris. Penniless, they had no idea where they were to spend the night (and that was one of the last metros).

I decided to bring the little flock home with me. Things might look clearer in the morning, and we would see. I managed to smuggle them into the hotel without too much noise and without attracting the attention of the hotelier. My room was none too big and held only a small iron single bed. No matter! The two young girls shared the mattress, and I took the box springs. The boys huddled, more or less at their ease, on top of the covers. They were not hungry but sleepy. The following morning, after a strong cup of tea and some honey cakes, I made it my business to find them somewhere more comfort-able. The hotel had one large room vacant. The other could stay with friends until something better turned up.

We became better acquainted with one another. In confidence, they told me that they had fled Sofia following a bomb attack in-side the cathedral there, during a mass attended by top-ranking ci-vilian and military authorities. It had left people dead and injured.

A crackdown on left-wingers followed. There was only one escape: exile.[7]

I bumped into them frequently after that. We spent many a long evening chatting at length about people and ideas with which they acquainted me and brought me to love.

Ah, the *cafés crèmes* and lightly buttered cakes of Montparnasse's La Rotonde! We spent hours there dismantling and constructing a better world. Dragui was one of us, of course! Others had done the same thing in that little smoke-filled café before us, as it was a gathering point for revolutionary youth.

Trotsky, for one, I had no doubt that we were going to get better acquainted.

What a splendidly fraternal ambiance!

When war was declared (in 1939), Vassia returned to Bulgaria; his sister, on the staff of a fashion house, was killed in an accident. Bouhov, it appears, met his end in Yugoslavia, at the hands of the Nazis. Itso and the others were making shoes and studying for a degree; Miloch, cousin to the king of Albania, was a law student and working as a sweeper for Borniol, always dressed to the nines. What became of you all? I lost track of you, but the memory of you endures and you have a place in my heart.

Our group included an excellent comrade, a good-looking boy who kept to himself and was a great admirer of the guys from the *"bande"* and for illegalists of every stripe. He worked at recovering weapons in the areas devastated by the war, places such as the Nord and the Somme.

He invited Dragui and me to spend a weekend in the little village where he was boarding. That evening, after supper, he brought us out to his work site. There were huge craters stacked with boxes of grenades, shells, and so on.

Climbing down into one hole, he opened a crate of grenades and, grabbing one of them, pulled the pin and hurled it far over our heads; it failed to explode. He had several more goes at this, opening a fresh crate each time. He slumped down on a crate in which the grenades were very dry and urged us to have a go at throwing them ourselves, after teaching us the procedure.

---

7 The bomb attack on St. Nedelya Church in Sofia was carried out by members of the Bulgarian Communist Party on April 18, 1925. Over 150 prominent officials and others were killed in the explosion and hundreds injured. Widespread round-ups of Communist Party members and other radicals took place and at least 450 people were executed without trial.

There was no danger of our being heard, as we were far from any housing, in a real wasteland. A Dantesque landscape where thousands of men had lost their lives.

As the comrade had brought a bag along, we packed it with a number of bone-dry grenades before heading back to the village to spend the night.

Dragui and I were loaded down like packhorses when we reached the Gare du Nord, carrying the famous grenades and clueless as to what use they might be put. But they could always serve some purpose.

Passing through the checkpoints (there was one in every station) was no bother, and the customs officials showed no interest in grenades.

Small though they may have been, these devices were very cumbersome; we were living in a hotel and keeping them in our room was out of the question. An elderly comrade, in whom we had every confidence and who really trusted us, agreed to store them at his little cottage and held them at our disposal.

One day, opening the newspaper, I spotted our arms-recovery comrade's name on the front page. He had attacked the cashier of a major daily newspaper in an attempt to seize his cash. But the cashier, a judoka, had subdued him and handed him over to the police.

Oddly enough, he showed up at the hearing as a defense witness, stating that the fellow had not had any intention of killing him, since he could easily have done so prior to being subdued.

Since his family did not want to hear tell of him, my friend Mado and I decided to take charge of him and, equipped with a visitor's pass, we took turns at going to see him in La Santé prison. An outstanding lawyer, Maître Berthon, agreed to defend him in criminal court where he was sentenced to a five-year prison term. He was sent to Fresnes and then to the penitentiary in Melun. His sister, who was living abroad, forwarded me her papers, and I was able to visit him while he served his time, except during my own trip to Russia, that is.

At the time, Gaston Rolland and Emile Cottin* were also being held in Melun. The former for having helped a deserter (who had then gone on to turn him in) and the latter for having shot at Clemenceau.[8]

---

8 Cottin had attempted to assassinate Clemenceau, president of France, on February 19, 1919 at the Paris Peace Conference. Initially condemned to death, his sentence was commuted to ten years imprisonment after a campaign for clemency spearheaded by *Le Libertaire*. Rolland's sentence to imprisonment in French Guiana for fifteen years was forestalled by a public campaign. His sentence was later commuted.

Every Sunday, we would meet up with the brothers of Rolland and Cottin at the station and contrive to synchronize our visits. That way, each of the prisoners got three visits in one.

5

MY TRIP TO THE USSR

We were too happy. It couldn't last!
Dragui's older brother, an officer in the Serbian army and military attaché in Germany, the man who paid for his studies and subsidized his every material need, somehow found out that Dragui was hanging out with anarchists and was very well known in those circles.

He sought him out in Paris and gave him an ultimatum: either give up on what he called his "craziness" and commit himself exclusively to studying or his allowance would be cut off. And he would have to manage for himself. There was a bitter argument between them. Dragui refused to give in to the blackmail. He would drop out of the university and find a job.

He was as good as his word. He was taken on as a laborer at the Renault plant. In the evenings, he would come home worn out, his hands all blistered.

Physically, he was up to it, albeit that he had never before done any manual labor. But the idea that he might not complete his medical degree was becoming more and more unbearable to him with each day that passed. He became bitter, aggressive, and distraught.

I could not bear to see him that way any longer. I could see how he felt torn. I was the one who urged him to back down. I wouldn't have wanted him to someday hold it against me that he had missed out in life.

His brother came to fetch him and took him off to complete his studies in Germany.

I was not there to see him go. I was in complete turmoil. I was torn. I was deeply in love with Dragui, and I lost him. It was awful to see the loss of his happiness! And he too was in despair. That he would have stood up to power or money, there is no doubt. But he just could not turn away from the profession he loved.

Separation did nothing to lessen his sorrow. He wrote me numerous letters that I returned without reading. I thought I would die. Then rebellion prevailed over grief. And I threw myself headlong into the struggle on behalf of our ideal.

I have never forgotten you, Dragui. . .

In 1922, the CGT held its National Congress in Saint-Etienne. I was there in my capacity as administrative secretary to the Metalworkers' Federation. The congress set the deal on the split inside the CGT and was marked by the birth of the CGTU.

There were two motions on the table: the motion tabled by Monmousseau* on behalf of the majority, "in favor of unconditional affiliation to Moscow's Third Trade Union International."

And the one tabled by Pierre Besnard,* representing the trade union minority, which demanded complete autonomy and utter independence in terms of administration, propaganda, the examination of organizational means in advance of any action and future struggle, and, finally, action itself.

The Monmousseau motion carried the day with 779 votes against 391. The majority endorsed affiliation, pure and simple.

However, Monmousseau was not formally a member of the Communist Party. Purportedly a free agent in his decision-making, he faithfully carried out the orders handed down by the CP, instructions to the effect that allegiance would be given to the Bolsheviks in Moscow.

At the national congress of the Metalworkers' Federation, the federal secretary Lucien Chevalier* was appointed to represent the Federation at the Moscow International Trade Union Congress (Profintern) and I was to go with him.[1]

---

1 The Red International of Labor Unions (Profintern) held its first Congress in 1921. May would attend the Second Congress held in November 1922 in Moscow, in conjunction with the Fourth World Congress of the Comintern.

The mandate from the Metalworkers' Federation was to oppose the CGT's affiliation to the Third Trade Union International.

I should point out that our comrades from the opposition line-up at the previous year's congress—Lepetit* from the Road Workers' Union and Vergeat from Construction—had "gone missing" at sea. Embarking on a wrong boat on the Murmansk peninsula, after having been held up in the USSR long after the other delegates had set sail (a ship had to be sent out to look for them, and that ship had never come), they were fated never to be seen again by us.

The poet and writer Raymond Lefèbvre,* a friend of Vaillant-Couturier and, like him, a communist (or perhaps he was no longer toeing the line?), was sacrificed, as was the interpreter, Sasha Toubin.[2]*

It was armed with a thousand recommendations from our comrades who came to accompany us to the railway station that we boarded our train. For instance, Pierre Besnard advised me, "watch your back, and count your fingers and toes." We were keen to learn what we were about to discover at the end of our journey as 1922 drew to an end.

Sharing our compartment were our good comrades Couture* and Lagache* from the Construction Federation, and we got along perfectly well together. Couture brought along a suitcase filled with victuals, including a huge ham, since we were on our way to a country where famine reigned. As for Lagache, he brought along some cocoa and sugar for the trip. I have to say that we really appreciated that beverage on the journey.

Since I had been refused a passport by the French authorities, for no particular reason, all I had on me was a pass, a safe-conduct note valid only as far as Cologne and issued by the police superintendent of my home district.

Of course, I did not alight in Cologne but continued on to Berlin. There, the Russian embassy blithely issued me with a Russian citizen's passport: I was a delegate.

In Berlin, I visited to some very well-known anarcho-syndicalist activists, including Rudolf Rocker, Augustin Souchy,* etc. I also

---

2 Jules Lepetit and Marcel Vergeat had been delegates from the CSR (Comité Syndicaliste Révolutionnaire) to the Congress of the Communist International that took place in Moscow during the summer of 1920. Openly unimpressed by what they saw in Russia and the nature of the Congress, the two, along with Raymond Lefebvre and translator Alexander Toubin, drowned on their way home. Their comrades argued that the Bolshevik authorities had put so many obstacles in their path to prevent them leaving Russia that they had been forced to hire an unsafe fishing vessel to get out of the country.

met up with Emma Goldman and Alexander Berkman (who I knew by their writing). Emma Goldman, who I will discuss later, and Alexander Berkman were both of Russian origin, although they had long been living in America, where they were very well known for their anarchist militancy. They had been deported from the USA to Russia along with some two hundred other Russians whose country was in the throes of revolution.

They had both just returned, disillusioned, from Russia even though they had been yearning for that revolution and, for hours on end, they told us of what they had seen and what they had experienced: the catastrophic situation in the country, most of their comrades shot, jailed, or deported to the camps that they had known under tsarist rule, in far off Siberia, whence they had been plucked to take part in the revolution. Famine, typhus, and counter-revolution. The peasants in revolt. The birth of the Cheka, established by Lenin, was responsible for the abrupt elimination, not just of the members of every party, but of workers, of those who would have given their lives for the revolution.

The terror enforced by the Bolsheviks who behaved like highwaymen "drunk on authority, channeling the Russian people's violent, spontaneous anarchy, and commencing a brand new bloodthirsty despotism," as Maxim Gorky had put it to them.[3] Homes raided day and night, people hauled away to who knows where, sentenced without trial, and never seen again. The dismal economic situation, the black market, the hunger-driven looting. . .

They had both witnessed the Kronstadt uprising, which they summed up like this:[4]

The Kronstadt garrison, plus the town's soviet, had stood in solidarity with the famished people of a strike-stricken Petrograd, which had run out of patience. On February 28 and 29, 1921, rumor had it that Kronstadt had been overrun by the Whites and that everyone should arm themselves and rush to its aid. But this was simply a lie by the official press.

The soviet and the garrison had drafted handbills that they distributed in the town. Their program was the following:

3 This appears to be from a conversation with Victor Serge reported in Serge's *Memoirs of a Revolutionary*.

4 Berkman's 1922 pamphlet, *The Kronstadt Rebellion*, had been published in Berlin by *Der Syndicalist*. He wrote a fuller account of his time in Russia in *The Bolshevik Myth* (New York: Boni & Liveright, 1925). Goldman also covered the events at Kronstadt in her book *My Disillusionment in Russia* (Garden City, NY: Doubleday, 1923).

Renewal of the revolution
Re-election to free soviets by means of secret ballot
Release of political prisoners
An end to requisitioning in the countryside
Abolition of the checkpoints that were preventing the popula-
tion from obtaining fresh supplies
Freedom for artisan production

And, finally:

Trade union freedom, freedom of speech and of the press for all
revolutionary parties and factions.

A delegation was dispatched to the Petrograd Soviet to brief the
populace there on what was happening. That delegation was thrown
into prison by the Cheka.

Emma Goldman and Alexander Berkman drafted a motion,
which they put to the "rebels" who adopted it unanimously; they set
up a meeting with Zinoviev,* and for two hours, Emma defended the
stance of the Kronstadters before the governing authorities; Emma
and Sasha were able to speak with some authority on behalf of a frac-
tion of the world proletariat. But they failed. They were advised to
"drop it" and were offered passage through Russia.

The sailors and the populace in Kronstadt sent a request for ne-
gotiations to the Politburo. In response, a poster phrased in these
terms appeared on the walls of the town: "Surrender or you will be
mowed down like rabbits."

The Red Army mounted attack after attack across the ice by soldiers dressed in white. The forts opened fire on the attackers, and
there was outright fratricide . . . The army secured the victory. Some
of the rebels fled to Finland, others fought on to the death. As they
perished, they cried out "Long live the world revolution! Long live
freedom!" Thousands of men and women were arrested and handed
over to the Cheka.

Those defeated belonged to the revolution body and soul. They
had articulated the people's suffering and will.

Trotsky bore the chief responsibility for this slaughter. And Lenin
allowed it to happen.

This was a short, too short, summary of the epic of Kronstadt.

Kronstadt is a dark page in the annals of the Soviet state! Not that there were not lots of others. The massacre of the Makhnovshchina, for instance! That evening in Berlin was a long one, but oh how intoxicating! It ended in the early morning. Friends handed me addresses and messages for what few comrades had managed to slip through the net of the Cheka (but for how long, alas!) and helped me to hide them among some old illustrated postcards that I managed to smuggle through.

This brought to my attention, in particular, the case of Mollie Steimer* and her partner Senya Fleshin,* who had lived in America and been among those people deported by the USA back to their countries of origin.

Both were members of the "Imprisoned Anarchists Support Committee," or Black Cross, which survived on donations from abroad, primarily from America. Their work consisted of delivering small food or clothing parcels to the prisons and certain camps.

This Black Cross had the consent of the government and was perfectly legal.[5] But one day, when in Arkhangelsk, they were arrested and jailed and then sentenced to deportation for life to the Solovietzky islands. A veritable hell, the islands consisted of a former monastery where Ivan the Terrible sent his supporters who had fallen out of favor and his adversaries. It had been shut down after the death of that tyrant. The Bolsheviks had reopened it for use as a holding center for "politicals," anarchists especially. The island was re-provisioned once a year, and most of the prisoners there died of scurvy.

I was asked if there was any way at all that I could lobby on their behalf and try to secure their release. I made a heartfelt promise that I would.

The trip was a demanding one, made over several days. After Berlin, we had to skirt Poland, crossing Lithuania, Latvia, and Estonia. Our first stop was Riga, a port on the Baltic where we were able to snatch some rest. The carriages in which we had made the long journey were ancient, with wooden benches, candles by way of lighting—and travelers who enjoyed even that luxury counted themselves blessed.

5 For the creation of the Anarchist Black Cross in Russia see B. Yelensky, *In The Struggle For Equality*, (Chicago: Alexander Berkman Aid Fund, 1958). (Note by M. Picqueray) [The organization was resurrected in England in 1967 by Stuart Christie and others, initially to provide support for imprisoned Spanish anarchists, before adopting a wider brief of supporting anarchist prisoners worldwide. —KSL]

We were stuffed in between huge bundles of laundry or blankets and male and female peasants, as well as whining, dead-tired brats. For where were these good folks bound? Those who alighted at stops along the way were replaced in an instant by others as heavily burdened as they were burdensome. The stink was unbearable, and loud snoring prevented us from getting a wink of sleep. Tired though I was! We managed to remain cheerful all the same. But we were eager to reach our destination . . .

After a night at the embassy and a generous breakfast, a few of us paid a visit to town. My preference was for the port area and, come noon, rather than heading back to the embassy for lunch, I invited my fellow strollers to join me for a fry-up at a shack frequented by the port's fishermen. The food was fit for a king, and the atmosphere very welcoming. We had no way of communicating other than by gestures, but there was human warmth aplenty and that did the job.

From Riga, we moved on toward Moscow. I ought to mention that it was freezing cold. We first encountered snow in Poland and, the further we traveled, the greater the chill we felt. We were dressed for warmth, but the carriages were unheated. My feet were unbearably cold. Luckily, from time to time, we had to alight from the carriage and, issued with spades, clear the tracks of snowdrifts! At every station, we were able to get ourselves some boiling tea or just some warm water.

Throughout the journey, there were magnificent forests of pine and birch, tiny villages blanketed in snow. I can't recall which town it was where we stopped to change locomotives and where we saw flocks of splendid geese, necks outstretched, and very much at ease among the passersby who, going about their business and so used to their company, paid them no heed.

And then we came to the Russian border.

There was a huge banner on display bearing this message:

Workers of the world, unite!

We had to alight and change trains and then pass through customs. I wasn't feeling any too confident, given the family photos I was carting in my bag, but they got through undetected. On the other hand, I was made to remove my boots (fine leather boots I had treated myself to in Berlin and had proven useless against the cold). They paid particular attention to the heels. These they removed. I never did find out what it was that they were looking out for. The comrade who searched me, after making me remove my hat, was very unpleasant and left me in a foul mood. I could not understand one damned word of whatever she was saying to me, other than *tovaritch* (comrade!), but her forbidding face was far from inspiring friendship, and I couldn't wait to be done with her. I had to insist before they handed me back my heels.

Next came the verification of our papers: obviously, and although Russian according to my passport, I stood like an idiot in front of the guard who asked me questions of which I could not understand a single word. He called for an interpreter, and after much ado, I was allowed to rejoin my comrades who were already sipping a reassuring cup of tea.

Couture sang out: "I'd much rather have a good glass of piping hot red!" A beverage unknown in that border canteen.

Some of our communist comrades seemed moved as they crossed the border. That I understood, as they were believers in all this. My own feelings tended more towards anxiety and a degree of fear of what lay ahead of us.

The revolution had sparked such enthusiasm, such high hopes of a better society! As far as we were concerned, this was the dawn of a new age that was going to radiate from Russia and flood the world. Certain anarchists, or anarcho-syndicalists, had let themselves be taken in by this and had joined the Communist Party (which, when all is said and done, was not as "rotten" as it is today). And discussions raged inside the groups and within the unions.

I should say that, like many others, I too believed that the "great day" had arrived over there. So why not back home? But I was and am still a libertarian. And I could not fathom why followers of Bakunin could have signed up to a party that followed his despised rival, Karl Marx . . . Fortunately, most of them quickly returned, having realized the error of their ways . . . But within the unions, the struggle was hot and heavy!

To make a long story short, we resumed our journey, bickering about that customs check that was barely distinguishable from any capitalist customs check.

And once more it was back into the splendid forests, snow-blanketed towns and villages, and heavy snowfall. . .

The French delegation (communists and syndicalists) was greeted with a degree of solemnity and then steered toward the hotels which had been set aside for us. My friends and I were assigned to the Lux hotel, which seemed comfortable. I shared my room with a Bulgarian woman and one from Turkestan, both communists. We might have gotten along very well, except that, every evening, they literally drove me nuts in trying to drag me along, unsuccessfully, to cell meetings somewhere that continued well into the late hours of the night.

On the evening of our arrival, all the delegations gathered in the Kremlin, a city within a city, in the grand ding hall of the tsars, in a sumptuous setting that defies description: gilded woodwork, huge mirrors, lights, chandeliers; the tables were laden with all manner of appetizers, and we reckoned they constituted our entire meal. Shortages and outright famine were raging across Russia at the time. We considered ourselves spoiled and tucked into the *blinies*, smoked fish, and other national tidbits. Imagine how dumbfounded we were when they then brought on the lavish servings of roasted meats, which I personally declined, as I had no appetite left. In my little head, I was thinking that this welcome meal was extraordinary.

The following morning, I stepped out with two friends and our "interpreter" and managed to slip away on some pretext in order to drop in on the Russian friends whose addresses Emma and Sasha had obtained for me during my short stop-over in Berlin.

The first was a literature teacher, as was his wife. They had no children. They were delighted to receive news from their "exile" friends in Berlin. They both spoke a pidgin French, but we managed to understand one another well enough. They were greatly moved upon reading the message I smuggled through. They let me in on a few of the details of their lives and how they were getting by. For instance, they were paid less than a workman at the Dynamo plant. And they were sometimes kept waiting for three months before they could access their wages. "But how do you manage to get by?" I asked them. "I do shoe repairs," he told me in what he intended as a jovial tone, but I could discern a blend of discomfort and sadness. They offered me the traditional *chai*, and I promised that I would be back with Lucien Chevalier in tow, taking the usual precautions to ensure that they were not detected and "bothered."

That same day, Chevalier brought me to the home of the brother of an engineer who lived on the outskirts of Paris, also an engineer himself, living in the heart of Moscow. We were welcomed with open arms. Then the children, a girl of fifteen and a boy of seventeen, both students at a technical school, showed up and, upon discovering that we were delegates, shook our hands effusively. They questioned us about life in the Communist Party in France, and when they found out that we were not communists but anarcho-syndicalist delegates, their faces dropped and, downing their tea quickly, they took their leave, wishing us a very chilly goodbye.

These two youngsters were members of the Communist Youth, and their devastated parents asked us not to call back, as they were in danger of being reported by their own children. To my astonishment, I found that this was apparently quite commonplace.

Besides, the couple who shared the apartment with them had not yet returned from work. It seemed vital that we should be off the premises before they returned. "Informers are everywhere," the father told us, "and we have to be wary of our own shadows, lest we be accused of anti-government activity and jailed."

That was a bad start. We had to be on our guard lest we create trouble for these good people through our visits.

So, what had become of the freedom for which they had fought?

The next day, there was the same gluttonous feast, again at the Kremlin, in gilded surroundings once tsarist but now communist!

Having a little insight into how the teacher and the engineer were managing for food, I bridled upon seeing the repetition of the previous day's meal. I clambered onto the table and, to the astonishment of those near me, although not of my comrades, who understood me well, I harangued the delegates who were gorging themselves, telling them how hateful it was that workers' delegates should be stuffing their faces when Russian workers were perishing of hunger. I described the circumstances of those whom I had visited, leaving out the details, of course, and I urged them to make do with meals more in keeping with their status and the circumstances of the country that was welcoming us.

A number of the delegates made their disapproval plain and shooed me away, not that I gave a damn. As for myself, I got up from the table, followed by a number of other delegates and friends who endorsed my opinion.

My outburst had caused a stir and attracted attention to little old me. I was kept under close surveillance and had to be doubly vigilant.

For instance, I could not set foot outside the hotel without being followed by an "interpreter" who was a member of the Cheka. They underestimated me. Again and again, I slipped through their fingers and carried on with my visits, alone or in the company of one or two comrades.

In this way, I came upon Nicolas Lazarévitch,* a mechanic who spoke impeccable French and was living underground. He pulled off the amazing feat of meeting up with us about ten times in his home, without arousing the curiosity of his neighbors. We chatted in a virtual whisper and left the house one at a time without drawing attention.

Nicolas provided us with priceless information and details about the lives of workers and intellectuals in the country. And about the rule of the incipient bureaucracy, the army and the police the new bourgeoisie, with their privileges, their very own food stores and rations provided by state cooperatives. To be honest, there was very little in the way of foodstuffs available: some hulled oats, herrings, a little sugar, all of which were accessible to workers. In the towns, there was hunger, cold, sickness, and typhus. In the countryside, requisitioning carried out by the army, which even seized seed and left the *muzhik* utterly bereft.

The trade unions were utterly subordinated to the party. Strikes were banned. Within the same trade, there was a wage scale reflecting the worker's productivity. The factory delegates, imposed by the party, and most of whom knew nothing about the trade, ruled over the workers like masters, spying on them and wielding the power of life or death over the worker, since they had license to insist that he be dismissed whenever they saw fit. Once let go, the worker also lost his accommodation and his dismissal, for a reason invented by his delegate, was recorded in his work card, making it all but impossible for him to find fresh employment. Consequently, he became a vagrant, liable to end up in a labor camp, wageless.

A number of us comrades had attended the election of a delegate at the Dynamo plant, a leading Moscow factory. He was a complete unknown to the factory workforce but was definitely a party member. The workers were asked to raise their hands to vote for the delegate. Every hand shot up. There were no votes against and no abstentions. Which came as something of a surprise to us.

"But," Nicolas said to us, "any poor wretch who might not raise his hand would have been dismissed on the spot, with all that that implies!"

An odd sort of trade union freedom!

We were appalled!

Nicolas Lazarévitch, who was a member of the "Moscow worker group," a minority faction that supported the independence of syndicalism from all political parties, while retaining the affiliation to the official trade unions, was arrested in 1924 and given a three-year prison term, a sentence commuted after two years to indefinite deportation. It took the intervention of the French anarcho-syndicalists to get that deportation order commuted to banishment from the country.[6] He came to France where, after trying his hand at a number of trades, he joined the proofreaders' union. Erudite and a very fine public speaker, he fought his whole life against the dictatorship of the proletariat and on behalf of freedom in Russia.

A few of us gathered together one evening at Victor Serge's* place. This was the very first time I had set eyes on him. (However, after his release from prison, after the Bonnot Gang affair[7] and prior to his departure for Spain, he had been living in Pré-Saint-Gervais, a mere fifty meters from me.) At the time, he was working with the soviet government and gave us the reasons why, as he later set out in his *Memoirs of a Revolutionary*:

> I would support the Bolsheviks because they were doing what was needed tenaciously, doggedly, with magnificent ardor and a calculated passion: I would be with them because they alone were carrying this out, taking all the responsibilities on themselves, all the initiatives, and demonstrated an astonishing strength of spirit. Certainly, they were mistaken on several essential points: in their intolerance, in their faith in stratification, in their leaning towards centralization, and administrative techniques. But, given that one had to counter them with freedom of the spirit and the spirit of freedom, it was among them. It could

6 Some accounts suggest that Lazarévitch may have been held in detention without charge. A campaign organized in France, primarily by the newspaper *La Révolution Prolétarienne* (Proletarian Revolution), led to his release and subsequent expulsion from Russia in 1926, after which he went to live in France.

7 For an introduction to the Bonnot Gang and Serge's role in their actions see Richard Parry, *The Bonnot Gang: The Story of the French Illegalists*, 2nd edition (Oakland: PM Press, 2016).

be, as it happens, that these evils had been impelled by civil war, blockade, and famine, and if we managed to survive, the remedy would come of itself.

There we have his very succinct answer to questions posed by his erstwhile comrades in ideas, startled to find him involved, even in the slightest, in a government that imprisoned and shot down anarchists.

Later, like many others, he acknowledged his mistakes.

The congress proceeded on its way, each delegation delivering its particular viewpoint on the matters raised and with more or less fire, depending on the trade union situation back home. Chevalier argued the position of the Metalworkers' Federation: trade union independence.

Most of the government leaders attended one or the other of the proceedings, some more regularly than that or more worried than the rest. Lenin alone put in no appearance, prevented from attending due to illness. We paid him a visit at his home: he was as lucid as ever and had all his critical faculties. I was rather impressed by this great fellow who had devoted his entire life to the realization of his ideal and had the courage to declare on a number of occasions: "It is a very great pity that the honor of launching the first socialist revolution should have fallen to Europe's most backward people." He pressed us on the situation back in France, and when he was asked about anarchists being imprisoned or shot, he told us that that was a necessary evil. Then, tiring and visibly spent, he summoned his wife, Krupskaya, who very kindly served us tea.

When the final session rolled around, the vote on affiliation to the Third International was due to be held. We were already aware that, insofar as the French CGT was concerned, the minority was facing a beating and that the Bolsheviks, headed by Monmousseau and Sémard, would win the day. They received a formidable ovation, whereas we, poor beaten curs, were leaving the hall with head held high, but with a heavy heart!

In the wake of the affiliation vote, the French trade union delegation was invited by the "old guard" to a private "get-together" in the Kremlin. Should we go, should we not go? It was our last chance to meet with the great figures who had fought under tsarist rule and who had made the revolution on behalf of what they believed to be "socialism" (and who all perished at the hands of that foul executioner, Stalin). We decided to go.

On arrival, I realized that the get-together was due to take place around well-appointed tables, which put me in a bad mood. I had sworn never to attend another banquet of the sort.

I was seated between Zinoviev and Lozovsky,* both of whom spoke passable French, especially Lozovsky who had attended several of our congresses in France and whom I had met previously in Saint-Etienne. I must admit, their conversation was light-hearted and colorful.

I let some of the courses go by, making do with the basics, and I explained the reasons why to my neighbors, which seemed to amuse them greatly. They suggested that I should spend some time in Russia. My answer was clear cut, dry, and categorical: I knew enough of what was happening there in regard to opponents (which I was) and that my Russian comrades (those who had not yet been shot) were rotting in the prisons or the camps, for life, and that were I to take them up on their offer, it would not be long before I shared the same fate. To this paradise, I would prefer republican rule with all its shortcomings, for there I could still speak my mind and fight on behalf of my ideal: anarchism.

After the meal, Trotsky called on me to give them a song "just like in France. After all, this has been a splendid meal among friends." Monmousseau came over to me and urged me to sing. They were no doubt expecting some love song or, at best, *l'Internationale*. This was one opportunity that I was not about to let slip! I did not need coaxing and, with all my heart, sang at the top of my lungs my old friend Charles d'Avray's *Le Triomphe de l'Anarchie*:

> Arise, arise, comrades in misfortune
> The time has come, we must rise up
> Let blood flow and redden the earth
> But let it be for our freedom!
> Standing still is going backwards
> The result of too much philosophizing
> Arise, arise, aged revolutionary
> And anarchy will triumph at last . . .

The face on the communists was a sight to behold. If they could, they'd have gunned me down on the spot.

But Trotsky had not flinched. He was even grinning. And he called out to me:

"See, comrade May? There is still freedom in Russia, since you were able to sing about anarchy in the Kremlin . . ."

To which I responded:

"Freedom for those who accept, who adapt, but as for the rest, it's off to the Butyrki [Moscow's prison] or the Solovietzky islands or elsewhere . . . My comrades Lepetit and Vergeat* were disappeared last year. Is there going to be a repetition of that feat?"

My comrades were terrified and wondered what was to become of me. Nothing could be ruled out. But I hadn't been able to hold myself back from shouting aloud what was in my heart. As to what was to come, we would see!

The communists sang the *Jeune garde* as a distraction.

Then there was some conferring between the Russians and their invited guests. Some delegates thought it revolutionary to take to the tsarina's bed with their boots still on. I said my farewells to my neighbors at the table and left with two pals. Pleased with myself but a bit anxious all the same, albeit I never let on!

Then it was time for the delegates to leave, each returning to his own country, by land or by sea. Having handed in my passport, I approached the Russian authorities for a fresh one, as promised. They made me call back day after day, to no avail. I grumbled, threw tantrums, but all in vain.

I would have to wait . . . maybe tomorrow . . . Given that his own papers were in order, Chevalier decided to stay behind with me until I received satisfaction.

I had not forgotten about Mollie Steimer and Senya Fleshin, serving life in the Solovietzky islands, and the promise I had made Emma Goldman back in Berlin.

To whom was I to turn?

The Cheka? Definitely not. I decided to ask for an audience with Trotsky "on an urgent matter." To my great surprise, a week later I was summoned to his office at the Kremlin. He was generalissimo of the Red Army by that point, in all his glory as Russia's No 2. I needed a witness. I asked Chevalier to go with me, none too sure that I would be leaving on my own two feet.

After screening by countless guards and trekked down long, wide corridors, I reached Trotsky's office where a guard ushered us inside.

There he was in a splendid white uniform, welcoming us with an icy courtesy.

I can't remember what color his eyes were anymore, but I have not forgotten his direct and harsh gaze. He rose to his feet, came up to us, and offered me his hand. Spontaneously, I thrust my hand into the pocket of my jacket and left it there. He turned to Chevalier and bade us welcome. Then he said to me:

"Unwilling to shake my hand, comrade May? Why would that be?"

"I am an anarchist, and we are divided by Makhno and Kronstadt!" I replied.

I was both blunt and imprudent. I was well aware of that, but I was acting on instinct upon finding myself face to face with this mass murderer. In an instant, I grasped the situation and was expecting the worst. Trotsky, smiling, took me by the shoulder and asked me to take my seat.

I told him the purpose of my visit and championed the cause of my comrades with all of the fire and heat of which I was capable. Having heard me out attentively, he sneered:

"You forget, comrade, that I myself was deported under tsarism . . . and, as you see, I still live . . ."

His abrupt tone unnerved me. I had a hard time maintaining my calm, and yet, had to . . . for the sake of Mollie and Senya.

Even so, I pointed out to him that if things had been so pleasant in Siberia, I could not understand why he had escaped from there.

"That was in order to make the revolution," he said.

I asked him if the anarchists who had been released and then shipped off to Siberia might not want to make the revolution themselves. And those who were still free . . . It might be better to cool their ardor than have them shot.

"I too am an anarchist," he claimed, "but the Russian people are an ignorant people. It is necessary to evolve, and, for that to happen, we must go through a transitional phase . . ."

"Which would last how long?"

"As long as it takes."

But he had not forgotten about the purpose behind our overture. "I will look into the files on these young people," he added.

"I'd really like to go to Arkhangelsk," I said. "Might I have a pass and a visiting permit?"

"We shall see about that."

Then he stood up. Our interview was over.

When leaving, I said to him:

"I would like very much to see my friends free before I leave Russian soil; could you, comrade Trotsky, give your word to do all in your power to see to that?"

"You are stubborn and . . . committed. As I have told you, we shall see about that. Au revoir, comrade May!"

Once again, he shook hands with Chevalier and then we left, none too convinced that our overture had succeeded.

I reckoned it would be at least a week before I had Trotsky's answer. I dropped by the office. My passport was still not ready.

Along with two comrades, we decided to travel out to Nizhny-Novgorod, a strange town, about which we had heard many things. It is an important port, but it is also renowned for its fur trade fair. We were able to tour a huge automobile plant, the equipment of which was very badly maintained.

There too we were able to see that the poverty was every bit as bad as in Moscow. In the shops, there were very few goods and queues were endless.

There was one amazing sight that I hurried to photograph: two guards on horseback escorted a boy of about ten years of age, dressed in rags and, on his chest, a wooden box dangling from a string around his neck and, inside that box, a few boxes of matches.

"Arrested and shackled for black marketeering," the interpreter told us. The sight was so grotesque that it might have drawn a smile, had it not been so pathetic! And we were in the land of freedom!

Snow was falling, and it was very cold: we headed back.

In the absence of the foreign delegations, there was a different appearance to Moscow. For instance, there was the long line of unemployed standing in the snow outside the labor exchange.

Thousands of abandoned children, the *bezprizorni*, carrying on them all of their earthly possessions, a bathing suit and ragged sweater, fill Moscow's streets. When you give them a crust of bread, they devour it, and some look as if they are about to pass out. They sleep wherever they can: in the doorway overlooking the embarkation dock, near Lenin's statue, or in the gutters or in cellars, anywhere they can find a space. How do they survive? On thievery and looting. And worse!

During the congress, there were only a few hundred of them around, and my comrades from the Construction Federation and I, who had just paid a visit to a rather well-appointed nursery, had put this question:

"Why, in a socialist country, are there so many children abandoned, perishing of cold and hunger? Shouldn't they be given priority?"

"There are children's homes," we were told by our interpreter, "very good and very comfortable ones where they are well fed, but they refuse to go there. They are too attached to their freedom!"

It struck me as bizarre that these children, in the midwinter, would rather freeze or starve to death when they had the option of some shelter.

I asked to visit one of the homes. But that was never feasible. Did they exist? I was told that, yes, actually, they did, but that the children there were mistreated and starving. So, they ran away to fend for themselves.

During the congress, they had had to be put out of circulation and were again thrown back on their own resources. I also found out that there was a very high rate of child offenders and that there was talk of shipping them off to the North, "to a settlement"... Poor kids!

At one point, me and some comrades were invited to visit the aerodrome. Decorations were being handed out that day. The hall was already packed by the time we got there. On the stage, delegates from every nationality were framed on each side by a soldier with his weapon at the ready. The proceedings opened with the inevitable *L'Internationale*, followed by a presentation address. Finally, there was a long-winded speech about an airman who was awarded a trophy and high praise. Then back to *L'Internationale*; it was rehearsed several times over. I had had enough by then and stood up, preparing to go outside. One of my Russian neighbors, who had spoken a few words in English to me during the proceedings, asked me if I had ever flown. No. Of course not!

He stepped outside, and I followed suit. He took me to a hangar where there was a number of small, two-seater aircraft, or "cuckoos." He must have been some sort of an officer: he issued orders to two soldiers who were there and they brought the plane out of the hangar and handed me sort of a bearskin (?) topcoat that smelled very strongly.

I clambered after him into the plane and once we had taken off he flew me over Moscow and its environs; there was some turbulence, the plane shuddered, and I felt nauseous. I don't mind telling you that I was very glad to be back on terra firma. All the same, I had the chance to marvel at the city of Moscow, ice-clad Moskva, especially the countless churches with their gilded and multi-colored domes.

And I had now been up in a plane!

In the hangar, we joined up with the delegates who, now that the proceedings had ended, were looking over the aircraft. Chevalier gave me a royal scolding over my escapade.

"What if something had happened! What if he had tossed you overboard?" What if. . . what if . . . ?

I was happy with my outing and safe and sound!

But, as you can see, there was not a lot of trust around.

Comrade Lazarévitch, with whom I had met up several times, was very pessimistic. He was not of the belief that comrade Trotsky would keep a promise that he had not actually made me. Not only would he not free our two friends, but I would not even be granted permission to visit them.

He was wrong.

I was issued with a pass for Chevalier and myself, plus an interpreter. I was out of my mind with delight. They were not free yet, but the wheels had been set in motion.

So off we went, bound for Arkhangelsk in a train with pretty rudimentary sleeping compartments. Our journey took three days. It was hellishly cold and about -50 degrees by the time we pulled into Arkhangelsk. I had swapped my leather boots for a pair of *valenki*, felt boots that made one's feet look like elephant's when they were pulled up over thick woolen socks, and exchanged my velvet hat for an astrakhan *shapka* that really protected my ears. A thick woolen scarf covered my lower face. My doubly lined rabbit fur coat was very warm. Only my eyes were left exposed.

We reached the Arkhangelsk camp by sled after downing a cup of very hot tea, as we were chilled to the marrow.

Our interpreter stopped us outside of a large, multi-story building. There was an armed guard on each side of the entrance. We had to present our papers to the guard post, then we were ushered into a big courtyard of huge red brick buildings, pierced by small square windows about twenty centimeters in dimension, furnished by bars. That, we were told, was where common law prisoners serving sentences of ten, fifteen, or twenty years were confined. There were armed guards at the entrances and police dogs kept a constant watch. We entered one of the blocks and found ourselves in a long corridor leading to a comfortable office; it too was well guarded.

A burly man, wearing glasses and a goatee, presided from behind a desk covered in papers. The shelves were lined with files. Two armed guards and a woman in a khaki dress, decorated with a red star, on her head a blue beret, were standing around the room.

As the interpreter explained the purpose of our visit, we were brazenly being weighed up by all these people. The exchange was taking forever, and the papers were painstakingly verified. Voices were raised. What was going on? On the instructions of the goateed fellow, the woman stepped outside. Had she gone to fetch our imprisoned comrades? We were left standing around for a time, then the woman came back and asked us to follow her. There was the same rigmarole in another office one floor down.

I questioned the interpreter who looked extremely uneasy. He knew nothing. We had to wait. This was not a good omen, and I felt anxious and losing patience.

After all the exchanges, the going back and forth, the interpreter told us that the prisoners were no longer in Arkhangelsk, but had been dispatched to Moscow the previous evening. I asked him to press the issue. We had our visiting permit and wanted to see Mollie and Senya. Nothing could be done. The staff member in charge did not so much talk as bark. He was emphatic: the prisoners were gone, and, without further explanation, he had us escorted back to the entrance gate.

We had enough time to spot in these corridors a number of small doors secured by huge padlocks and guards coming and going. A squad of about fifty men trooped into the yard. These men were coming back on duty. Some were wearing long capes in a somewhat sorry state and *valenki* tied to their trousers with scraps of cloth and cord. They looked frozen and in foul mood. Some women, in equally dire condition, carried huge cooking pots. Armed guards escorted both groups. The atmosphere was oppressive and I could not wait to leave this inhospitable place.

The interpreter told us that the men had to work in the nearby forests or on construction sites. Other squads showed up, in the same condition. That really got to me. I was beside myself, unable to speak or take action, and I was itching to get out of there. We sought shelter in a sort of a canteen where there was borscht and smoked fish, washed down by traditional tea.

And then we caught the first train bound for Moscow. What else could we have done? Other than get out of the sinister place where we had arrived with high hopes.

The stubborn rhythmic rumbling of the wheels started its noisy chorus that accompanied us throughout our entire journey.

The corridors were populated by Red Guards, most likely officers, children running and crying, and lots of civilians whose unbearable carelessness is revolting.

At times, the train slowed to less than twenty-five kilometers an hour. Throughout the journey peasant women arrived, hawking butter, eggs, and milk. What an odd uniform these women wore! A shabby *caraco* overlaid with woolen fabric, making them look like a tower.

There were young women, caught up in the demanding toil of laying track. Flat faces, snub-noses, slanted eyes, their Mongol ancestry was obvious in their features. Just like their male counterparts, they loaded stones onto some wagons, helping to shift a rail, checking the fishplate, securing anchor-plates. To them, equality at work was more than an empty phrase.

At stops, famished and frightened local children would turn out in search of whatever scraps they could get.

Samovar in hand, the passengers swooped on the man doling out the boiled water for the tea that they could not do without.

Our second night appeared to be uneventful. The snow was falling relentlessly. I was just dozing off when footfalls on the carriage roof piqued my interest. And then a volley of gunshots rang out. Frightened, people timidly opened the door to their compartments, while the fellow in charge of the berths darted outside. This is what had happened: an influential member of the Stalingrad central committee had dozed off . . . He had been so imprudent as to leave his window ajar. His overcoat, holding his wallet, was in use as a pillow. All of a sudden, it was snatched right from under him. He was just in time to see a hook skillfully harvesting his coat. The ingenious young thief was standing atop the carriage and, seeing a shadow flash by, had rashly opened fire.

Two hours later, one raincoat was gone and my bag very nearly went the same way. We had been urged to lock doors and windows, but a Russian man had opined a few hours earlier:

"No more thievery over here. What would be the point? Everyone can make an honest living. Thievery is peculiar to bourgeois societies where greed rules the roost!"

Alexander Berkman had told me that he had tied his briefcase to his ankle before going to sleep, by way of a precaution, but when he woke up, it was no longer attached to the cord.

As for me, an expert relieved me of my purse along with my delegate's card, both lifted from the pocket of my overcoat, and I had felt nothing.

"We take money wherever it is!" is the motto of all pickpockets, be they in Paris or in Moscow!

The most humane explanation I was offered came from a Russian worker.

"There are so many poor wretches without a thing!"

Was he right?

Back from our trip, worn out and disappointed, I headed for the Hotel Lux and found a letter there that had been left for me by a young boy. It was from Mollie and Senya. They were no longer in Moscow but in Leningrad, where they were under house arrest pending their departure for the West. For they had been sentenced to banishment. And banned from communicating with delegates. They asked me if I might come out and see them. Each day, they would be in X church at a given hour.

In agreement with Chevalier, we informed the interpreter that we wanted to visit Leningrad to see its museums. That request proved acceptable, and we were off on our travels. We again ran with the usual snow, ice, and cold. We had to be patient. It looked as if we were close to our goal. We passed through magnificent forests of snow-covered pines and birch trees. I took a few snapshots, even though the weather was scarcely suitable. We had to stop every so often, and men would dismount brandishing spades to clear away the drifts blocking the track. There was no shortage of tea and boiling water in the stations we were passing through.

On reaching Leningrad, off we went to book a room and have breakfast. At the hour appointed by my friends, I stood up from the table as if about to go to the toilet, leaving my overcoat on its peg.

Then, spotting an *isvotchnik* (sled-driver) at the door, I hailed him and got him to take me to the church, the name of which I had problems pronouncing. Fortunately, he was able to understand me and, seeing me so lightly clad, handed me a smelly old buckskin blanket in which I wrapped myself tightly against the very sharp cold. Having left my overcoat hanging on a peg, I was confident that the interpreter would not suspect I was off on an escapade . . .

I gestured to the driver to wait for me and stepped inside the church, still wrapped in my blanket. I walked around and stumbled upon the little duo standing in front of magnificent paintings that they appeared to be appreciating greatly.

I took a pew near them and struck up a conversation in English. I told them about my travels and my disappointment and how delighted I was to see them free. Their sentence had been commuted to banishment from Russia and their departure should not be far off. They seemed much affected by this. But surely such banishment was better than deportation to the Solovietzski islands? On that they agreed, but they were sorry to be leaving their comrades-in-arms behind, some of them in prison, others in the camps away in the North.

I had to leave them rather quickly, so as not to draw attention to them and expose them to other trouble. They clasped my hands and squeezed them tightly. "Bye for now! See you in Paris!" was our goodbye.

I did indeed meet up with them again in Paris a few months later. They had stopped over in Berlin to pay a visit to our comrades Rocker and others.

Once back in Moscow, we decided, after some rest, to visit the city that we had only viewed superficially. Then we met up again with our underground friends, taking huge precautions. Lazarévitch was delighted with our success. He had not been any too sure about it.

I was surprised to find a letter waiting for me at the hotel's office; it contained a poem that came from the Butyrki prison. It had been dropped off by a recently released prostitute. I stuffed the poem into my purse and had it translated on my return to Paris. In fact, my friend Marcel Body,* Bakunin's translator, translated this cry for help emanating from a prisoner, Féodorovna, who later died in prison.[8] She announced her delight to be freed in 1917 and to be able to

8 Marcel Body translated Bakunin's *Etatisme et anarchie* (Leiden: J. Brill, 1967).

take part in the revolution; then along came the Bolsheviks and her return to prison, her despair, like so many anarchists who shared the same fate:

"For the Anniversary of February 25, 1917"

I remember that day, freedom's great day
When, rising up, the humiliated slaves
Hoisted the banner calling for struggle
The struggle for life, happiness, and freedom
Ahead of the new dawn
The prison slept the sleep, laden with nightmares, of the martyr
Sans dreams, sans thoughts, sans luminous dreams
Amid the noise and clatter of rusty chains.

But lo, we hear the terrifying thunderclaps
Of the great storm . . . closer . . . clearer.
And the victory song of zealous men.
And the call to battle on the barricades:
"Save the prisoners—pioneers of freedom!"
Who were the first to tread the dark path to victory
In return for all those years of martyrdom
Let them see and pluck the ripe fruits.
And the prison collapses and the solid bolts
Creak, shatter, and the chains fall away,
And beneath the rays of a glorious dawn
The prisoners cast off their heavy shackles
O minute, o divine hour of freedom!
On every side, the free world, marveling, is overcome with joy.
I would have wanted to embrace the whole world.
But this is not the time for sentiment and meditation.
And the yoke of tsarism melts away: the broken thrones
Lie in bits in the dust.
Supports of power and of the crown, the prisons blazed
And the laws were burned in triumph
And the people rejoiced, drunk on freedom,
Celebrating the great victory day.
Already, we forgot vengeance for long years of torment
The liberated people forgives all its enemies.

And now five years have gone by since those great days
The gods and the tsars have changed several times over.
And the light from burning fires has long since burnt out
And days and nights become darker and darker:
The hurricane of bloody terror has blown
Not for freedom but for power and thrones,
Beneath the red flag that hides infamy
And on this anniversary day,
I languish once more in the shadows of the prison
And for me it is so hard and bitter, yes bitter,
That once again reign other masters,
That once again death stalks the prison.
That once again rights and freedom are trampled underfoot '
And that the groans, the deep groans of a people bereft of rights,
Fill Greater Russia as they did in bygone times.

—Féodorovna
Written in the Butyrki prison,
Moscow, February 28, 1922

6

BACK IN PARIS

My passport arrived at last. This time it was a British one. A passport valid for two people: husband and wife. This was nonsense, since Chevalier did not speak a word of English, but there you have it, and there was no point hanging around for anything else. So, I accepted it.

We bade farewell to the friends we were leaving behind in Moscow, in a very dire situation, happy to have secured the release of Mollie and Senya. Happy to leave Moscow and return to France to carry on the fight.

We were issued with tickets for Warsaw. At the station, we bumped into a small squad of delegates who had had their own problems and, like us, held made-up passports. We traveled together as far as Warsaw.

On arrival there, we were directed to the Russian embassy where they served us tea and sandwiches and cakes. Then Chevalier and I were driven to the station and issued with tickets for Berlin.

This train was comfortable and had berths. Farewell to candle-lit wooden carriages! We had the compartment to ourselves and we settled down for the night. Goodbye, candlelit wooden wagons! Very shortly after the train pulled out, I started to have stomach cramps, nausea, and cold sweats. Really, this was not going well at all! I made for the toilets. On my return to the compartment, I discovered Chevalier in the same condition as me, pale and clutching his stomach with both hands. Obviously, we had no medicine likely to ease our plight. All night long it was trips back and forth in the carriage.

"Bastards!" Chevalier was saying. "What did they feed us?"

To which I replied:

"Maybe they poured something into our tea!"

What a night!

But in the end, we were still alive and kicking!

It took two or three days in Berlin before we were back in form.

I had to go to the Russian embassy to pick up a new passport, as the British one was only valid as far as Berlin. There I was issued with a safe conduct pass like the one I had used on the outbound trip, but that one had been genuine, whereas this one . . .

We were also handed train and berth tickets as far as Paris. The train was an international service, packed with passengers. Our adventure in Warsaw ought to have left us wary, but poor innocents, good "apples," it never occurred to us that we would be played here as well.

The trip went swimmingly as far as the French-Belgian border, where there was no checkpoint.

But after that, there was a change. In Jeumont, two plain-clothed policemen strode directly to our carriage, then to our compartment, checking the numbers and the berth numbers against the copies they had. We were told to collect our luggage and alight. They took us to the police post at the station to check our papers.

Slick, well-coordinated work. I was accused of traveling on a phony pass of safe conduct. Which was the truth. As for Chevalier, when he was searched, he was found in possession of the phony British passport that he had been careless enough to hold on to rather than destroy back in Berlin, as he should have done. And now here we were in the "slammer," each in a cell of our own. And it was still freezing cold! Naturally there was no way of grabbing some shut-eye because, not only was it freezing, but the cell stank, the mattress was vile, and I was afraid of catching lice.

In the morning, we were offered a cup of foul coffee, then taken to the prison in Avesnes-sur-Helpe and each of us placed in a different block. The director allowed us to order in our meals from an inn near the prison, and the rabbit served with prunes that they brought me seemed delicious. Nevertheless, I was still not over the trick that had been played on us. Who had fingered us? Who had supplied them with our berth numbers? Much obliged, my dear "*cocos*" (commies), for all your attention!

On arrival at the prison, I was placed in a filthy shared room, into which were packed about twenty women of all ages, whose work was to stitch millers' sacks: the flour and the dust made them look like clowns. The air was unbreathable.

I carried out a quick survey: convicted and remand prisoners were thrown together to save resources. That meant using one stove-heater instead of two, as there was a second room for "remand prisoners" awaiting trial, and it was clean and led into a tiny garden. I made a request to the director, who granted it immediately: that other room was opened up, light was set to the stove, and three or four of the women joined me there; a young maid who had stolen some trinket from her mistress, and some smugglers, mothers, repeat offenders who had been on their way to Belgium to buy their coffee and ... tobacco.

Our comrades from the Federation came to visit us and brought us some newspapers carrying the reports from those attending the congress. We were visited, not in the prison, but in the criminal court where we were found guilty: Chevalier got a three-month prison term and I (what was the difference?) forty-five days' imprisonment.

Time drags in prison. They had actually offered me some work: making flowers for funeral wreaths. It seemed an easy task: stringing pearls on some iron wire. But we had to break the wire using our fingers as the prisoners had no access to wire-cutters.

I decided to give it a go ... One day of this "work" was enough for me, my fingers were bleeding. Besides, one had to build up a certain rhythm.

Not being under any obligation to work, I handed in my apron.

To occupy my time, I turned to the prison library. But the books were unsuitable and repulsively dirty. They were illustrated with obscene graffiti, which had nothing pleasant to offer.

Every day I used to make several circuits of the garden, humming away in mechanical fashion. On this particular morning, the chief guard overheard me and banned me from singing.

"And those little birds yonder, can you ban them from singing too?"

"For insolence," that remark earned me four days in solitary, to which I was removed immediately.

The isolation cell held only a board with no mattress or blanket. The sole window was broken, and the breeze, freezing at that time of the year, was getting in. They removed my "civilian" clothes, which I had held on to up to that point, and I was issued a loose cotton blouse that reached to my ankles and a home-spun habit of no particular color. I must have been a sight in that get-up. Hopping mad, I started singing at the top of my lungs, rehearsing my entire revolutionary catalogue. What more could they do to silence me? Fit me with a muzzle?

The meals sent over from the inn were knocked on the head and replaced by half a bread roll and a pitcher of water. I did not take kindly to this and skipped them. I decided to go on strike and, without touching them, piled up the bread rolls as they arrived. On day two, I had to stop myself from nibbling on the bread. It might have been stale, but my stomach was rumbling! On day three, I was feeling a little feverish . . . and was feeling cold. What wouldn't I have given for a blanket! I cursed the chief guard and resented the whole of humanity.

But I held firm.

On day four, the chief guard himself showed up with a very greasy bowl of soup with a cabbage leaf floating in it. He teased me by offering me the bowl like I was a dog.

"Good soup today! Good sou-soup!"

I asked him to set the container on the floor and relieve me of his presence. The moment he set it down, I kicked it over and the liquid got all over his trouser leg:

"That's what I think of your soup!"

He grabbed me by the neck, despite my kicking, and told me:

"Get out. You're free. But what a stubborn sow!"

I told him to mind about his manners and, once back in the hall, I ordered a bowl of bouillon fetched from the restaurant, best bouillon I've ever had. Then I settled back into a more comfortable regime.

Next day the chief warder had me brought to his office and asked me if I would take charge of the library and draw up a list of books to refresh the stock. Of course, only a few of them turned up. I had time to read them all before I was discharged from prison.

On the day I left, I met the Procurator of the Republic, who walked up to me and asked me how my stay in the prison had gone.

He offered to carry my luggage (!) and traveled with me to the railway station, where he himself was going!

Chevalier had managed to get one of the guards to pass me a little note wishing me a good trip back: he still had half his sentence left to serve.

In a few hours, my travels would be over: I had started out enraptured, in the company of comrades, with a glimmer of hope in my heart, and now here I was ending it, alone in the corner of my compartment, thinking back on days spent among people who, even having made the revolution, were impoverished and wretched and living every day in fear of losing what little freedom they had left.

I thought of all my anarchist comrades who had been arrested, tortured, shot. Of the ones dying a slow death in Siberia, in the Far North, in Solovietzki. I thought about the horror of the totalitarian machine, which grinds down the individual, and about the system whereby the power of decision-making over an entire people is concentrated in the hands of a few.

My trust in man had been somewhat shaken. I was sad! Things would get better. We had to fight on for an ideal in which we had placed all our trust, all our hearts, all our faith.

What a joy it was to be back on the Parisian asphalt after those months away! And back among comrades! I was bombarded with a thousand questions. They wanted to know all . . . And Besnard said to me: "You minded your Ps and Qs and now here you are, back again!"

Then it was back to work at the Federation, pending the return of its secretary who was moldering in prison.

Several groups asked me to tell all about the trip. Others had done so before me. Chazoff* who represented the jewelry-makers' union, for one, but he had been over there only for a very short time and had only seen one side of the coin. . .

During my time in Avesnes, I had often felt nauseous and chalked that up to lack of fresh air and poor living conditions. I decided to go see a doctor who told me what I already suspected somewhat, that I was pregnant. Due to various circumstances, my close friendship with Chevalier had turned into a loving partnership and the results of that were about to make themselves felt.

Having read my Malthus* and the newspapers and pamphlets of our good friends Jeanne and Eugène Humbert* and the works of

Marestan* and G. Hardy,* I could have resorted to an abortion, which would have been a very easy option for me. But since the child was there, I would keep it and raise it on my own. For me, it was an immense joy and a great experience. Besides, the opinion of the "father" barely mattered: he was not free and already had one child. I had no intention of doing anything to wreck that home, even if it was already under strain. But that was no concern of mine. Besides, later on, he found my decision perfectly acceptable and we remained close friends.

I went into labor one Saturday evening while I was at Charles d'Avray's "Grenier Gringoire" along with several friends. The elderly pianist was retiring and lots of singers had turned out to say their farewells and the evening dragged on forever.

I wanted to hold on for as long as possible, but the contractions were accelerating and I stood up to go.

"Stay with us," my friends said.

"I'd love to, but I can't. I have to be off to bring a child into the world!"

There were great cries of joy, and they escorted me all the way to the nearest hospital, the Lariboisière, singing all the while.

Sonia was born at five o'clock that Sunday morning into jovial surroundings, as the intern, a cheerful lad, was forever cracking jokes and, despite the pain, I refused to be outdone. How beautiful my daughter was, and how I loved her even then!

I gave up my job with the Federation and started working from home, which allowed me to focus entirely on the baby and to meet our needs. The Italian comrades with their newspaper were a big help to me.

I was still active, albeit I avoided dragging the baby into rough spots, but at demonstrations, one often saw a little girl in golden curls perched on the shoulders of my comrades who, by the way, adored her.

She was only a few months old when our friends Poncet* and Clot[1]* were murdered in Grange-aux-Belles. I had left her fast asleep in her little bed, intending to pop out for just a few minutes, and I almost failed to return.

The battle between the "bolshies" and the anarcho-syndicalists was at its height. On January 11, 1924, there was a meeting at the

---

1 This was in fact Nicolas Clos who was a member of the minority tendency in the Metalworkers' Union.

Grange-aux-Belles. Sonia was calmly asleep (as a rule she slept the night through and did not stir until the early hours, but I rarely left her and, then, only for short periods). I was going to poke my head in out of curiosity, as a neighbor. The supposed topic of the meeting was anarcho-syndicalism.

At the door, I bumped into Bernard, secretary of the glove-makers' union. He was wearing his great black hat and his cape. He was no longer young. In his sixties, maybe? There was no way of telling. Up on the platform, "Captain" Treint[2]* was spouting his bile and launching into a violent attack on anarcho-syndicalists.

All of a sudden, a voice rang out from the rear of the hall, near the rostrum, a voice I knew well . . .

"Long live anarcho-syndicalism!" followed almost immediately by a cry for help:

"To me, comrades!"

It was Boudoux,* a militant from the SUB. The youngsters guarding the rostrum swooped on him with fists flying.

Followed by Bernard, I made a beeline for where the brawling was, pushing aside all in our path. We found about fifteen comrades in that corner and managed to pull Boudoux free. Using the front row seats, whose occupants we shooed away, we threw up a barricade and from the top of that fought back against the young guards wielding batons. I came empty-handed; but I took off my leather belt, wrapped it around my fist, and took my place in the brawl.

Close to me, a big guy dressed in corduroy velvet and wearing a cap was swinging punches. I caught sight of Lecoin, Chevalier, and other familiar faces.

Abruptly, Treint was heard ordering the young guards to stop fighting.

"Stop! That will do!"

The young guards scattered and, from the podium, shots rang out and whistled past our ears.

There was panic in the hall as people raced for the exit or milled around; there were broken chairs and smashed glass. It was not a pretty sight.

Over in our corner we took stock. There were about fifteen of us. Some comrades were stretched out on the floor. All of a sudden,

---

2 "Captain" Albert Treint was at this time General Secretary of the Communist Party.

Poncet, known to us as "the plumber,"[3] slumped next to me along the wall (a draft-dodger, he was living under an assumed name, and it was only after he died that I found out his real one).

I patted his cheek, thinking that he had taken ill.

"I'm hit, May . . ."

I could not see anything. I opened his jacket; over his belt, blood flowed . . . He had taken two bullets in the belly. Then he slumped over to the side. He was quickly ferried out to the dispensary in the courtyard and, given the seriousness of his condition, an ambulance was fetched from the Saint-Louis hospital, a couple of steps away. He died overnight.

Clot, the big guy in the cap who had been near me while the brawling was going on, had made a bolt for the rostrum from which the shots had emanated. On reaching the foot of it, he too collapsed, killed by a bullet fired from above that penetrated his cap and then his skull. His body was to be removed by the police shortly afterwards.

Other comrades had sustained wounds. Charlot,* concierge of the CGT hall in the Avenue Mathurin-Moreau, a one-time steel erector, who already had a limp from an accident at work, took a bullet in the thigh. We evacuated the wounded and argued heavily about what had just occurred.

Their dirty deeds done, T[reint] and his acolytes had left the hall in the midst of the confusion. The hall was cordoned off by the police when they arrived, with a superintendent at their head.

The following day, *L'Humanité*[4] [*Humanity*] gave its version of events and accused the anarcho-syndicalists of having turned out in force to sabotage the meeting and of having used firearms against them. Unfortunately for them, and according to the investigation, the only bullet markings found were in the corner where our comrades had been huddled, and they were all at head height.

Some of us were summoned before the Police Judiciaire (they tried to get me to provide the name or names of the shooters, to which end they tried all sorts of stratagems). It was not my place to turn anyone in. Let the culprit or culprits turn themselves in. Let them have the courage, or let the police do their job and unmask them. No one was ever arrested and no charges ever brought.

---

3 Adrian Poncet was a member of the Union Anarchiste.
4 The newspaper of the French Communist Party from 1920 onward.

I used to cross paths with one of the shooters virtually every day and I called him a murderer. He did not react, but did he feel remorse? It looked to me as if his hair was turning white.

It was not only in Russia that the Bolsheviks were killers!

With consummate cynicism, a delegate from the CP went to see the Clot family, gave his side of the story, and the CP held a magnificent funeral for Clot . . . this after murdering him!

It was all about saving face!

I received a telegram from Emma Goldman and Alexander Berkman. They were coming to Paris for a time and were keen to meet up with me. At their request, I booked a room for Emma in the Place de la Sorbonne and another for Alexander (we all knew him as Sasha) in the Rue Royer-Collard near the Luxembourg gardens.

Emma only stayed forty-eight hours, as she was expected to give a series of talks in England. Sasha had a lot of work. He asked me to spend a few days helping him out with the drafting of his *Memoirs*. I felt greatly at ease with this kind, generous man who carried inside him the stigma of the fourteen years he had served in prison.

Contrary to what I read about him later, about the pessimism that is supposed to have prompted his suicide, Sasha was a playful character and very agreeable to be around. We often dined in one of two restaurants facing his hotel, one Russian, the other Polish. Musicians and Russian singers used to drop by and enlivened our meals. And Sasha could be found humming the traditional tunes they played.

He had a visit from a young Russian-American shirt-maker who was off on holiday to Israel. That was the excuse for a few comrades to gather over some borscht in a restaurant in the Rue Racine; we were joined by Mollie, Senya, and Schwartzbard,* who had a small jewelry and watch shop in the Boulevard de Belleville.

We were chatting happily over lunch when a gang of men burst noisily into the restaurant: their loud voices attracted the attention of the customers. All of a sudden, the blood drained from Schwartzbard's face; he had just recognized the erstwhile *ataman* of the Ukraine among the group. This was Petliura,* who had been behind many bloody pogroms against Jews and who had made his reputation with countless murders, rapes, and looting. Fifteen members of Schwartzbard's family had been hanged on Petliura's orders.

He returned to the restaurant the following day, but this time, Schwartzbard was armed; and so, on May 25, Petliura was gunned down by Schwartzbard, intent on avenging his loved ones. Seriously wounded, Petliura was rushed to the Charité hospital where he was dead on arrival. Schwartzbard was hauled up before the Paris criminal court on October 18, 1925, and his trial lasted a week. Monsieur Henri Torrès mounted a brilliant defense. It was one of the most celebrated trials of the age.

Numerous personalities testified on Schwartzbard's behalf, such as Séverine, the countess of Noailles, Maxim Gorky, Joseph Kessel,* Professor Langevin,* Victor Margueritte,* and they all exposed the pogroms and Petliura the murderer.

At the time of his trial, Schwartzbard declared: "I am content to have done what I did. I avenged my people and killed a murderer!"

He was acquitted.

7
MY SAINT-TROPEZ!

Emma Goldman and Alexander (Sasha) Berkman were to be an important part of my life from then on. While not yet personally acquainted with them, I already admired them tremendously and knew all about their past activities. But it is right that you should know more about them.

Emma Goldman, for starters. The daughter of Jewish small merchants, she was born in Russia in 1869 and studied in Petrograd. In 1886, she left Russia to join her sister in America, where she started out as a confectionery worker. In New York, she quickly became caught up in the workers' movement, which at the time was in the midst of agitation on behalf of the eight-hour day.

She met up with some anarchists, including a German outlaw by the name of Johan Most, a very well-known militant and outstanding public speaker who, finding Emma extraordinarily receptive, took charge of her revolutionary education. A born orator herself, she gave lecture tours and fought ardently for women's liberation.

It was at that point that she made the acquaintance of Alexander Berkman, a Russian like herself, and became his partner. In 1892, during the lock-out at the Carnegie ironworks in Pittsburgh, she stood by her comrade's action when he shot and wounded Frick, the manager of the foundries who had ground hundreds of workers into poverty.

Sasha Berkman received a twenty-two-year prison sentence for that act. He would not be released until 1902. Emma struggled for fourteen years for his release.

She was to sample America jails several times herself, as her energy and relentless dynamism in defense of human rights turned her into a fighter of the first order. She collaborated with a range of anarchist newspapers—like *Freiheit [Freedom]* and *The Anarchist*—and launched an anarchist review of her own, *Mother Earth*.

During the First World War, she fought with all her might against militarism and American entry into the war: she served a further two years in prison.

The outbreak the Russian Revolution roused all sorts of hopes in revolutionaries across the world. Hers was a generous spirit but dangerous to the capitalist world: America deported over two hundred "agitators" back to their countries of origin. The convoy bound for Russia included Emma Goldman and Alexander Berkman.

Swiftly disappointed by what was going on in their homeland— the complete absence of freedom, the backlash against tried and tested revolutionaries, the extermination of workers and sailors in Kronstadt, the extermination of anarchists—Emma and Alexander left the country after numerous difficulties. Emma set off on lecture tours across Europe and Canada.

Our two friends settled in Saint-Tropez.

Alexander Berkman was born in Vilna on November 21, 1870 and arrived in America at about the same time as Emma.[1]

Immediately after his arrival, Berkman integrated anarchist circles in New York, made up mostly of German and Russian émigrés. He followed the teachings of John Most, which were very close to the ideas of Kropotkin.

Then he ran into the woman who would at first be his companion and, then, his life-long comrade-in-struggle. Emma Goldman was Jewish and Russian, as he was. They lived in common with Helen and Fedya (two anarchists). They parted company from Most and joined the Autonomy group.

There was much talk about the Homestead affair: steel magnate Carnegie had made up his mind to liquidate the metalworkers' trade

---

1 Berkman arrived in the United States on February 18, 1888. Goldman had arrived there on December 29, 1885.

union with its several hundred members in his plant. And then to slash the pay of skilled workers. The workers would not agree to these plans and went on strike. The manager, Frick, promptly ordered a lock-out and called upon the police, who sent him three hundred armed officers. The workers armed themselves as well: when the police approached the plant, they were greeted by sustained gunfire. Many were wounded on both sides: seven dead for the workers, three for the police.[2]

Emma and Sasha were monitoring developments closely. On her return from work, Emma handed Berkman a newspaper that read: Pregnant women cast into the streets by sheriffs, strikers' families evicted . . . They looked at each other and were of one mind: something had to be done.

"I have to get to Homestead," Berkman said.

And they set about raising the cash needed to buy a gun and his fare.

Eight thousand National Guardsmen entered Homestead. Workers were hunted down. Martial law was instituted and two thousand scabs began work in the plants. Of the four thousand workers employed there previously, only eight hundred were to be rehired. The union was decimated.

Berkman managed to get inside Frick's office and to shoot at him, wounding him only lightly. Immediately seized, Berkman was handed over to the police.

When Berkman was taken to court, he declined the services of an attorney and wanted to present his own "defense," turning it into an indictment against society and against exploitation of the people. The judges refused to hear him and sentenced him to twenty-five years in prison.

He was to serve fourteen of those years in Pennsylvania prison. What he was to endure over those fourteen years is indescribable. He was to be freed on April 19, 1905 and reunited with his comrade Emma and some of his former comrades-in-struggle who had supported him during his long lonely days.

Upon his release, he found things different than they had been, and one of his good friends explained to him:

"We are the same as before . . . only made deeper and broader by years and experience. Anarchism has cast off the swaddling bands of

---

2 May's account of the events at Homestead is a little awry, leaving out the role of the private Pinkerton Detective Agency and other matters. For a detailed account of events there see Alexander Berkman, *Prison Memoirs of An Anarchist* (Chico, CA: AK Press, 2016).

the small, intimate circles of former days; it has matured and become a factor in the larger life of Society. . . the philosophy of Anarchism is beginning to pervade every phase of human endeavor. . . Even in this socially backward country, the seeds sown are beginning to bear fruit . . . a great inspiration to renewed effort."[3]

And Berkman, gradually returning to life, resumed his fight on the people's behalf.

When revolution broke out in Russia, Berkman, Emma Goldman and about two hundred Russian nationals were shipped back to Russia. They debarked there with hope in their hearts, but little by little they witnessed the revolution falling short; their anarchist friends jailed, banished to Siberia, if not shot out of hand. They witnessed the rebellion of the workers and sailors of Kronstadt and saw them massacred. Their intercession with the new masters came to nothing. They left this country that had become so inhospitable and sought refuge in Germany, then in France, where Berkman made a living from his writing and drafted his memoirs. He died in Nice in 1936.

I met Sasha Berkman and Emma Goldman in Berlin in 1922, and I had dealings with them right up until they died. Contrary to what the [French] translator of Alexander Berkman's memoirs claims,[4] when he portrays him as an "anarchist leader,"[5] Sasha never "surrendered politically." He remained an anarchist until his death. Characterizing him as a "die-hard" is quite gratuitous; as to his "ineffectiveness," that remains to be proven.

What is true, on the other hand, is that a huge number of pages were dropped from his book and that the translator's paragraph below is an entirely baseless view, at which Alexander's friends cannot help but bridle:

The mythology of those who would like to inject conscious-ness into *the proletariat carries connotations all too obvious to minds like ours* (de)formed by psycho-analytical suspicion for there to

---

3 These words are spoken to Berkman by "Philo" (probably Max Baginski, German revolutionary anarchist and member of the Mother Earth Group). They are from *Prison Memoirs Of An Anarchist*, 451.

4 The first French edition of *Prison Memoirs* made it into print in 1977 as *Mémoires de prison d'un anarchiste* (Paris: Presses de la Renaissance). It was translated by Hervé Dénès, who was rather cavalier in his translation. He omitted one chapter of the original and words, sentences, and paragraphs, are also left out throughout the text. His introduction to the book, from which May quotes, is none too complimentary toward Berkman.

5 There is no such thing. (Note by M. Picqueray.)

be any need to say more. Which is why this present edition is harmlessly seasoned with certain refrains about the Cause and a few letters that duplicate those which feature here. It is not a matter of locking Berkman a second time into some interpretive discourse. Let us say simply that this book is primarily an account of the gradual softening of an ideological and character armor. By the end of his memoirs, when he is freed, Berkman stops writing the word people with a capital P.

Completely absurd!

But let's find the two of them again in Saint-Tropez.

They had rented a small cottage there, lost in the midst of the greenery, on a hillside, where the view encompassed the entire gulf and the coastline as far as Saint-Raphaël.

In those days, Saint-Tropez was both a fishing village and business center, and lots of *"tartanes"* (boats) with bright-colored sails filled the port, shipping sand (from Pamplona), salt (from the islands off Hyères), and wine from the hills above and around Saint-Tropez.

Each day, the fishermen with their strong accents landed generous catches, which they hawked in the old fish-market.

It was a small village where the living was easy and basic.

Besides the natives, a quiet English clientele turned up for a short while in the wintertime. The only hotel in the port not being plush enough for their liking, they would stay in Beauville or in La Croix-Valmer.

From time to time, a yacht would anchor in the port—belonging to Vanel or the Prince du Ligne—and that was pretty much it.

There were painters, like Dunoyer de Segonzac, Luce, Manguin, and Signac.

Writers such as Colette, staying at *La Treille muscatel*, Lichtenberger, Vildrac, Joseph Kessel, etc.

Moviemakers like René Clair,* Valentin, and a few performers would winter there.

Paul Poiret bought the dyes for his dresses there.

It was a far cry from the nonsense that has turned the adorable little port into one of the biggest brothels in France!

Three Americans—Barry Jackson, Arthur Leonard Ross, and Mark Dix—came to Saint Tropez to spend a few days with Emma and Sasha, and made them a gift of three thousand dollars to buy the cottage that was baptized *Bon Esprit*, so that this eternally wandering couple from "nowhere," as they were known, might have a roof under which to rest and seek refuge.[6]

Emma, beginning to write her memoirs, set to work on *Living My Life* and asked me to work with her and one of her friends and to type up the manuscripts.

Working alongside her was fascinating, although she could be difficult; the life of this woman, this feminist, anti-militarist, and anarchist radical, was genuinely extraordinary and so very rewarding.

That task took six months.[7] Sasha Berkman revised the whole thing, making various amendments and corrections.

Lots of friends dropped by to visit them: Eugene O'Neill, Upton Sinclair, Rebecca West, Frank Harris, Eleanor Fitzgerald . . .

And then one day whom should I see debarking but my friends Mollie and Senya.

Mollie and Senya, who had set up a photography studio in Paris, were invited down to Bon Esprit for a "vacation." On that occasion, I asked them to drop in on my concierge and pick up any post that might have been left for me.

Let me digress here to say that the comrade jailed in Melun had returned to me, having read them all, the books I had had sent directly to him by the publisher. And, along with some letters and newspapers, they found a parcel of books from the prison, forwarded on from Melun prison by a "leaver."

I took careful note of all this and arranged the books, about which there was nothing untoward, on top of the chest of drawers in my room.

Yet, in the early hours one morning, two plain-clothed policemen showed up to search the premises: this concerned me personally. They spoke to me about the famous books, had I taken delivery of them? And so on. When I pointed to them on top of the chest of drawers, they leapt upon one of them, a hard-backed English grammar, and, mad with joy, waved it under my nose:

6 In fact, quite a few people gave Goldman money to purchase Bon Esprit. As well as Ross (her lawyer), others such as Peggy Guggenheim, Theodore Dreiser, and Van Valkenburgh (editor of the anarchist journal *Road To Freedom* under the pseudonym Walter Starrett), provided the funds necessary to buy the property in 1928—where she wrote her autobiography, *Living My Life*. Berkman lived in St Cloud, a suburb of Paris.

7 Goldman began work on her autobiography in 1928, completing it in 1931. *Living My Life* was published in two volumes by Alfred A. Knopf in 1931.

"Do you know what you have there? A treasure! A real treasure!"
Taken aback, I replied jokingly:
"Really? I didn't know I had a treasure in my possession. But what's this all about?"

They refused to let me in on the "secret," and it turns out there actually was one.

After they showed me the arrest warrant made out in my name, I had to go with them to Marseilles where, after a visit to the prefecture, I was locked up in the Présentines prison, a verminous, sinister former convent.

I spent several days in a communal cell there, surrounded by all sorts of women of all ages. The rumor immediately spread: "she's a political," which the women immediately translated as "she's a spy!"

Some of them threw it in my face, with the air of offended patriots. It made absolutely no difference to me. Besides, I had absolutely no idea why I was there. Maybe I was a spy, after all!

My dispossessed and wretched companions were awash with contradictory sentiments. Sisterhood and mutual aid, sure, but mischief-making too, perhaps due to their incarceration, which had never done anything to improve them.

We had been given sacks of dried beans to be graded, beans that were destined for our plates. There were two of us to a sack, and we had to work in silence. A sort of a shrew, perched on a desk raised a few steps, policed us: "Such-and-such, shut up or I'll mark you down for punishment." A sort of a litany called out in a shrill voice that grated the nerves.

With a wink of the eye, I showed my partner the beans, of which three quarters were to be thrown away. We had to place the good ones in a separate sack, and there were so few of them that the work was making no progress.

Just a few steps from me was a poor woman who looked dazed, also working her way through the beans; she was the butt of teasing from some girls. I was aware of her story: she came from the Nord; her fifteen-year-old daughter had run away from home, she had tracked her down, to Marseilles she said, and came down to fetch her, thinking that she might locate her as easily as she would back in the village. Having used up her money, she was sleeping on a bench where the police had gathered her up, then released her, several times over. She was in jail for vagrancy.

Not only did the poor woman look lost, but she appeared to be afflicted with sleeping sickness. Her head would regularly flop on to her chest. She made a splendid target to amuse some of the girls.

From where I sat, I could see the set-up. One of them would pinch her, another would pull her hair, tug at her clothing, all done gently and feigning innocence. And they were getting on my nerves! Having had enough of this, I called out to them:

"Leave her in peace!"

One of the girls got up to hit me, but I deflected her and gave her a couple of loud smacks.

"You're it now, girlie!"

Mayhem! The policewoman blew her whistle, the girl and I were taken away to a cell (not together, luckily!), and the following day we were brought up before the board, before the director, who gave us both four days in solitary where we were both taken immediately.

It was every bit as uncomfortable as the one in Avesnes, plus it had bugs. Ah, the bugs of Marseilles! Fat, huge, yuck!

I had spent only a day and a half in solitary when two detectives arrived from Paris to collect me and bring me to the prison in Melun—not the main prison, to be sure, but the town jail. They found me in a sorry state. I was allowed to wash and change my clothes. My suitcase was quickly packed.

I must have been a sight to behold as we boarded the train, handcuffs on my wrists like some grand criminal and people who caught a glimpse of me must have thought:

"What could she have done of such importance to have her cuffed like that?"

As it happened, my detectives had some sense of decency, and they removed the handcuffs in return for my word that I would not try to escape. After that, we shared a cold, but very appetizing meal which they had brought along, and it was a change from the fare at the Présentines.

They then advised me to get some sleep (we had a reserved, three-person compartment). I lay down on one of the benches, not all that reassured. One of the men propped himself up "to sleep a little" and the other stood guard!

Because of the bugs, I hadn't had a wink of sleep in solitary, and, wary or not, I fell asleep.

On arrival at Melun prison, and after the usual formalities, my traveling companions wished me luck (thanks, sirs!) and handed me over to a female chief guard, a Corsican like themselves, who led me to my cell down some long, deserted corridors.

This would be my home from now on, I would be alone, held in "secret." But I do not hate the solitude.

My cell was quite big, lit from a barred window; the furnishings were very basic: chained to the wall, there was an iron bed frame that I had to fold down to sleep on; there was a shelf and a stool chained to the wall, plus a wash-bowl and a jug of water on the shelf. And a rudimentary toilet. What a world!

The wardress closed the heavy door, and I was left alone with my thoughts. A barely audible whisper reached me from the adjoining cells. I unpacked my odds and ends and quickly settled in. Then I paced backwards and forwards in my "cage."

At noon, I heard some noise coming from the corridor. This was lunch, trundled along on an unappetizing cart pushed by some prisoners. The spy-hole slid open. I was to reach out my bowl, which was then filled with a ladle full of unappetizing liquid. I was passed a crust of bread several days old. And that was it! I was hungry, but the menu was less than captivating. I tried the soup. No, definitely not, it did not pass muster! I poured it down the toilet. I gnawed on my crust of bread.

In the afternoon, I heard some women in clogs being led out for exercise. They came to fetch me too, but I was on my own. I had to cover my head with a hood made from coarse cloth, with two holes cut in it so that I could find my way. What a sight I must have been! I was to don this piece of nonsense every time I left my cell. Mandatory!

The yard was a few square meters in size and surrounded by high walls. To let off steam, I raced around it and performed a few stretches. I breathed deeply. Recreation was brief, barely fifteen minutes of it. Then back to the cell.

I caught sight of a few silhouettes being bundled into the cells. They were dressed like medieval peasants.

That evening, there was more noise in the corridor, and it was time for supper: same rigmarole, not that the soup seemed to have improved any. I found a few half-cooked beans in it and chomped on them. I was going to have to get used to this regimen.

True, from the canteen one could buy a few items, up to a given sum. For the following day, I'd take a little butter, some chocolate, and a kipper.

The bell rang out, gloomily, and it was bed-time. It would also ring out very early to wake us up. I wasn't sleepy, but I was able to stretch out on my more or less clean mattress, to which two coarse sheets and a blanket had been added. In the seams, I spotted some dead lice that had perished in the disinfection process.

The silence was unbearable. Night had not yet fallen. I gazed at my little patch of sky and became lost in thought. What am I doing here? Buried alive; I had done nothing to deserve this! And how long am I going to be here? Why had A. B. played this trick on me? He was only a comrade, and I had done my best by him. What was so important in the book that had been borrowed and returned? When will I ever find out? That morning, I sent out a letter for Suzanne Levy, my lawyer friend, asking her to visit me. When could she pay me a visit?

I could not close my eyes; there was too much going on in my head. I was chomping at the bit and . . . the hours ticked by. Now the bell was ringing! A new day was about to begin.

Carts trundled along the corridor bringing a vile mixture described as coffee. It was warm, and I gulped it down with pleasure.

At the end of a week, I had a visit from my lawyer and walked through the corridor, still wearing my mask, which I removed as I entered the room set aside for us. We were alone and could speak freely. Suzanne had wasted no time and had already had a look at my file, and, as it happened, the examining magistrate assigned to me had been in the same year as Suzanne. He would soon see us. She told me that the note slipped inside the cover of the book was the Afno Code, the War Ministry's secret cipher, no less!

Suzanne brought me some newspapers mentioning the matter, with my photo on the front page, which I scanned very quickly and found other reports regarding a few comrades who were concerned for me: Emma, Sasha and others. This was going to be a drawn-out business. I had to be patient. But Suzanne knew that I was brave . . .

And life carried monotonously onwards . . . I read and answered the letters I had received. News about my little one: she was fine and believed that I was in hospital. My heart aching, I read and re-read the letter which my darling had touched with her little lips. From friends came encouraging words, reproaches . . . Just as there was from family members who talked about dishonor! I was seething! Didn't they understand that I hadn't done anything reprehensible and was in prison all the same? That's what infuriated me. To gamble and to lose, that's another thing!

On the outside, stories were being concocted! Some nark had spotted me in Wiesbaden (where I had never even set foot). I had been trying to haggle with the Germans over the secret cipher . . . etc. They had to issue letters rogatory and look into my timetable, day by day, right from the day I received that book.

I was called in front of the judge who turned out to be an understanding sort, we were able to speak freely, and, without any bother, he filled me in on the entire story, beginning to end. They already knew that A. B., while working in the prison print-shop, had slipped the code into the back of the book. To what end? They still had no clue! He had not tipped me off, not wanting to compromise me. Bravo! Mission accomplished! And if I had been up to date, what would I have done with the code? Would I have hidden it? Or destroyed it? There was some doubt about that.

And how was it discovered that the code had gone missing?

Through a fellow prisoner and co-worker, who uttered these fine words during an administrative visit:

"We can get anything we want into or out of this place!"

That put a flea in the ear of the supervisor who, after investigation, unearthed a few anomalies. A beating and time in solitary for the printers had done the rest. The bluffer-cum-nark was the notorious Serge de Lez, a run-of-the-mill burglar who, under the Occupation, ran a torture office on the Champs-Élysées and was knocked off come the Liberation. Lovely guy!

The judge stated that he regarded me as blameless and that I had had no hand, act, or part in the matter and that I would be released just as soon as the findings of the rogatory commissions were made known.

I would spend the entire winter in that none too well-heated cell. Time dragged, and my morale was not always high. Sometimes at night, I could hear shouting and moaning and pounding on the door. Unfortunate wretches who just could not take any more! The jingle of keys, scuffling in the corridor, recalcitrants being dragged away to solitary. Here, calm had to prevail, and we had to suffer in silence.

I had known solitary in Marseilles, they all resemble one another: a foul hole giving off an unbearable stench, where one endures hunger, cold, loneliness, and, on occasion, beatings. No water in the basin and a couple of flush toilets. Human degradation in all its splendor. And we are in a civilized country in the twentieth century! What a disgrace!

The guards had lost all their femininity. They stood for everything ugly, stupid, and harmful, smarmy and pretentious.

On Sundays, depending on their religious persuasions, the inmates were able to attend services. They were divided by a partition. Some of them were only there for a break in the monotony.

The Sunday fare was better: bouillon with meat. I never did get to taste it. No sinews, no fat, no bones, no beef. The stuff in the canteen was vile, like everything on sale there. This was shameless exploitation in every regard: the butter was rancid, and yet it was the best thing on offer along with sardines, herrings, and chocolate. Even the bread was low quality.

The lentils contained more grit than lentils; the beans, most of them worm-eaten, stank of naphthalene!

One day, unwrapping my packet of butter I found a note booking me into a fine restaurant on some undetermined date. It came from the canteen manager, a former mayor from X in the Paris area who, using a mallet, had murdered his mistress, the beautiful Gaby, in her cellar over money. Left for dead, the poor woman, who had merely been injured, had dragged herself for a matter of days until she reached a sewage grate, which is where they found her with face and body partially eaten by rats. She had just enough strength left to name her murderer before she died. He was serving five years. Sickened, I tossed my butter into the toilet.

For Christmas, the wardress handed me a small package containing some jellied fruits and iced chestnuts.

"That," she informed me, "is from a guard who would like to remain anonymous."

I never did find out his name. A sympathizer, perhaps? I was really touched by his gesture.

One day I had a female visitor whose mission it was to boost the inmates' morale and catechize them. I told her that my morale was just fine and my conscience was easy and that I needed no help, especially not religious comfort, I being an atheist. She puckered her lips and angrily slammed the door behind her. I heard her say:

"She's a savage! You were right, Madame!"

Another visit, which took place in the visiting room, was from an old friend, Sonia, and my little daughter. I positively ran to the grille where I could see my visitors. My heart was pounding:

"You're sick, Mama, but when are you coming home?"

The grille stopped me from squeezing her to my heart. I exchanged a few words with my friend, my heart in my mouth, and I had difficulty getting the words out as the tears rolled down my face. There was so much noise there that we could hardly hear one another. The guard was pacing back and forth between the two grilles: my neighbors were shouting very loudly. And then the visit was over. My little girl blew me kisses. I smiled at her:

"See you soon, darling!"

I shuffled back to my cell, losing my mind, and collapsed onto the floor, drunk with pain.

My lawyer came to see me several times; she kept me up to date with the progress of the investigation. She was a ray of sunshine. She brought me news of the outside world, of the movement and of friends, and newspapers and books from a few friends who did not forget about me. I would be out soon! If only it were true!

That was also the opinion of the judge who sent for me a second time. The matter was making progress, and now it was only a matter of a few days before the charges would be withdrawn.

And at last the day came!

"Gather up your things, you're getting out!"

I took the steps four at a time, not daring to believe these glad tidings. There were formalities to be concluded and clothing to be retrieved, and there we were headed for the main gate and freedom beyond. The open air came like a slap in the face. I was none too steady on my feet.

There was a hairdresser nearby: I stepped into his shop with my clothes bundle. The hairdresser looked at me, aghast: he knew where I had come from but he asked me no questions. I was thankful to him for that. I looked at myself in the mirror: I was ashen, my features drawn, and I had definitely lost a few kilos.

With my hair styled, I was feeling better, and I made for the railway station. My head was spinning a little. Paris! The bus . . . and then I was at my friend Sonia's place. My little girl threw her arms around my neck. I was finding it hard to take in. The nightmare was over.

After a few days, I was back home and there were some friendly letters from Emma and Sasha waiting there for me, plus one or two less friendly ones! One letter caught my attention, it was from China. It was François, asking me to come down to Saint-Tropez; he would be there for a few days. He had found himself an apartment overlooking the beach: I could move in there with my little Sonia.

Sickened by what I had gone through, I decided to agree to the offer of a safe haven and a place to rest. How I had made François's acquaintance is a story easily told:

With my good friends Emma and Sasha, some evenings we went out "on a tour of the town," which meant having a glass of something at the *Café de Paris* down by the docks; that was the main café in Saint-Tropez back then, where the crème de la crème—notaries, businessmen, estate agents, and passing commercial travelers—used to hang out ...

We had two other preferred meeting places: one was the *Café du Phare* at Meloni's place near the jetty, which was patronized by fishermen and their families who dropped by for some fresh air. To the strains of an elderly crank-operated player-piano, some youngsters would be jiving and waltzing to old airs familiar to all.

Meloni's competitor was Palmyre, which had a smoky bistro at the foot of the citadel. Around a cemented area about the size of a pocket handkerchief, there were tables and benches to seat couples who dropped by after work for a bit of entertainment and flirtation. It was cool and nice there, and it was very pleasant to sip on a glass of pastis or Saint-Tropez rosé while listening to the sing-song voices of the *Tropeziens*.

Boules players used to meet up in the splendid Place des Lices with its hundred-year-old plane trees.

I think it was in Meloni's place that I first met François, a good-looking boy with that rolling gait one finds in those who live by the sea. His father skippered a *tartane* from Saint-Tropez to Nice and right along the coast. François, though, preferred "long range" sailing and had traveled the seven seas.

Saint-Tropez was a breeding ground for merchant marine commanders who, at every opportunity, sponsored young men attracted to long-range travels. This is what happened to François.

He had invited me to go dancing once and then several more times, by way of our getting acquainted. He used to talk to me warmly about his travels, about China, about Japan, and the Islands and wanted to hear all about me and my friends. His stop-overs in Saint-Tropez were rather short, amounting to one or two weeks, and then he was off again to Marseilles and the enchanted lands.

In prison (how did he know this?), I received several letters from him, all simple but warm, plus a little parcel of dresses for Sonia that he had bought in China or in India, or wherever. I was deeply touched by that. Only somebody familiar with the loneliness of prison can comprehend the joy and emotion that can be stirred by the slightest sign coming from the outside world.

Those short, simple letters, sincere when set against the attitudes of certain anarchist comrades who had criticized and castigated me, without quite knowing what they were talking about, meant that my mind was quickly made up; I gathered up my clothes and my books and, after one last visit to my friend Sonia and a few farewell calls, I caught the train for Saint-Tropez where François, who was waiting for me, welcomed me with open arms.

I had no idea of the whereabouts of my friends Emma and Sasha, and Bon Esprit was shuttered up; I left a message for them letting them know I had been there, which they would find upon their return.

Whereas François had been warm and his father charming, I have to say that my initial contacts with my "in-laws," meaning his mother and sister, were a bit on the chilly side.

These two women looked askance at my becoming a part of their lives. The old prejudice against the "outsider" still lingered.

The pair ran a tight ship and reckoned they could steer me in whatever direction suited them.

I was hurt and disappointed, but very determined not to be pushed around. Yet, out of attachment to François and partly out of cowardice, I let that go on . . . Although I earned the occasional sweet smile, I knew that, deep down, they did not like me, and I was faced by almost daily evidence of that.

François decided to call a halt to his deep-sea travels and take up fishing. He had his savings and would buy a boat and some nets and . . . become his own master. We would be happy, the three of us!

He quickly became disillusioned and his savings were exhausted. I had to find work.

I did not know anybody in Saint-Tropez likely to give me a job. Moreover, I was "the outsider."

Luckily it was mushroom season. Every morning we set out with our baskets over our arms on a "mushroom hunt" through what were then magnificent hills. We were upbeat and happy despite the unfavorable circumstances in which we starting out: at noon, we would lunch on a sandwich and drink water from a stream. In the evening, we would ferry our day's harvest to the traders and could purchase whatever we needed. That was it for a while. We got by.

I applied for a job with a British bank, which had just opened its doors, but I was none too hopeful, for there were two local men after that job as well. It was in my favor that I knew English: the manager and the "postulants" did not. "The outsider" had carried the day. This was a topic for local gossip.

François had borrowed money to buy an engine-less boat and nets and had begun fishing. Our circumstances improved. I saw Emma and Sasha again whenever they were in town.

The "affair" plus the attitude of certain comrades had wounded me deeply. Saint-Tropez was a haven of peace. The simple, quiet lifestyle gently healed me, and I was back on an even keel. The bank's clientele, some of them foreigners, were pleasant. I made the acquaintances of people who went on to become friends: Marcel Olivier, René Clair, Joseph Kessel, etc.

Like every fisherman's wife, I had to go to the market every morning to sell the catch to the fishmongers by auction. Initially, not being too knowledgeable about fish, I was driven down on the price, but I was very quick to learn. Then, after a good wash, I made my way to the bank. Sonia was attending preschool.

And then Lucien came into the world! François was delighted and all proud to have a son . . . and so was I!

René Clair became his "godfather."

While I was at work, a kindly, sound Piedmontese woman took care of the baby.

Life was going along nicely, with some good days, some bad.

Then Head Office shut down the Saint-Tropez branch.

The proceeds from fishing covered the outlay on fishing equipment. What was I to do?

René Clair and one of the bank customers, Valentin, offered me a grocery store. That sort of work held scarcely any charms for me, but what was I to do? How could I refuse their kind offer?

The business was going quite well but there were lots of

customers who shopped "on account," fishermen and many other families, whom I could not refuse (which made Bronja Clair say that I was like the Salvation Army!).

I let my heart soften and was soon unable to cope and pay the bills. I could hardly appeal to my friends, and I was terribly annoyed. So that was the end of the store! And of our household!

There were too many things driving us apart: our tastes, our outlooks on life, the life of the housewife, which I found oppressive after having lived the life of an activist. François just did not want to hear talk of politics. Open or hidden conflicts with the in-laws had undermined the bond between us. Add to that the failure of the shop, the responsibility for which was mine alone. All of these things were the cause of our separation, which was quite painful, primarily for father and son.

Yet we came to a suitable agreement whereby François could see him whenever he liked and that we would part on good terms.

And so, I had to begin again from nothing: with two mouths to feed and no job.

A magnificent hotel, the Latitude 43, had just been built. A marvel of luxury and comfort, meant for a choice clientele. The manager, nephew of the king of the arms-dealers, Zaharoff, presented it to his wife for some birthday or other!

I stuck in an application and was hired as a receptionist.

Most of the staff (apart from kitchen and housekeeping) and the management was Russian. Prince Obolenski, scion of one of the oldest aristocratic families, was handsome and imposing in his splendid lift-operator's uniform! Merezhovski, both hotel manager and a prince, was a great pal of Joseph Kessel's! A little uppity and pretentious baron was pool-boy; the cashiers' names were Denikin and Wrangel. There were lots of other illustrious names from the days of the tsars . . . and the receptionist was anarchist May Picqueray, friend of Makhno!

Some of the staff (kitchen and housekeeping) took their meals in the office; the remainder of the staff had their own dining room. Needless to say, the meals could be a bit animated at times. We would talk revolution and Makhno; they detested the Bolsheviks, of course, who had as dispossessed them.

At the height of the season, with the hotel sold out and turning away bookings, a strike erupted. I had not been informed, let alone consulted. So what lay behind the strike, which had spread from the kitchens, I had no idea. I found out later that the staff were mostly communists and that the strike had been anticipated ever since the opening of the hotel.

The manager absolutely refused to discuss, and there was a complete and unremitting lock-out.

I was jobless again!

A portable typewriter that had been offered to me proved my salvation. I offered my services to the summer residents whose numbers were on the increase. I placed an ad with the agencies. I learned to feel at home on the yachts, which were by then invading the port. I typed up these ladies' and gents' correspondence.

Joseph Kessel, who was working on *Macao, enfer du jeu*[8] at the time, had work for me to do nearly every evening, sometimes until late in the night, which allowed him to head out to sea with his friends during daylight hours.

Jeff, as I called him when it was just the two of us, was a charmer, and we got along famously but his drinking binges were—alas! —on an unimaginable scale! Whenever he happened to drop into a café and was in the "mood," he could easily down a bottle of vodka. After which he would toss around all he could—glasses, bottles, the windows, smashing up tables, chairs, and leaving the café a scene of devastation.

Since they knew him, it always ended up pretty much the same way: he would spend the next day sorting out the breakages or would dispatch me to pick up the bill. And, apparently, he offered his apologies.

In Paris, I carried on working for him at his home in the Porte Dauphine, and our collaboration was only interrupted by the war in Spain when he had to go there to cover it as a reporter while I busied myself with other things.

Rejected by the fishing community for having walked out on one of its own, I struck up relations elsewhere. For instance, I had become acquainted with the editor-in-chief of the newspaper *L'Echo du Littoral et du Var* and his wife; we used to see one another frequently and he had asked me to write items that I would regularly forward to the paper. It was, for me, a much-appreciated source of income.

---

8 This novel was actually written by Maurice Dekobra and published in 1938.

My friends Emma and Sasha urged me to go back to Paris. As they waited for me to make my decision, they often invited me to Bon Esprit where I met their friends, mostly Americans, writers, painters, sculptors, and activists.

One of them, Fernando Gualdi, a sculptor at the Bosc studio, was regarded by the local police chief as a "potentially dangerous anarchist"; he had something against him, for some unknown reason, and made up his mind to be rid of him. He took steps to have him deported. All of the artists and writers in Saint-Tropez, who held him in high esteem, drew up a petition taking exception to this—baseless—expulsion of one of their own.

I was commissioned to bring it to Draguignan, to the prefect of the Var department. An antiques dealer brought me there in her car, and we very nearly did not get there.

The car door was opened from the inside by means of a wire. On one sharp turn, I was thrown to the side and my elbow caught on the wire. The door flew open, and I took a few tumbles along the roadway before finding myself sitting in the dust and tar, which was melting beneath the summer sun.

Some people who had been working in the vineyards and who had witnessed the accident, although they could not fathom what had happened, came over to help. I shook my legs and arms. There was nothing broken, but I was covered in bruises, and my clothing was in a pitiful state; my white blouse and skirt had lost their sparkle.

My traveling companion had pulled up a few dozen meters ahead and, believing me dead, was frozen in her seat, not daring to turn her head. She was reassured when she saw me and started up the engine again.

On arriving in Draguignan, I walked into the first pharmacy we came to and had my scratches and bruises rubbed down with alcohol, which was not a pleasant experience! And so, wounded and grubby, I arrived at the office of the prefect, to whom I handed the petition. Curious to know what had happened, he was briefed on the entire matter of the accident, which might well have turned out worse.

Despite all the efforts made, the expulsion order stood and Fernando was forced to leave Saint-Tropez and his friends. He lived for a while in Marseilles then sought refuge with me in Paris, up until the day when (who had fingered him?) he was given a six-month prison sentence and taken to the jail in Poissy.

On my return to Paris, I reestablished contact with certain good friends of mine. Louis Lecoin, for one.

On June 28, 1936, I had a phone call from Emma, bringing me the awful, ghastly news in a broken, barely audible voice: Sasha had just died. In the depths of depression, he had shot himself with a revolver. Knowing him well, I could not believe it and, to this day, if I cry over his death, I have a lingering doubt in my heart.

I set off immediately for Nice where Sasha had been living on and off for the previous few years with a young Austrian woman.[9] Relations between them were not the best; sick and given to hysteria, she created a number of painful scenes for him, and he often sought refuge in Bon Esprit near Emma.

I found the two women distraught. I shall never forget the pain in Emma's eyes; the woman had just lost her comrade-in-struggle and, without a word, she clasped me tight in her arms.

I took it very badly myself . . .

The first stirrings of revolt erupted in Spain, and, for Emma, a new hope of seeing her ideal realized.

Invited by A. Souchy to come to Spain and take part in the revolution, she arrived in Barcelona in September 1936, gave a number of broadcast radio addresses, addressing the workers and militiamen, and then paid a visit to the Madrid front where she found her good comrade Durruti.

She was able to appreciate what had been accomplished, the collectivizations carried out by the peasants and workers in a number of provinces. She then left for London where she set up an office for mutual aid for the Spanish comrades.

But the international reaction, the treason of Russia, won the day; the revolution was defeated. She moved on to Canada where she mounted a campaign for the release of jailed comrades. On February 17, 1940, Emma suffered a stroke; she passed away on May 14. On May 18, her body was brought back to Chicago where she was buried in Waldheim cemetery, near to her Haymarket comrades (the Chicago Martyrs).

Fernando was freed after serving his time in Poissy prison (La Santé was overcrowded and even comrades sentenced to short terms were being directed to the central prisons).

9 Berkman's companion, Emmy Eckstein (1900–1939), was born in Germany.

Freed may be going a bit far! The day before, I was in Poissy where I spent the night in a little hotel near the prison. I wanted to be there to greet him on his release. It was bitterly cold, and I had brought him something to cover himself: a snug pullover and a warm overcoat.

The gates opened before seven o'clock, and out came ten or so prisoners surrounded by numerous guards. Fernando threw himself into my arms, his eyes filling with tears. For six months, he had been completely isolated and denied all correspondence (remitted to him on his discharge). He ate little and badly, strictly absolute basics. He was terrifyingly thin.

I managed to get the guard who freed him from his handcuffs to let him have a piping hot coffee with croissants bought from the local bistro, and I handed out croissants to the other guards.

I had thought that all the men [were] all due for release. Not a bit of it. Their release was due to take place at the prefecture . . . and I watched as the heavy van with its cargo of sadness and wretchedness disappeared.

I caught the train and headed straight for the prefecture; the prisoners had been driven to the Roland-Garros stadium (which Monsieur Daladier* would later convert for use as a concentration camp).

I knew Madame M., the prison visitor who was also in charge of the Roland-Garros camp. I dropped in on her: she introduced me to the camp commandant, a polite, but inflexible fellow. Visits were forbidden, and all I could do was spot Fernando among the inmates and give him a wave of encouragement.

I made all sorts of overtures to get Fernando released and by the time when success was in sight and the release order arrived at the Roland-Garros, Fernando had already been transferred to the Le Vernet d'Ariège camp with its vile reputation.

8

THE ROUT AND THE OCCUPATION

When I arrived back in Paris from Saint-Tropez, I sought out Louis Lecoin, firmly resolved to help him with his propaganda and also to make my own tiny contribution to the Spanish revolution.

At that point, Louis and some other comrades were busily shipping arms, provisions, medicines, and all manner of stuff to our Spanish comrades. Certain pacifists had been taken aback by his stance: they were forgetting that while Louis was a pacifist, he was also a revolutionary, and could not refuse assistance to those fighting for their freedom.

With Nicholas Faucier, he also launched the SIA (Secours International Anarchiste/International Anarchist Aid).

As for me, I was eager that my contribution to the revolution should be directed into taking care of the children. I joined the Spanish Children's Aid Committee under the guidance of Madame and Monsieur M., who were renowned for their selfless humanism bereft of any political denomination. They had set up colonies for the Spanish children.

We went out in trucks to look for stray, wounded, orphaned children, whom we would bring back to the various colonies where they were cared for and treated with love.

Later, I was put in charge of the family reunification service at a time, following the Rout, when husband, wife, and often the children found themselves separated and sometimes in entirely different camps or regions. It was work for the long haul. So many Spaniards bore the same name, like us French with our Duponts and Durands!

Further, the very young did not know their own names at all. We had to go back to the location, date, and time when the child had been found and make further inquiries. This was a mammoth and, in many respects, exacting task. And one not always crowned with success.

The Germans were closing in on Paris. The Quakers had withdrawn to Toulouse and asked me to accompany some Spanish children down to Marseilles. We were to collect them from Bordeaux. Even as the Germans were entering Paris by one gate, we were leaving by another. A veteran from Spain, a tall hearty fellow who had lost his right hand, replaced with a hook, was to drive the truck that carried us, along with Sonia, my daughter, Purita, my assistant, Illa, the renowned photographer of animals who had just lost her husband at the front, and Ratou, a young lad who had been entrusted to me by his parents. My own son was in a colony in Arcachon at the time, one of M.'s colonies. I knew that he was safe and sound.

The roads were terribly packed; our truck had great difficulty forcing a passage through the men, women, and children, burdened with the most motley baggage, which they often just dumped by the side of the road when they did not have the energy to carry it any further.

Italian planes flew overhead and sprayed us with machine-gun fire, sowing suffering and death with each pass.

Scattered bands of French soldiers also fled southwards. Civilians challenged them and insulted them:

"Why are you running away? It's your fault we are here! You have deserted your posts! Cowards!"

Some carried on their way, dragging their legs and making no response. Others, however, hit back:

"We were given our orders to fall back, and we are carrying them out! Shit, we've had just about enough of their lousy war!"

We reached Limoges and tried to grab a little sleep either inside the truck or by the roadside. We had picked up few poor wretches, lost and harassed, who no longer knew whether they should press on or retrace their steps.

Day was just about breaking; our driver roused us, and we were off again for Bordeaux where Miss Pye welcomed us warmly. We were each able to get some rest in a proper bed and have a hot meal.

The children were already en route to Marseilles where the Mexican consul would take charge of them.

We arrived in Toulouse where the Quaker mission had already set up shop and was reaching out into the whole region. Rooms had been reserved for us at the *Capoul* hotel.

It would be my job to feed and water the refugees passing through and to house those stopping in Toulouse.

Off I went in search of premises. We were allowed to use the cereal market, a huge hangar that could house several hundred people. It needed conversion, like a number of other buildings, for use as a welcome center. We sought out mattresses, beds, baby carriages, blankets, and bundles of straw and hay.

And our customers came flooding in. In huge numbers.

These unfortunates needed help settling in. They were especially in need of rest . . . Then there was tending to the mothers, caring for and feeding the infants, the elderly, readying meals for everyone. There were not that many of us and, after a few days, we were utterly spent.

War, that disgrace to humanity, has several faces. The face of exodus is pitiful; there is the fear and the headlong flight before "the enemy." The sort of fear that grabs you by the innards, makes you abandon everything and rush headlong until you fall, exhausted. There were dramatic incidents: old folks dumped along the way because they could not keep up any more, children who had lost their parents . . . The sick and the injured laying by the side of the road, waiting for help that might never come.

Refugees? They were pouring in from everywhere, some from the Belgian border, from the Nord, from the Somme, from the invaded areas. Their homes, their farms had been destroyed and torched. And each of them was entitled to rise up against or weep over what had become of his life.

In between the dramas, there were funny moments. A little old man came to us, carrying on his head the only baggage he had, an armchair. Another held a caged bird, someone else a chamber-pot. Two little old ladies cried hot tears. We did our best to comfort them: they had forgotten their false teeth and could not chew their food.

But there were tragedies, of course, and they dominated. I was particularly touched by one:

A village had been evacuated just as the Germans were arriving and setting everything ablaze. The last truck was ready to pull out. People scurried. A woman carrying a baby in her arms climbed down from a truck, having forgotten the baby's nappies, and she made a dash for the house, returning after a few minutes. They pressed her, we must get going, step on it! And the truck raced away as fast as it could. A few meters further on, the woman let out an animal-like scream and made to leap from the moving truck. She was restrained, the village was in flames. She had quite simply forgotten her baby, which she had set down on the bed while she was packing.

There she was prostrate, clutching in her arms a bundle of rags that she rocked while shaking her head. She had gone out of her mind.

"She's not dangerous," said those with her. "She spends the whole day singing a lullaby . . ."

Damnable war!

It was long past time to eat and I wasn't feeling hungry, so I decided to head back to the hotel for some sleep. I was downcast, sickened by all the suffering, all the horrors. There was a lump in my throat, but, rather than tears, it was rage that mounted and overtook me. I hated the warmongers, the guilty parties, whatever their nationality or the part they played. Statesmen, capitalists, arms manufacturers, be they the Krupps, the Wendels, or the Zaharoffs,[1] who built their enormous fortunes on the deaths of millions.

I hate statesmen who regard a war as the only way to nip social upheaval in the bud, inevitable when the misery was such that victims can no longer fight back and succumb to fatalism. War was therefore the only way to avoid all revolution and even major reforms and safeguard those fortunes and vested interests.

They say and they write that war is the only solution to resolve crises.

It makes it possible to cash in on stocks of weaponry, raw materials, and even the stock of human material surplus to the requirements of the labor market.

---

1 The first two were major arms manufacturing companies while Zaharoff was a famous, and notorious, arms dealer.

What a disgrace! What infamy! How long until a mobilization of consciences demanding disarmament and shouting:
"Up with lives! Down with arms!"

Noë is a small hamlet with a population of about 1,800, situated between Toulouse and Muret. There was a camp there for "undesirables" of Spanish, Italian, and other nationalities. I was in charge of supplying that camp with provisions, clothing, and blankets, as well as medicine. Life there was not luxurious. They lacked everything. I visited once a week.

There, I had the joy of stumbling upon my old friend Meschi,* a one-time syndicalist propagandist from the construction sector whom I had often welcomed to my home in Paris and who adored my little Sonia. When I say the joy, what I mean is that I immediately thought about doing all in my power to improve his lot and get him out of there.

His internment was taking a heavy toll on him. He wasn't a young man anymore, and his rheumatism often kept him pinned to his cot. I fetched him the medicine he needed so that he could get back on his feet and walk around a bit.

In the course of my work, I had made the acquaintance of the chaplain. Not unpleasant company, for a priest. We might be able to work with him. After I had "worked" on him for a while, he was eventually ready to help me get Meschi out of that Hell, as he described the camp. But when I filled my good friend in on the plan, he put his foot down: he did not want to be indebted in any way to a priest. I insisted but was unable to change his mind.

He was obliged to spend long months there before he got out. Of course, I fetched him whatever I could: correspondence, newspapers, extra rations. But none of these made up for his freedom.

In terms of camps, I was to see worse!

Le Vernet.[2]

Its reputation was dire. Certain Spaniards whom I bumped into in Toulouse described it to me as an unspeakable convict colony . . . And they were not exaggerating in the slightest.

Arthur Koestler wrote:

2 An internment camp/prison in the Arige department that was initially used to house POWs during the First World War. Later, in 1939, it was used to house refugees from the Spanish Civil War.

It was the only disciplinary camp in France to which prisoners from other camps were transferred for punishment, a sort of a Devil's Island north of the Pyrenees. It was originally created during the Spanish prelude to this war to bestow French hospitality upon the defeated Republican militiamen. In those early days, accommodation in Le Vernet consisted of trenches dug into the frozen earth, in which the wounded were allowed to die and the healthy to get sick.

The first installations in the camp were the barbed wire around it and the cemetery next to it, where the first rows of wooden crosses all bear ... Spanish names. There are no inscriptions ...

Later, a number of wooden huts were built, each to provide two hundred men with a living-space of twenty-one inches in width; and when they were completed, the whole camp was evacuated because some inspecting commission found it uninhabitable for human beings. For a few months, it stood empty except for the rats and bugs; then war broke out and it was filled again with a strange crowd of men from all over Europe whom the French newspapers had graciously labeled the Scum of the Earth.

They were partly the last Mohicans of the International Brigades and partly politically active exiles from all countries under Fascist rule ... who had drunk of Mussolini's castor oil and had lain on the torture racks of the Siguranza in Bucharest and sat on the ghetto benches of Lvov and known the steel whips of the SS in Dachau; who had printed secret anti-Nazi leaflets in Vienna and Prague and, above all, had fought through the prelude of the Apocalypse in Spain.

To make this private anti-Left pogrom of the Sûreté more palatable to the public, the "Scum" was given a fair sprinkling of about twenty per cent of genuine criminals, pimps, dope-peddlers, nancy-boys and other types of the Montmartre underworld.

After the Armistice treaty, the men got together and appealed to the Commander, asking him to let a few of the most exposed escape before the Germans got them. The Commander refused. As an officer, he probably disliked the job he had to do; but after all, he had a salary ... to lose. Next, a delegation of the prisoners asked that their files in the camp office be destroyed before the Gestapo arrived. This the Commander promised: but when the first German commissioned arrived, the lists of prisoners were complete ...

Paragraph nineteen provided for the extradition of any German-born subject the authorities asked for—In other words, the handing-over of anti-Nazi refugees to the Gestapo ...

What they were after instead was human labor ... volunteers for their labor camps, to work on fortifications, in factories, mines, etc. So desperate seems to be their need for labor that they took anybody, regardless of political faith, "provided that the candidate was of Aryan descent, medically fit and willing to work hard," promising a fantastically high pay of one hundred and twenty francs ...

Well over a thousand desperate men enlisted. Most of them belonged to the criminal and non-political element. The International Brigaders refused en bloc ... Another thousand or so were shipped by force by the French authorities to North Africa to work in the modern slave gangs of the Trans-Sahara railway ... men dying like flies from under-nourishment, exhaustion and epidemics in the murderous climate ...

Constant menaces [hung] day and night, week after week, month after month, over the heads of the men in Le Vernet. They had no hope for the future ... yet, not more than a dozen of them went insane and not more than a score committed suicide ... the cemetery is probably the most cosmopolitan collection of skulls since the mass graves of the crusades. [What lingers] is the smell of the latrines during an epidemic, the smell of the damp straw in the huts and the smell of the men who had been rotting on it for years; the hunger, the cold, the beating, the fear; the look in the eyes of men the day before they go mad and the look in the eyes of a gendarme when he puts on your handcuffs ...

And crusaders they were ... pioneers in the fight to safeguard the dignity of man. But perhaps future historians will unearth their story ... and perhaps they will alter the label attached to them, and call them what they really were, "The *Salt* of the Earth."[3]

---

3 This quote is taken from Arthur Koestler's memoir *The Scum Of The Earth* (London: Jonathan Cape, 1942).

Fernando was being held in the Le Vernet camp, an hour's train ride outside Toulouse. I decided to go and pay him a visit there.

One Sunday morning, off I set with the kids, with snacks for the day. I reported to the camp gates and bumped into a sentry who, after much negotiating, agreed to take in the package meant for Fernando, then asked me to move along rather abruptly.

So, the kids and I did a slow circuit, shuffling with defiant sluggishness from guard to guard.

The camp covered several dozen hectares on which wooden huts had been erected for about six thousand men split up into three camps: the first held International Brigaders and Spanish fighters who had crossed the border into France in the wake of their defeat. The second held politicals from every nation and persuasion, including Degrelle's* (Belgian) fascists. I spotted some famous faces there like the writer Arthur Koestler, some Italian syndicalists, my Russian friends Sacha Piotr* and Nicolas Lazarévitch, and some Spanish activists such as Liarte,* Sans, and Vivancos* the painter, as well as an Argentinean journalist and lots of others.

Sector No. 3 (C) ran along the Ariège river. Using binoculars, I strained for a glimpse of Fernando; I caught sight of him several times, but he had absolutely no idea we were there. He later found out that I had been there, once he had been given that package, which had been opened and most of the food contents pilfered, food that I had had a lot of trouble gathering together.

I made the Toulouse-Vernet trip on a weekly basis, but I had never as yet managed to gain entry. One Sunday, I resolved to try my luck and ensure delivery. Presenting my card as a Quaker delegate, I asked the guard if I could see the camp commandant. The guard coarsely replied that he was not available and that, in any case, he would not see me. He ordered me bluntly to keep moving along.

"Hurry it up!"

I told him that I was off to the village to get lunch for the kids and would be back. And that he should pass my calling card on to the commandant.

I was back an hour later. Spotting me from some distance away, the guard beckoned to me. He had a change of attitude: the commandant would see me. He escorted me to him.

The commandant was a small, red-faced stocky man, and a bit of a tyrant. After introducing himself to me, he took me on a tour of the camp. First, to see the food stores: beans, chickpeas, and potatoes, all of them of rather poor quality. There were no blankets, no shoes, no clothing of any sort. And no medicines.

He took me to the infirmary: when I entered, I choked on an unbearable stench. I sighted a number of skeletal creatures sprawled on some pallets, some of them even on boards. What an abomination! Their poor eyes were eating their faces. Staring, unseeing . . .

The doctor, himself an inmate (who I later helped to escape) told me he was powerless to care for these men due to lack of the most basic medicines. A large number of the bedridden waited for death.

An atrocious pain tore at my chest at the sight of this distress. I felt nauseous and had to get outside very quickly, mumbling vague promises. I had absolutely no idea how I was going to live up to them.

Around the camp, men were dragging themselves, half-naked, some possessed no more than a scrap of sackcloth between their thighs as their only garment. I registered the eyes of these living dead. The commandant, as he walked me around, told me also of his powerlessness. All his requests were being shelved. The only reserves they had were helmets and gas-masks!

The Le Vernet camp had a foul reputation as a death camp: it was well deserved.

I had sworn that I would be back. I could not go on living without doing something for those unfortunates. I pleaded their case to my committee. I was not sure that I had convinced them. In fact, they included people sympathetic to the Right as well as to the Left and professed to be wholly neutral.

The picture I painted of the camp was dark, very dark, but I hadn't exaggerated a thing. It was truly what "life" in Le Vernet camp was like. I managed to secure the sponsorship of the committee and was authorized to keep that damned camp supplied with food, medicine, clothing, and blankets.

Four days after my visit, I was back with a truck filled to bursting point, not that it amounted to very much per inmate. Huge wheels of Gruyère cheese, long slabs of lard, milk, medicines, blankets, and clothes. The commandant seemed delighted. I had promised him that I would be back each week with a similar load.

In his enthusiasm, he asked me what I would like. A cup of tea in the mess perhaps? I told him of Fernando and asked if I might see him.

An office was promptly made available to us. We were very happy to see each other again. He squeezed me very tightly in his arms, saying: "I just knew you would come, that you'd walk back into this Hell!" And tears, of joy, streamed down his face.

For a few moments, I was free to spend time with him. In this way, I learned of all the details about life in the camp where men who had fled their homeland or fought for their freedom rotted. Freedom! Deaths from lack of hygiene and under-nourishment were commonplace.

I saw men squabbling over the privilege of emptying the camp's huge latrines into the Ariège river. I followed them. What I witnessed horrified me: out of the fecal matter the men were separating out half-digested beans, washing them off, and devouring them gluttonously. How famished did they have to be! And what a disgrace for human beings to be treated that way, no matter whether they were "common law" or "political" prisoners! And this was happening in my homeland, in France, thanks to Monsieur Daladier's good offices!

I was as good as my word: every week a huge lorry pulled up to the camp laden with everything I was able to get my hands on. Furthermore, I asked Fernando to draw up a list of what was most sorely needed in his hut and, on Sunday, I would bring personal parcels.

One Sunday, the commandant invited me to have a cup of tea in his mess. I accepted the invitation, as I was keen to put it to him that he might make a hut available to family members who traveled far and were unable to see "their prisoner," a hut where they might spend a little time with their kids, their father, brother, or husband.

After some argument, he agreed, and on the next Sunday, I, along with the kids, was able to call upon Fernando and share lunch with him. I had fetched a generous meal from the hotel. And I was able to spend time with him until it was time for the return leg of the train journey.

In this hut, the commandant had placed some tables and benches: even, were my eyes deceiving me? . . . an old piano! Now, where did he get that machine? The hut filled with more and more visitors: all those who had managed to alert their families.

In addition to Fernando, I was able to drop in on another pal of his, sometimes Italian, sometimes Spanish, sometimes Russian, happy not only to share a good meal but also to receive news from the outside.

One day, behind the barbed wire enclosing those "on punishment detail," I spotted my old friend Sacha Piotr, the Russian nihilist with the amputated hand. He jumped for joy when he saw me. I was able to slip him some food and clothing without being spotted, for he was still undergoing punishment and banned from communicating with anyone. And then, one day, he was gone, and I discovered that he had died . . . of disease?[4] I had been able to take a snapshot of him behind the barbed wire (still secretly, as this was banned) and some years later was able to forward the forbidden snapshot to his engineer son living on the outskirts of Paris.

To get ahold of the identity papers I had in mind for Fernando to get him out of there, I decided to head back to Paris for a few days and crossed the demarcation line in Orthez with my son.[5] This was without problem and, a little later, I crossed back over the line near Vichy. Back at the camp, I found out that, in my absence, the Italian Commission had visited and had taken a number of Italians away with it, Fernando being one.

I carried on supplying the camp, sad to know that my comrade was in the clutches of the fascists. What would become of him?

But that was no reason to ease up on my activities! Quite the contrary!

On one of my supply visits (my last), a non-commissioned officer whose humane treatment of the inmates had been pointed out to me (oh yes, there are exceptions everywhere!)—which permitted me to slip him the occasional bit of chocolate for his children or some soap, which he visibly appreciated—took me to one side and let me know that the Gestapo was due the following day to take charge of several German inmates. He feared for their lives. I told him of my surprise that he was confiding in me.

"I trust you," he said. "We have to do something."

"Have you no one inside the camp who might help you?"

"Unfortunately, no. I don't trust anyone here!"

I shall skip the details. What counts is not how I went about it but the outcome.

---

4   Piotr was transferred from Le Vernet and later died in Auschwitz.

5   The demarcation line was a boundary between the part of France run by a German administration (the Occupied zone) and the so-called Free zone, run by the French Vichy government. Set up by the Germans after the fall of France in May 1940, one usually needed papers to legally cross this line.

In any event, when the Gestapo showed up the next day, they had to ask a few questions. As did the commandant. Nine of their "clients" had gone missing.

Issued with train tickets and some cash and clean clothes, those inmates went wherever fate might lead them. I never did know their names, and I never set eyes on them again.

The very next morning, two men showed up at my hotel. They absolutely had to see me. I had to follow them to a building that bore no resemblance at all to a police station. I spent a number of hours there and was subjected to a regular interrogation.

"If I was to have helped anyone escape, I'd have started with my friend Fernando."

That was a pretty solid argument. There was no need for them to know that it was not my fault if he was moved in my absence . . .

I was released and advised to waste no time getting out of town, as the Gestapo might well be less indulgent.

I did just that. When questioned, the Quaker supervisor told the police:

"I don't know if she did it . . . But she is quite capable of doing so!"

With the children, I fled to a little village near the border with Andorra and rented an old house by the river's edge. The house was very ramshackle and by no means luxurious. Not even comfortable. The ground floor was used by the farmer as a wood-store. Access to the first floor was by means of a ladder: a big room containing two old-fashioned, elderly beds, a table, a bench, and a great chimney. We made the best of things. There was a draft everywhere blowing through the gaps in the floorboards and cracks in the wall, but it was home, and we were, for a time, at ease.

We got our wood supplies from a nearby saw-mill and provisions from the only local grocery—*cum* bar, *cum* restaurant, etc. Snow was beginning to fall and so the countryside was magical, and we shivered around the fireplace. I managed to get hold of some heavy feather eiderdowns, and there was milk aplenty from neighboring farm.

Once a week, we would sit down to a fine meal at the grocery-restaurant. The soup there was superb, and the large Godin stove in the center of the room radiated great heat. Peasants would often drop in to warm themselves and have a hot drink at the counter, while chatting about the news.

Sonia and Ratou left us to rejoin their friends, but they were not gone for long. One day, a telegram came for me signed "Sonia and Ratou" that had taken eight days to reach me and stated:

"We are starving to death!"

I sent them some money, but what they really lacked was food; they had managed to find an elderly nanny-goat, which, after several days in the oven, was still inedible!

They retreated to Toulouse, had a Pantagruelian[6] meal at Elvira's place, and then came down to rejoin us in our hideaway.

Elvira was a school-mistress, a Spanish refugee who ran a restaurant with her elderly parents in a working-class area in Toulouse. Her customers were exclusively working-class. Her meals were copious and good. A number of refugees from Paris had stumbled on the restaurant where one could eat well but at reasonable prices. It became our rendezvous.

There, one could bump into Albert Bayet,* Charles Wolf,* who had one of the finest discotheques in Paris, Violette[7]* and her friend Edgar Morin, Pierre Dac (who was soon to travel on to England), Temerson,* a movie actor, Clovys, from the *Muse rouge* who sold newspapers, and many others . . . who were in the resistance. We were at home at Elvira's place and the after-dinner conversation was mighty.

During that period, when no one could be sure of what lay in the future, we found in Elvira's wonderful establishment not only nourishment but an unrivaled human warmth. At her place, we felt safe.

Once winter had passed through our village, I headed back to Toulouse. My comrade Lazarévitch who was in Le Vernet had brought to my attention the presence of his brother-in-law Isaac, who had fled Paris and the round-ups there. Isaac found himself in what was from any angle a dire situation. I managed to locate him and took him under my wing . . .

He had managed to get a couple of retirees on the outskirts of Toulouse to rent him a little two-room shed in some gardens. It was very spartanly-furnished, but it was a roof over his head, and in those uncertain times everything was very precarious. I managed to get him some bona fide papers, which meant that he could move around in complete safety.

Finally, almost!

6 This is a reference to the giant Pantagruel, a character from the works of François Rabelais. The implication is that Sonia and Ratou ate a gigantic meal.
7 Violette Chapellaubeau.

I decided to seek out Pucheu* in Vichy. Trotsky had once upon a time granted me a meeting. There was no reason for Pucheu not to receive me!

I wanted to try and see to it that a few comrades got released from Le Vernet camp. I was banned from there, but my place had been taken by another "Quaker." I used my Quaker identification card to make my way into Pucheu's presence. He gave me a very amiable welcome. He congratulated me on the work we were doing. He just wanted to know how he might be of assistance to us, but a certificate of sponsorship would be required. I could get one pretty straightforwardly from a comrade in the Var department.

Lazarévitch was promptly released. He was the only one to get out of Le Vernet camp legitimately. At the same time, his partner and their son,[8] who were in a different camp, were able to join him in Marseilles, and the family was reunited in the Var.

A pretty sizable batch of "politicals" were shipped off to North Africa.

Sonia and Ratou left for Paris once again. I remained in Toulouse where I made contact with folks of the resistance and did what I could to help out one or the other.

I had left the hotel, it being too expensive, and was living with Pat (aka Isaac) in a shack in the suburbs. There we managed to more or less get by on vegetables grown in his garden.

I was due to give birth soon. It might seem thoughtless to bring a child into the world in such troubled times. Yet I had done nothing to avert it. For me, it was a kind of protest.

The Jewish question was one that had never really arisen as far as I was concerned. It had taken that ignoble war and the persecution of the Jews, that manhunt, to open my eyes to it. And here I was, expecting a Jewish child! Isaac (known to us as Pat) had never had a child before and could not quite take account of what was going on. He was simply happy, regardless of the risks of all sorts! And so was I!

His pal Rainer, a Romanian writer, would often drop by on a visit (one day he brought along Lanza del Vasto*), and we passed marvelous evenings in his company! One evening, he left us on the platform of the railway station, off to fetch his wife and daughter in Romania.

---

8 Lazarévitch's partner is best known as Ida Mett (1901–1973), the Russian anarchist and author.

He was worried about what might happen to them. I had a foreboding that we might never see him again:

"Don't go," I said, "I'm afraid for you!"

But off he went and was dispatched to a camp in Russia, from which he was lucky enough to escape. That foreboding of mine had been mistaken. We all met up again in Paris where he published his memories of Russia in *Mon ami Vassia*.[9]

Of course, following the escape from Le Vernet, I had had to cut my ties with the Quakers.

The birth of the child went very well. But our funds were shrinking. We needed to come up with a solution. Pat found some work with a peasant in a different department. And I made up my mind to head back up to Paris with my two kids, Lucien and Marie-May, and to look Sonia up.

That meant crossing the demarcation line. I was provided with some contacts. In Mont-de-Marsan, there was a smuggler who could easily get us over the line. So off I went to the appointed place. On meeting him, I found the smuggler reluctant. Not only was he asking for a substantial sum of money, but his wife was against him doing it at all, as it was too risky . . . I decided to make the crossing without his help. I had him point me to the approximate spot and plunged into the woods. Night was falling. We came to a big farmhouse; dogs were barking, the peasants came out, and, at the sight of us, realized what we were doing. They invited us inside to spend the night under their roof and would get us across the following day, as the dogs were off the leash in the forest that night; arrests had been made, and the Germans had a post on the railway line a couple of steps away.

After a very comfortable night, we were ready to leave; but still they were putting us off. The timing was not right, we should hang on and have lunch at the farmhouse. We had stumbled into some pretty extraordinary company who bent over backwards to be nice to us. We were served homemade confit of duck, an unforgettable delicacy, especially in those times of scarcity . . . After which it was time to go!

On all fours, we slipped across a low railway bridge and disappeared into a forest. I had my bag slung over my back, my gurgling

9 This early account of labor camps in Russia appeared in 1949, published by Sulliver Editions in Paris and written by Rainier Biemel* under the pseudonym of Jean Rounault. It was later published in English as *My Friend Vassia* (London: R. Hart-Davis, 1952) and as *Nightmare* (New York: Thomas Crowell, 1952).

baby in my arms, the noise audible in the forest. I placed a rusk in his mouth, as the German sentry was just fifty meters away . . . My son strode boldly by my side, and he too had a bag slung over his back. There was a pottery just where we emerged from the forest. We left our bags there and skedaddled in the direction of Mont-de-Marsan, which was several kilometers away. Our bags would be brought to us at the railway station. That way, we would not attract attention to ourselves. We ran across a small German bicycle patrol; it cycled right by. Everything went well. We caught our train for Paris.

I shall never forget those good people, to whom we wrote the moment we reached our destination; I forwarded them the underclothes they so sorely needed. They had gambled their freedom in a display of great solidarity! Something rare enough to deserve appreciation.

Before leaving Toulouse, I was able to give Mollie and Senya a hug on the station platform; after having been interned in the Gurs camp, they were getting ready to leave for Mexico. I had managed to procure from a Mexican anarchist comrade an affidavit in which he agreed to host them and see to their needs. And so they were freed and for many a year carried on with their activities in Mexico.

On arrival in Paris, I discovered that Louis Lecoin had been arrested over his leaflet "Peace Right Now," of which he had disseminated several million copies; from La Santé he was moved to Angers and to the Gurs camp, to begin with, and then to Djela fort in North Africa, along with Louzon* (a veteran syndicalist activist who ran the review *La Révolution prolétarienne*).

Other comrades had been interned too. These included Huart* and Haussard,* outstanding militants. Out of weakness, some people had gone to the front lines. Others had skipped the country. So I bumped into very few comrades.

As an anarchist, what was one to do in Paris in wartime? Propaganda? Newspapers, banned! I made up my mind to do what I always had done: help those who were in straitened circumstances. There was no shortage of them!

In order to survive, I joined the Alkan press as a proofreader and, along with a few other workers, set about producing forged documents. There was a great market for these (served out of solidarity, be it understood), both among Jews and STO workers.

One friend of mine, back from Germany and demobilized on health grounds, provided us with an excellent model, which we hastened to reproduce. A friend who was a drawing teacher did the stencils for us. Our only difficulty was the paper. It was a sort of an indescribable hue, something akin to goose shit.

A number of young and not so young people conscripted for STO service found themselves demobilized, thanks to our care.

I looked up my friend Thérèse, whose German journalist partner, who had fled Hitler, was a wanted man. I discovered that he had managed to get out to Mexico along with the last leaders of the Spanish revolution.

Thérèse was working for a daily newspaper and had been selected to go to Germany on STO service.[10] It was vital that she wriggled out of this. She came up with the best hiding place in the world by throwing herself right into the wolf's jaws. With her flawless command of German, she was taken on at the German censorship office. It was there that I found her upon my return.

I decided to make the best of the situation. I would drop by every day to see my friend Thérèse, despite the repugnance I felt towards those displaying swastika armbands. Her "colleagues" had to get used to my face and to my presence. And it was in her office that I composed most of my phony papers and hid my rubber stamps.

It was without its risks. One day I was very nearly caught at the typewriter where I was busy demobbing an STO conscript. I almost shit myself, but I kept my cool and carried on and saw my task through. I was in a sweat. Thérèse was green with terror.

Of all the censorship officials, there was only one who took us into his confidence and offered his opinion on the war, which he detested. He was a musician. When his bosses got wind of his views, he was dispatched to the Russian front. We offered to help him out of his bind, with phony papers and a safe haven. But he declined our help for fear of reprisals against his family. We never heard another word about "poor Paul," as he referred to himself.

I made contact with a number of comrades belonging to resistance networks. We did them favors, swapping their papers, but I was never willing to sign up with any of their networks. I wanted to be

10 The Service du travail obligatoire (Compulsory Work Service) was initially created by the Vichy government and was used by the Germans to fill in gaps in their workforce. It often meant compulsory transfer to Germany and a life of forced labor in special work camps there.

free to make decisions and responsibilities for myself. I believe it was that that was my salvation, whereas so many other women and men found themselves being rounded up and deported.

Saint-Nazaire had been bombed and destroyed by the RAF, which targeted a huge concrete installation, a safe haven for German submarines, which suffered hardly a scratch. I brought my mother home to live with me, as her home had been burned down. Once the Germans occupied the Free Zone, Pat/Isaac also sought refuge in my home until the war ended. I had plenty of mouths to feed and little to offer in the way of food.

A good friend of mine was in charge of the ration cards service at his suburban town hall. One day, that town hall was raided by us both and a number of ration cards were carried away. Every month, I used to call back to renew my small stock of cards. That enabled me to save a fair number of people from starving, and no one was harmed.

Besides supplying phony papers, I had to come up with maids' quarters, inhabited or otherwise, where radio sets could be set up. A real obstacle course, German cars were forever on the road and sometimes to great effect.

As luck would have it, I found myself working in concert with an escape network, smuggling French prisoners out of Germany and, from my base in Paris, aiding and abetting the escape of Alsace-Lorrainers drafted forcibly into the German army.

The work was infinitely varied.

The pick-up point for the phony papers was in the gardens at the Palais-Royal, under Colette's windows. One day I watched as the lad I was waiting for approached, his face distraught. The Germans had been waiting for him at home. He just had time to whip the door open and escape. He had not had the presence of mind to turn the key in the lock, so the "Jerries" who had come to arrest him shot at him as he took the down staircase four steps at a time. It was a miracle that he had not been killed. Be that as it may, he kept our appointment after taking countless detours. He collapsed onto a bench.

After that he was in possession of papers from me that were "in order" and, some time after that, he got out to England.

I was very nearly pinched myself on my way to the home of an architect who lived on the Champs-Élysées, to whom I was to pass on some documents. As I arrived at his door on the second floor (it opened onto a broad corridor), I spotted that the door had been forced. I continued on my path without stopping. Luckily for me. As I passed his lodge, the concierge, who had seen me there several times, told me that the Gestapo were up in the apartment and were waiting for the tenant in question. I waited around a long time for him and was able to tip him off. He escaped their clutches that day. But he was later arrested at the home of some friends where they used to gather, after a tip-off, and was deported to Germany.

There were lots of such anecdotes with more or less happy outcomes.

The Germans were getting ready to pull out of Paris, taking with them everything they could carry. I was bicycling home from work and saw a crowd gathering outside the department stores in the Rue Petit. A truck loaded up with boxes was ready to pull away. And on every side, there were people objecting:

"They're making off with our provisions, and we haven't a bite to eat!"

I dumped my bike in a hallway and, along with one young lad, clambered onto the truck and set about emptying it of its cargo.

We had lots of "customers." Every one of them made off carrying a box in his arms or on his shoulder as he made a beeline for home. The truck was all but empty when the German troops in the inner courtyard caught on to what we were up to. They lobbed a grenade in our direction. There was a flight of sparrows. My accomplice and I did not hang around. They simply reloaded the truck.

As I recovered my bike, I saw that someone had set one of the boxes in question in my luggage-basket. I returned pleased by the little trick we had played on them.

When I opened the box at home, it was to cries of delight. I held little cans of Breton tuna in oil, a real treat for us and our friends.

Then came the end of the war. The procession of De Gaulle and friends along the Champs-Élysées to the Hôtel de Ville. The tanks of Leclerc, and the delirious crowds.

There was also—sadly!—the dismal and shameful spectacle of vengeance at work: women and young girls, hands in the air, under the escort of exultant FFI members who were jabbing them in the ribs with rifle butts.[11]

11 The Forces Francaise de l' intérieur (French forces of the interior) were comprised

Other naked, shaven, roughly painted unfortunates were paraded through the streets to a chorus of hoots, slaps, and spittle from a witless, imbecilic, heartless mob. While the real culprits sipped champagne in utter impunity.

F. B., a staffer from a right-wing newspaper who had "collaborated," found himself in a pickle: I furnished him with the ID he needed to get out of it. Not that he enjoyed his freedom for long; he was placed in Fresnes prison where he rubbed shoulders with Brasillach.[12*] Even though he and I did not think along the same lines at all (his beliefs horrified me), as an anarchist, I had a duty to throw him a line. After he was released, he ignored me and I, him.

One friend of our comrades, Maurice W.,[13*] director of a left-wing review, discovered during the Occupation that he held some pro-German sentiments. One of our people in his memoirs accused him of having worked for the police. I didn't think he had gone quite that far. Friends of his adamantly denied the accusation and everyone, myself included, respected him even after he passed away.

Pat was reunited with his nearest and dearest. We parted as good friends. He saw his daughter very frequently and spent his holidays with her. He died of cancer in 1960.

My Sonia was coming back to Paris, back from the Dordogne *maquis* where she had served as a liaison agent, with all of the attendant risks. She was deeply depressed.

To banish her dark mood, I decided to take her to Italy to look up some friends, among them Fernando, from whom there had been no sign of life since the fascists took him out of the Le Vernet camp. The border was closed to civilians. Some contacts I had in the Army's Ordinance Survey Commission slipped me two orders sending us on a mission to Genoa. And so off we went, our bags slung over our backs.

Down in Nice, an old friend, Nonore,* an anarchist activist, grinned at the sight of our army papers. She recommended against using them and promised to find us a people-smuggler to get us through the minefield.

Of course, we ignored her advice and headed straight for the

of French Resistance fighters.
  12 The right-wing writer Robert Brassillach (1909–1945) was executed even though many intellectuals, across the political spectrum, lobbied for clemency.
  13 Maurice Wullens.

military in Beaulieu who had to give us the authorization to cross the border. We ran into a regular army officer who made a face when he saw our papers and refused to recognize our Commission, it being a body established by the Resistance. We had to head back to the Nice base, which we did begrudgingly.

There, a commandant rubber-stamped our mission orders. Returning to Beaulieu, we were informed that was not enough, that this required the stamp of the Nice Resistance. How come? I was running out of patience:

"You know, lots of things got done during the war . . . without your authorization and without your rubber stamps; with or without your leave, we are going across that border!"

And it was said in a certain tone!

And was the colonel impressed? Maybe not! But he promptly issued us with the requisite paperwork, so there we were, all perked up and bound the Italian border.

At the French border crossing, no bother!

But the Italians eyed our papers and called out:

"What's this? What's this? Female soldiers!"

Being under the authority of the Americans, they were in no position to go making decisions. So, we had to wait in no man's land for the arrival of an American officer who was filled in on our position. Not only did he rubber-stamp our papers, but he offered to take us in his own car as far as Bordighera, where we caught the train to Genoa.

We managed to trace Fernando through the good offices of an anarchist group whose address we had. He had been mistreated by the fascists and had teeth knocked out. Jailed right up until the Liberation, he had then been freed by the resistance. He was making a gentle recovery from the abuse inflicted upon him and his delight at seeing us again was plain to see.

We spent a month in Genoa. The anarchists and anarcho-syndicalists were resuming their activities after protracted and nonsensical civil war that had pitted people against one another, some millions of individuals, when they had no real reason for hating and slaughtering one another.

My Sonia's partner was Georges Malkine,* who was twenty-five years older than her; he was a writer and, above all, a surrealist painter who had been part of the renowned *Révolution surrealiste*[14] team, a friend of Antonin Artaud and Desnos. He had dodged the Gestapo by some miracle and had turned to proofreading as a means of survival.

He had two children by Sonia. When the second was born, grandfather Malkine, a celebrated musician who had settled in New York, eager to get to know his grand-children, brought them to New York where they were to stay for a few months. They later settled there.[15]

In turn, I was invited to New York for the birth of the third child. New York was unfamiliar to me; it was a great discover. That city—dirty, fantastic, frightening—grabs you by the guts when you become truly acquainted with it.

It was unthinkable that I should come to New York and not drop in on the newspapers and trade unions!

I paid a visit to *The New York Times* in the heart of New York and saw the building from top to bottom and, on my return, was able to present a report to my own union about the work practices of our American comrades, which were quite different from our own in terms of pay rates and all things concerning our occupation.

I visited various anarchist groups—Italian, American, all women, Jewish, etc. A friend of Emma Goldman, Rose Pesotta,* was then secretary of the very important Garment Workers Union affiliated with the CIO; she introduced me to a series of trade union personalities.

An international trade union delegation was on a visit to New York and to the trade union organizations; Rose Pesotta welcomed them with the radio in attendance. Everyone was free to speak his mind, myself for one! That was some evening!

Feminist groups that looked up to Emma Goldman asked if I would speak at one of their meetings. I was able to gauge the work effected by Emma in these circles, not to mention her work in various New York anarchist groups.

Emma Goldman's niece and the latter's two sons, well known New York publishers, invited me to pay a visit to rural New York

14 The journal *La Revolution surrealiste* (Surrealist Revolution) was published in Paris from 1924-27. All in all twelve issues were published.

15 Sonia Malkine (1923-2014) had worked with various elements of the French resistance, including Spanish Republican exiles. In 1948 she and her husband, the Surrealist artist Georges Malkine, traveled to America where they settled in Brooklyn. After visiting Emma Goldman's niece Stella Ballantine, in Woodstock, they moved there in 1953. Sonia would go on to become a well-known folksinger and radio host. In her later years she gave interviews discussing her time in the Resistance.

and Woodstock, where they lived year-round.[16] Woodstock blanketed in snow was well worth a visit. The bulk of the population there was made up of all manner of artists, musicians, singers, composers, stage or movie performers, artisans working in wool, leather, or metal, painters, and sculptors. That is where I met, among others, Joan Baez, Bob Dylan, and Sam Eskine, who owned the finest collection of folk music discs and recordings from all over the globe. After her husband passed away, Sonia lived in Woodstock with her children. A musician in her own right, she toured America earning her livelihood.

I wouldn't like to live in the USA, where life is so different from ours here, but I went back there on several occasions and made the acquaintances of unionists, anarchists, and simply ecologists. American youth seem to be waking up to all these issues. Demonstrations against nuclear power stations are frequent and well attended. But for the outward appearances of liberalism, America also has its prisons packed with all manner of refractories. Alongside its billionaires and small and great bourgeoisie, there is enduring poverty, especially in certain states.

Whereas we in France have our own prisoners, poor, and vagrants too, I have never seen anything as pathetic as the living dead of New York's Bowery, the quarter of diamond merchants and bums, its stark clash of the very rich and the very poor, where limousines and the dregs of New York society rub shoulders, with "men" famished to death stand on the edge of the pavement, stripped to the waist, trying to hawk their shabby shirts, or, in bare feet, their hands clutching a pair of shoes with holes in the soles, just waiting for the equally impoverished buyer to offer them to.

America too is in need of its revolution.

16 Stella's son Ian Ballantine (1916–1995) created Ballantine Books with his wife Betty in 1952 with a policy of producing simultaneous hardback and paperback editions of novels. Later they went on to specialize in publishing paperback science fiction and in 2008 were jointly inducted into the Science Fiction Hall of Fame.

A la MATERNELLE 1902
Châteaubriant
Avec Ernest

2

3

1: May's father
2: May's mother
3: May with younger brother Ernest at nursery school, 1902

4: Louise Michel
5: Gaston Rolland
6: Emile Cottin
7: Charles d'Avray

8: Séverine
9: Dragui Popovich
10: May on her return from Canada
11: Sébastien Faure

12

12: *Le Libertaire*'s editors, 1921. Louis Lecoin on the left

13: Saint-Etienne congress
14: "Lost at sea" off Murmansk (Lepitit, Lefebvre, Vergeat, Toubine) 1921
15: Nestor makhno in 1922

16

17

16: Germaine Berton on trial
17: A working session in Moscow, 1922–23

20

19

18: Friquet, Fleshin, Mollie Steimer, Voline, and his family in 1924
19: Stein, Emma Goldman, Sasha Berkman, and Mollie (May was in jail in Melun at the t
20: May with daughter Sonya after she was freed from Melun

21

FARO

, bravant les méchants, je me presse
…urer. » (BEAUMARCHAIS).

faire de Silésie
glée, sans l'être

rence des ambassadeurs a te
ngues séances hier, au cour…
elle a terminé ses travaux su…
de la Haute-Silésie. L'accor…
tre les Alliés, c'est-à-dire que…
glaise a été adoptée.
s brièvement qu'on soutenai…
… : Le Conseil de la S. D. N.
é de fixer une frontière ; i…
celle frontière est acquise.
arrangements économiques…
ent être que proposés et no…
la Pologne et à l'Allemagne…
… conventions et les conven…
ent être librement consenties…
le traité de Versailles n'au…
Alliés qu'à fixer une frontièr…

UN ATTENTAT
contre M. Myron Herrick
ambassadeur des Etats-Unis

Un attentat qui rappelle la manière
des nihilistes russes a été commis hier
contre M. Myron Herrick, ambassadeur
des Etats-Unis à Paris. Fort heureuse-
ment, cette tentative d'assassinat contre le grand ami de la France a échoué
et la « machine infernale » que des
mains criminelles avaient préparée à
son intention n'a fait que blesser légè-
rement quelqu'un de son personnel.

Voici dans quelles circonstances cet
attentat a été commis.

A 9 h. 1 2, un facteur apporta, com-
me chaque jour, le courrier à la chan-
cellerie de l'Ambassade, 5, rue de
Chaillot. Tous les plis et les paquets

23

21: Nicolas Lazarévitch
22: *Le Figaro* reports on May's parcel bomb sent to US ambassador
Myron Herrick, 20 October 1921
23: A demonstration following the execution of Sacco and Vanzetti

24

25

26

27

28

24: François Niel, with his and May's son, Lucien (aka Lulu)
25: May and children in Saint Tropez
26: Pat and May's daughter Marie-May in Toulouse
27: May's three children (Sonia, Lucien and Marie-May) in Paris
28: Xavier

29

30

31

32

29: Viaud and Chalard
30: Jeanne Humbert
31: Eugène Bizeau
32: A get-together of militants: (left to right) Nicolas Faucier and Alice, René
   Boucher, Charles d'Avray, Georges Cochon, Rirette Maîtrejean, Louis
   Lecoin and May Picqueray

33: *Le Refractaire* colleague Margot
34: *Le Refractaire* colleague Elisabeth
35: *Le Refractaire* colleagues Anne and Christèle

36

37

38

36: May in New York
37: Protesters in Le Larzac
38: In the Place de la République in Paris

9

MY COMRADES-IN-STRUGGLE

"No God, No Master"; we need not go over that again.

Yet those of whom I am about to speak, I'm going to call them my "masters." Not that they ever gave me any orders, but their work and their lives made me what I am.

Sébastien Faure* was the first of them. Others have pursued his work.

Some have merely passed through my life, but such was their impact on me that I wanted to know everything about their lives and their actions.

Makhno is one case in point. The premises 114-120, Boulevard de La Villette, belonged to the old CGT. For the most part, they were inhabited by anarcho-syndicalist activists. There you might have found Marie Guillot* from the Teachers' Union, general secretary of the CGTU (she refused to pay the tax on her salary and the tax collector had her furniture impounded. There was some fun that day!). There was also Pécastaing* from the Garment Makers; Olive who came in from the Hérault along with Férandel, Soustelle, A. Viaud, Respaut . . . all of them outstanding militants. There was Albert Guigui* who arrived from Algiers and went on to make a career for himself with the ILO in Geneva. Or Broutchoux* from the Miners'

Union, who "bunked on to the railways" rather than dip into union funds. He had a trick: according to the railway regulations, the ticket inspector was supposed to wear white gloves while checking one's ticket. Broutchoux used to tackle them on this point every time, and the poor flummoxed inspector, who had no gloves, was therefore unable to check his ticket. Job done! Broutchoux had a son who was killed by the gendarmes "by mistake." The man went out of his mind as a result.

And there was also Charlot, from the Iron Workers' Union who, following an accident, was no longer able to climb to the rooftops and became the concierge at No. 118. Not to mention Henri Ferré* from the Syndicalist Youth, or the Lemoines,* or Jacques Guillot,* conscientious objector. Or Marion, who became a turncoat; or Louise Heuchel* or Louise Pohu* and her partner Toto Allende* and others whose names escape me. We used to bump into one another often in one or another's house, to debate pressing matters or simply to enjoy one another's company. Larger meetings took place at the Magnaval restaurant in the Place du Combat, or in the Rue Saint Maur, at the Fraternelle where the members of the Social Defense Committee* or Black Sea Sailors* Defense Committee used to meet.

I lived at No. 120, two minuscule little rooms, but there was always a good broth simmering on the cooker or coffee ready for serving. Indeed, it was my "privilege" to welcome the waves of immigrant comrades arriving from pretty much all over back then: the Russians fleeing from dictatorship, the Bulgarians likewise, then the Italians who had managed to dodge Mussolini's castor oil and prison. After being restored, they would be directed by me to the home of this or that comrade who had a room or a bed, or some corner where they might rest, be it in Paris, in the suburbs, or out in the countryside.

It is in this way that one morning a couple showed up with their girl, all three worn out and disheveled. Especially the man, whose entire body was covered in wounds. They had some refreshment and stretched out on the only bed where they very quickly dropped off to sleep. I sent for a comrade who knew Russian, whereupon I discovered that my guests were Makhno, his partner Galina,[1] and their daughter. I was greatly moved in the presence of the "great man"

---

1 Galina Kuzmenko (1894–1978) was a strong advocate of the rights of women and was chairperson of the teachers' union in the liberated Makhnovist areas.

whose epic I knew only from hearsay. Epic, the word is not too strong a description of Makhno's exploits.

I listened to him talk for nearly an hour, but, realizing that he was very weary, I entrusted him and his family to some friends in the suburbs who took him in and where a doctor who was also a friend offered him the care he required for his condition.

We bumped into each other often, and a firm friendship grew between us. Even though he managed to have frequent contacts with exiled countrymen of his and to argue about the issues he held dear— revolution, the anarchist society, the anarchist platform—he was out of his element. He simply ached for action, and it pained him to see how the revolution had degenerated in Russia. He could not forget his former comrades from the Makhnovshchina who had been slain and decimated by Bolshevik troops. He suffered in his flesh and in his whole being.

To survive, he did odd jobs and wound up working as a laborer for Renault. As if all that was not enough, the French police harassed him and wanted to see him deported. It required intervention by Louis Lecoin and the assistance of certain establishment figures to thwart the deportation plans.

Tuberculosis, a disease he had contracted in prison in Moscow, was eating away at him, and at the age of forty-six, Makhno passed away, nearly destitute, in July 1935. The comrades who escorted him that day to Père-Lachaise cemetery, where he was to be cremated, carried in their hearts, not the picture of the long-suffering, embittered, disappointed little man but the image of the *Batko* (Little Father), victor of Denikin and Wrangel, victim to the Bolsheviks whom he would have considered his brothers.

Who was Makhno?[2]

He was born on October 27, 1889 and raised in the village of Gulyai Pole in Ukraine. The child of poor peasants, he was only ten-months old when his father passed away, leaving his mother to look after him and four young brothers. From the age of seven, he was a herder, looking after cattle and sheep for the peasants of his home

2 Black Cat press in Edmonton have published three volumes of Makhno's autobiography in English: *The Russian Revolution in Ukraine* (2007); *Under the Blows of the Counter-Revolution, April–June, 1918* (2008); and *The Ukrainian Revolution* (2011). For a lively account of his life see: Alexandre Skirda, *Nestor Makhno: Anarchy's Cossack, The Struggle for Free Soviets in the Ukraine 1917-1921* (Edinburgh and Oakland: AK Press, 2004).

village. At the age of eight, he entered the local school, attending only during the winter months and working his summers as a herder. At the age of twelve, he was placed with some German *kulaks* (rich peasants)—there were lots of German settlements in Ukraine back then—as a farmhand. Even then, he nurtured a deep-seated hatred of exploitative bosses and dreamed up ways of settling scores with them, for himself and others, if some day that were within his capability. Later on, he worked as a smelter in a factory in the village.

Up to the age of sixteen, he had no contact with the world of politics. His revolutionary and social thinking was shaped within the narrow compass of fellow proletarian peasants. The 1905 revolution suddenly yanked him out of those circles and plunged him into the torrent of great revolutionary developments. By then, he was seventeen and full of revolutionary zeal and ready to tackle anything just to set the workers free! He joined the ranks of the anarcho-communists and, from that point on, was a tireless militant.

In 1908, he fell into the clutches of the authorities, who sentenced him to hang for his anarchist associations and his part in terrorist activities. Out of consideration for his young age, his sentence was commuted to life imprisonment in Moscow's central prison, the Butyrki.

Although he had no prospect of release from prison, he learned Russian grammar there and mathematics and literature, cultural history, and political economy. He had an outstanding instructor there, a fellow prisoner by the name of Arshinoff. Prison was the only school from which he drank deeply of historical and political learning, and this was a great help to him in his subsequent revolutionary activity. Life and deeds were a second schooling whereby he learned to "read" and understand people and social developments. It was in prison that Makhno compromised his own health. Obstinate and unable to countenance the complete crushing of personality to which he was subjected, like everyone else in penal servitude, he still bridled at the prison authorities and was forever being sent to "the hole," where, due to the cold and damp, he contracted pulmonary tuberculosis. After nine years on the inside, he was forever clad in irons for bad conduct. Along with other political prisoners, he was rescued by the uprising of the Moscow proletariat in 1917. He spent some time in his home village, where he was the only political convict. And he earned the esteem and trust of all the peasants. He was now an accomplished militant, having powerful momentum of passion and a determined idea about social struggle.

By the time the Ukraine was occupied by the Austro-Germans, Makhno was commissioned to raise peasant-worker battalions to take on the invaders. He was obliged to retreat, and the local bourgeoisie put a price on his head. By way of reprisal, the Ukrainian and German authorities set fire to his mother's home and shot his older brother Emilian, a disabled war veteran.

Then he made for Moscow to meet the anarchists there, and he paid a visit to Lenin with whom he had lengthy talks:

"Anarchists are always full of self-sacrifice, ready for sacrifice of any sort, but they are blindly fanatical, ignoring the present and thinking only of the distant future," Lenin told him.

To which Makhno replied:

"I ought to tell you, comrade Lenin, that your allegations regarding anarchists are wholly mistaken. In Ukraine, the entire campaign was waged by anarchists. You Bolsheviks have no foothold in our country areas. Where there are Bolsheviks, their sway is minimal.

"Nearly all the townships and peasant associations in Ukraine were established on the prompting of anarchists, and the armed struggle by the laboring population against the counter-revolution was undertaken under the ideological and organizational leadership of anarcho-communists alone. These are facts that you cannot contest. I take it for granted that you are perfectly well aware of the manpower and fighting capabilities of the Ukraine's revolutionary irregulars? It was not without reason that you cited their courage in defending our revolutionary gains.

"All of this sufficiently demonstrates how much, Comrade Lenin, is your allegation erroneous that we do not have our feet on the ground, that our position on the present is pathetic, albeit that we love thinking about the future. We stand four-square in the present and work there to seek out whatever brings us closer to the future, to which we give serious thought."

Whereupon Lenin, throwing his arms open said:

"Perhaps I was mistaken . . ."[3]

Makhno returned to his village where he raised a detachment, which, after three weeks, had become the terror not just of the local

---

3 This exchange is reported in Makhno's memoirs and was translated into English as *My Visit to the Kremlin* (Edmonton: Black Cat Press, 1979).

bourgeoisie but also of the Austro-German authorities. Makhno's theatre of operations was wide-ranging. One feature of Makhno's tactics was rapid movement. He would always turn up out of the blue where he was least expected.

Within a short time, he had thrown an iron noose around the entire region where the local bourgeoisie had dug in. With the speed of a hurricane, Makhno's men, dauntless and merciless towards their enemies, would fall like lightning upon their enemies and vanish just as quickly. The next day, Makhno would start up all over again a hundred kilometers away. Then, the day after that, he would pop up another hundred kilometers away, cracking down on a Magyar detachment that had been repressing the peasants.

Battalion after battalion was sent in to crush Makhno. To no avail. Makhno's partisans made it their general rule to kill Austro-German officers while letting soldiers taken prisoner go free. They were urged to head for home, recount there what the Ukrainian peasants were doing, and to work to bring about the social revolution back home.

"Victory or Death. That is the dilemma facing the workers and peasants of Ukraine at this present point in history. But we cannot all perish, for there are we are too many of us. We are humankind. So we shall win. But we will not win just to repeat the mistakes of the past and place our destinies back in the hands of new masters. We shall win in order to take control of our own fates and arrange our lives in accordance with our own wishes and our own truth." (One of Makhno's earliest appeals.)

I could fill page after page with Makhno's actions, but here is a summary of them: as Makhno liberated a village, it was reorganized along fresh lines, and it was left to the villagers to determine their own fates and live their own lives without leaders or authority; he created the *Commune libertaire*, just as they did in Spain in wartime. If they so wished, the communes were free to establish connections with one another, always long the same lines.

In military terms, he had to drive the Poles, the Austro-Germans, and all the rich landowners out of Ukraine, and their lands were distributed to the peasants.

And then he had to contend with the "White" armies, Wrangel's army, Denikin's army, driving them out after ferocious fighting.

What the soldiers of the Red Army had not been capable of doing, Makhno's men did.

Once they had entered some village as victors, the first concern of the Makhnovists was to dispel any possibility of misunderstanding: the Makhnovshchina was not to be taken for a new *power*, for a new *political party*, for some sort of *dictatorship*.

It started by rescinding all bans and lifting all prohibitions and restrictions, imposed by any political authorities, whether upon the press or political factions. Unfettered freedom of speech, of the press, of assembly, and association was proclaimed for all. Berdyansk prison was leveled with dynamite, as were the prisons in Alexandrovsk and Krivoi-Rog. The working population everywhere acclaimed these actions.

In the course of the Russian revolution, the Makhnovshchina era in Ukraine was the only one when genuine freedom for the toiling masses found full expression. For as long as the region was occupied by Makhno's troops, the urban and rural workers could, for the very first time, say and do everything they wanted and how they wanted. And above all, at last they had the opportunity to see to the organization of their lives and labors themselves, in accordance with their own understanding of the meanings of justice and truth.

Especially deserving of note were the *keynote ideas* on the basis of which the originators set about the task to rebirth the work of education and grounding that work.

1. It was left to the workers themselves to oversee the proper handling of the training and education of younger generations of workers.

2. School had to be not only a source of essential knowledge but also a means of shaping the *conscious and free human*, capable of fighting for a truly humane society and of living and acting within it.

3. If it was to meet these two requirements, the school had to be independent and therefore divorced from *Church* and *State*.

4. The teaching and education of the young had to be handled by those so inclined by their penchants, aptitudes, and knowledge. This endeavor was to fall under the effective and watchful supervision of the workers.

In Gulyai Pole there were a few intellectuals enamored of the principles of Francisco Ferrer's Free School. At their instigation, a vigorous campaign arose, resulting in an interesting pilot scheme for a wide-ranging educational effort. A mixed commission made up of peasants, workers, and teachers was set up and commissioned to cater to all the economic and pedagogical needs of school life. The peasants and workers took charge of the upkeep of whatever educational staff were required by all the village and district schools.

In record time, that Commission produced a free education scheme, inspired by Francisco Ferrer's ideas.

At the same time, courses for adults were organized.

And so, the drive to education was relaunched on a fresh footing.

All this passionate creativity of the masses was brutally ended by a fresh, thunderous Bolshevik onslaught mounted throughout the length and breadth of the Ukraine on November 26, 1920.

The situation just described had not been to the liking of the Bolshevik leaders who tried to harness Makhno and to get him and his men to join the Red Army. Makhno refused. Ambushes were set for him by Lenin and Trotsky; but he thwarted them. From some captured Bolshevik spies, Makhno learned that a massive attack by Red soldiers was in the offing against him and his men. But, by way of a pretext for it, they would have to deploy slander and lies. Lenin claimed that the Makhnovists and anarchists were hatching a plot and a massive uprising against the soviet government.

Sheer repetition meant that the Bolsheviks managed to get lots of people inside the USSR as well as abroad to swallow these lies.

Makhno opened up contacts with the Kharkov government which informed him that it had all been a simple misunderstanding, that a special commission would be charged with clarifying the whole business, etc. That conversation took place by direct line at nine o'clock on the morning of November 26. Now, six hours before that, in the middle of the night, the Makhnovists' representatives in Kharkov had been rounded up, as had all the anarchists in that city and elsewhere.

Two hours after the conversation, Gulyai Pole was overrun from every side by Red troops and subjected to fierce shelling. On that very date and at that very hour, the Makhnovists' Crimean army came under attack. There, the Bolsheviks, resorting to trickery, managed to capture that army's high command and its commanding officer and put every last one of them to death.

On November 27, Makhnovists found this proclamation on prisoners belonging to the Red Army: "Forwards against Makhno! Death to the Makhnovshchina!"

This was evidence that the onslaught had been a long time in the making.

The treacherous attack quickly spread to every region: however, lots of anarchists had been arrested in Kharkov and other towns. While the Makhnovists' commanding officer in the Crimea had been seized and executed, the cavalry commander, Martchenko, though cornered and under ferocious attack from detachments from the Bolshevik 4th Army, managed to break loose and force a passage through the fortified checkpoints. Taking with him what men he still had left, he succeeded through forced marching day and night to join up with Makhno, who again gave the Bolsheviks the slip; what anguish it must have been for him to witness the arrival of the little band of 250 riders (all was left of his 1,500-strong cavalry). Martchenko then said: "Now we know what these Bolsheviks are made of!"

With that handful of men, numerically insignificant yet exasperated and undaunted, Makhno, just about recovered from his illness (typhus) and in appalling pain from his wounds (the latest a broken ankle), went on the offensive. He managed to rout the Red Army cavalry regiment closing in on Gulyai Pole from two sides.

He succeeded in slipping through and raising around 2,500 men (1,000 cavalry and 1,500 infantry, Makhnovists and Red Army deserters combined). He launched a counter-attack and routed the 42nd Red Army Division, taking 6,000 prisoners. Two thousand wanted to join Makhno's troops, and the remainder were sent home. They were merely advised to stop acting as instruments of power in the subjugation of the people. He delivered several consecutive blows to the Red Army and took tens of thousands of prisoners.

But then news came that the Red Army was about to dispatch entire regiments of cavalry and infantry to wipe out the Makhnovshchina.

That would spell the end of the insurgent army. The Council of Revolutionary Insurgents thereupon decided to evacuate the region for a time, allowing Makhno complete liberty as to the direction of the movement.

For upwards of three months, an unequal struggle was waged, with nonstop fighting by day and by night. After he reached Kiev in the depths of the freeze in an area strewn with boulders, Makhno was obliged to dump artillery, provisions, and munitions. Two divisions of Red Cossacks added to the massive armies pitted against Makhno. It looked as if any chance of escape had evaporated. Yet no one considered dispersing in a shameful flight.

The sight of that handful of men, alone among the boulders, the sky and enemy gunfire, and ready to fight to the finish and doomed to perish was unspeakably sad.

A harrowing suffering, a mortal angst took hold, prompting cries of despair, screaming to the entire universe that a chilling crime was about to be committed and that whatever greatness there was within the people, that the most noble, the most sublime produced by a people at this heroic time in its history, was about to be annihilated and perish forever.

Wounded yet again, Makhno was brought to the Dnieper, arriving there in a farm cart. There followed wrenching farewells to his men. The latter then turned to face the Red divisions, where most of them lost their lives. That was the end of the Makhnovshchina.

There was one particularly vile defamation among the slanders hurled at the Makhnovist movement generally and against Makhno personally. It has been reiterated by many writers of every persuasion and by gossips of every hue. Some spread it deliberately.

They claimed that Makhno and his men were awash with *anti-Semitism*, that they hunted down and slaughtered Jews. Others contend that Makhno tolerated, "turned a blind eye," to the acts of anti-Semitism carried out by "his gangs."

We could spend dozens of pages listing the times Makhno cracked down, unsolicited, on the slightest display of anti-Semitism, on the part of some lost soul in the general populace or within his army. In such cases, Makhno had no hesitation in reacting on the spot, personally and violently, just as he would to any injustice and blatant crime.

One of the reasons why Grigoriev was executed by the Makhnovists was his anti-Semitism and the enormous pogrom he had mounted against the Jews in Elizavetgrad, a pogrom that had claimed the lives of nearly three thousand people. One of the reasons why Grigoriev's former followers were disbanded and initially absorbed into the insurgent army was the anti-Semitic mentality that their former leader had managed to inculcate into them. Let us put a few points on record:

1. Within the Makhnovist army, revolutionaries of Jewish origin played a rather significant role.

2. Members of the Education and Propaganda Commission were Jewish.

3. Besides the many Jews who served in that army's various units, there was a battery manned entirely by Jews, plus a Jewish infantry unit.

4. The Jewish settlements in Ukraine supplied Makhno with lots of volunteers. And, broadly speaking, the very large Jewish population played an active and fraternal role in the movement. Rich and reactionary Jews certainly had a hard time of it, as did non-Jewish reactionaries, but that was solely because they were reactionaries. The myth of an anti-Semitic Makhno is false and needs to be dismantled (to quote Arshinoff).

One cannot speak of Makhno without mentioning one of his comrades, Vsevolod Eichenbaum, better known by his pseudonym, Voline. He was born in the Voronezh region on August 11, 1882.

Invited by Sébastien Faure to contribute to the *Encyclopédie anarchiste* [*Anarchist Encyclopedia*], Voline landed at my place with his wife and four children, at pretty much the same time as Makhno.

Unlike Makhno, he came from a well-to-do family; his father and mother were both doctors and had provided him with a sound education. His brother, Boris, and he had been entrusted to the care of governesses who had ensured that they were properly educated and taught them French and German.

Voline was educated at the high school in Voronezh and then joined the Saint Petersburg Law College, before very quickly dropping out, drawn even then by Social Revolutionary ideas. This prompted him to play a very active role in the events of 1905.

It was on the occasion of that great upheaval that he was picked up by the tsarist police, jailed, and eventually banished. In 1907, he managed to escape from banishment and made his way to France. It was in Paris that he completed his education in the social movement.

He then left the Social Revolutionary Party and developed an interest in emigrant Russian anarchist groups. In 1913, he became a member of the International Action Committee and specialized in French propaganda against the looming war. By 1915, such was his activity that the Viviani-Millerand government had him arrested and interned in a camp up until the war ended and then tried to expel him.

Tipped off about his expulsion, Voline went into hiding and, with the help of French comrades, set sail from Bordeaux for the United States. He left his wife and four children behind in France.

Voline was welcomed with open arms by the Federation of Russian Workers Unions of the United States and Canada (a powerful organization with ten thousand members), which published *Golos Truda* [*The Voice of Labor*], an anarcho-syndicalist weekly paper to which Voline contributed. He lectured on the Russian revolution of 1905; an outstanding public speaker, he was highly regarded.

In 1917, the editorial team and Voline left for Saint Petersburg where there were rumblings of revolution. The Russians who had lived in the United States were reunited with those in Russia itself. The paper switched to daily publication, with Voline as editor. But our friend resigned from the paper following the breakdown of the Brest-Litovsk peace talks.

Voline traveled to Brobov to rejoin his wife and children, who had made it to Russia after countless adventures. In Brobov, Voline worked in the city soviet, in the people's branch, trying to get the populace to understand the revolutionary events. Shortly after, he switched to the *Nabat* [*Alarm*] newspaper, where he was charged with rallying all of the various strands of anarchism and devising his own anarchist "Synthesis." He traveled on to Moscow where he carried on with his work as a staffer with the main *Nabat*.

But along came the Bolshevik backlash. The free press was done away with and the anarchists were persecuted. Voline was elected to the chair of the Insurgent Military Council, throwing himself into that task for six months.

Afflicted, as Makhno also was, with typhus, he was arrested by the 14th Red Army, hauled back to Moscow, and handed over to the Cheka. And then Makhno signed a military treaty with the Bolshevik government to secure the release of Voline and all the arrested anarchist comrades. Voline was freed in October 1920. He made for Kharkov to lay the ground work for an anarchist congress scheduled for December 25. But Voline was arrested the day before that, as were the anarchists who had been working in conjunction with Makhno.

The anarchist movement was decimated by appalling repression and the portion of Makhno's army that could be reached was wiped out. Voline was locked up in the Butyrki prison in Moscow before being moved to the Lefortovo prison.

He and his comrades were subjected to despicably brutal treatment. By way of protest, they mounted a hunger strike that lasted ten days and which ended thanks to the unexpected intervention by delegates from European trade unions, there to attend the International congress. They managed to ensure the release of the of the prisoners, Voline being one, on condition of a lifetime banishment. They were allowed to leave Russia with their families.

Moving to Germany, he received help from the Frei Arbeiter Union and was able to pen an excellent pamphlet it published, entitled *The Persecution of Anarchism in Soviet Russia*; he also translated Arshinoff's book *History of the Makhnovist Movement*, while editing the important Russian-language weekly paper *The Anarchist Worker*.

Then, for Sébastien Faure's *Encyclopédie anarchiste*, he wrote some remarkable entries that were often reprinted in pamphlet form and translated for the foreign press, notably in Spain. At the suggestion of the CNT, he edited the French-language paper *L'Espagne antifasciste*.

Later, he quit Paris for Nîmes and then Marseilles, where World War Two found him; more than anyone else, he had reason to fear repercussions as an anti-Nazi, an anarchist, and a Russian.

By some miracle, he avoided the dangers surrounding him. But he did not escape the wretchedness of war entirely, enduring all sorts of privations, which softened him for the tuberculosis to which he eventually succumbed. He died in Paris in the Laennac Hospital on September 18, 1944 and was cremated in Père-Lachaise surrounded by numerous friends.

I last bumped into him in Marseilles in a youth hostel, where he was working on his book *The Unknown Revolution*, a book dear to his heart and published thanks to the loyalty of his friends.[4]

At the start of 1929, I happened to be on the premises of *Le Libertaire* when a thickset fellow of indeterminate age introduced himself as the Marius Jacob* who had been sentenced to convict labor for life in 1905 for one hundred or so burglaries.[5]

His black, expressive eyes plunged right into one's own, as if probing right to the heart; his face was craggy, a hint of the suffering he had endured during the twenty-three years of Hell he had just "lived" through.

I was familiar with the tale of this artist-burglar who had provided the inspiration for the fictional character Arsène Lupin, and

---

4 Voline's book, *La Revolution inconnu* (*The Unknown Revolution*), was published after his death by *The Friends of Voline* in 1947.

5 For more information on Marius Jacob in English see Bernard Thomas, *Jacob* (Elephant Editions/Ardent Press, 2013).

everything that I knew about him endeared him to me. I hugged him and gave him a big kiss. We made a great fuss over him; like a child, he was astounded at the changes that had taken place during his long absence: the metro, the trams replacing the horse-drawn carriages. Most of the comrades from his younger days were gone. Police repression had played its part in that.

Together with two or three pals, we took him out to lunch and, not much given to talking—understandably enough—he told us how happy he was to be out and to have been reunited with his mother, who had defended and supported him throughout his time in Hell.

During these twenty-five years, two months and eight days spent in French Guiana, he had spent nine years in solitary, shackles on his feet, and thirteen years in the cells. Nineteen times he tried to escape. His mother sent him law books, which he devoured. He adored such reading material, which enabled him to support and help his comrades in their legal difficulties.

His mother, whom he loved deeply, was his sole reason for living. He never succumbed to any of the many vices inherent to prison life.

Some reporters and writers showed an interest in his case. Marie was like a dog with a bone as she moved heaven and earth and explained it and pleaded for the return of her good little boy, who never had any luck . . .

In France, the comrades launched a press campaign that bore late fruit. Monsieur Gibert, the examining magistrate in the Bonnot Gang case, having become chancellor for Criminal Cases, signed off on his file, cutting his sentence to five years to be served in France.

He was loaded onto the "Biskra," bound for Saint-Nazaire. They had to remove his shackles, and he was no longer able to walk. With his hair all white, he looked like an old man with one foot in the grave. He was taken to Rennes and then to Fresnes and to Melun. On June 19, 1926, a presidential order slashed his sentence to two years. And on December 30, 1928, the gates of the prison were opened at last. He had not set foot on the streets, nor breathed freely, nor hugged his mother for nearly twenty-five years. Mother and son embraced each other as if they had parted only the day before. Marius's fiancée, Rose, had passed away five years earlier.

He lived in a small apartment with his mother, working in a workshop where he kept his head down. Back from the blackest of night after all those years (he was about to be fifty years old), it was up to him to claim his place in the sun. He found Paris oppressive. The busy crowds frightened him. One *sou* at a time, Marie had set aside the sum of a thousand francs for his use. He bought a lottery ticket, pulled on his army boots, and, with his knapsack on his back, off he went, first to the Yonne with Marie and later to Bois-Saint-Denis, a small hamlet near Reuilly.

He happened to discover that the doorknocker of one property at the edges of the Loire was made of gold, and he considered this an insult to poverty. He removed the golden knocker and substituted a metal one. That was to be his very last theft.

He also found out that the anarchists in Russia had been decimated by the Bolsheviks and that authority ruled the roost around the globe; in France, the members of the Bonnot Gang had left minds befuddled. Collective forms of action had overwhelmed individualism. The unions had made headway among the toiling masses, but the libertarian CGT had fallen under the sway of Marxists.

Those who had not been infected with the notion of dictatorship had banded together into the Union Anarchiste, around Louis Lecoin. Anti-militarism, conscientious objection, anarchism—that was their fight. Plus, the liberation of unjustly convicted comrades, such as Sacco and Vanzetti in America, or Durruti, Ascaso, and Jover in France.

Jacob was delighted to make the acquaintances of them. They served the ideal that he had been pursuing in his own idiosyncratic way.

He was saddened to see the cause defeated everywhere, or almost everywhere. Mankind must have lost its reason if it believed in the virtues of indoctrination.

So, he had a go at building himself a new life in the countryside. He bought himself a large tent to house his goods and then a donkey cart and a small shack. Business was good. He dreamed of settling down, but the attempt proved disastrous.

And then Marie, the only woman in his life, passed away at the age of seventy-five.

But was Jacob finished? Did he give up? In July 1936, he went missing for a few months. There were rumblings of revolution in Barcelona. The old beast stirred and off he went in a search for gold to buy arms; there was gold everywhere, dormant gold that might be used as a war chest. He went to Barcelona; Ascaso was dead by then, killed in the course of an attack. Durruti was dead too, Camillo

Berneri had been killed by the communists along with his comrade Barbieri.[6] The anarchists were fighting on all fronts.

He realized that the International Brigades had been a jolt of the world's conscience in the face of the ascendancy of "totalitarians" of all persuasions. "I am a utopian," Jacob thought to himself. "History is not a matter of sentiment but of the balance of power. Until such time that the individual consciences of men are more evolved, the will to power of the few will succeed."

Then, he climbed back into his donkey cart and returned to his stall in the market in Issoudun. He met Paulette, fifteen years his junior. They fell for each other and were married. Happy days!

Sadly! Paulette died of cancer shortly after the Liberation. The loss devastated him. He carried on living with his dog, Négro, and his cats.

He mingled with his friends, the ones who had followed Lecoin or Pierre Berthier* or the ones he had made in Issoudun market. He wrote articles for them under pseudonyms. He lobbied on behalf of certain fellow inmates: and harbored some in his home in Neuilly. Some of them stole from and swindled him . . .

"Well, me, I need nothing!" he said . . .

In 1952, he felt inevitable old age coming on. He drew up his will. He did not have much, but he was afraid lest his enemy, the state, knowing that he had no heir, reap a penny of benefit from his legacy. While still living, he bequeathed the shack, the land, and a few thousand francs to his friends. All his affairs were in order. His heart and his head were intact. Only his body was beginning to weaken. He procured the products necessary to end that. He held a little banquet for the village kids. All nine of them. Then he took them a long walk. He laid out his linens, tidied the house. Scribbled a few words for his pals, leaving them two bottles of rosé to drink after his death.

At daybreak on Saturday the 28th, he covered his bed with a blanket and sheet. He laid there his blind and ailing dog, Négro. He injected him with some morphine.

Then he lay down himself, having checked that the coal-burning stove was leaking carbon monoxide aplenty to complete the work of the injection. Beside his dog, he took the syringe. By the time his friends dropped by a few hours later, he appeared to be sleeping.

---

6 The Italian anarchists Camillo Berneri and Francisco Barbieri were murdered in Barcelona on May 5, 1937 shortly after being arrested by "police" on charges of being "counter-revolutionaries."

I have already mentioned Lecoin lots of times.

But there is so much that I have yet to tell you! He was without a doubt the man alongside whom I worked hardest for the cause.

In December 1956, my friend Louis Lecoin was stricken by a huge misfortune. His wife, Marie, died suddenly, leaving him utterly at a loss and crushed by the pain.

He then determined to sell his house in the Midi and move to Paris to mount a campaign on behalf of conscientious objectors, a number of whom had been languishing behind bars for almost a decade. He also wanted to embark on a campaign to force the government to vote through a conscientious objector status that might spare whoever was refusing to bear arms only to rot in prison for years without end or to flee the country, with all that implied.

As he put it to us with his customary bluntness: "In wanting to rescue the objectors, it is myself that I also want to rescue!"

After having stepped back from the struggle, here he was back with renewed vigor to join the active minority, "the only force that pushes societies out of their ruts and in the direction of salutary developments."

This was a big undertaking at the beginning of 1957, coming as it did after the efforts of Henri Sellier,* Jean Gauchon,* and Émile Véran,* who had been tireless in their concern for imprisoned conscientious objectors for upwards of a decade.

He was very well aware that the battle would be long and tough, as the general staff was not at all prepared to "let itself be walked all over" by pacifists, whose struggle would consist not only of securing the release of prisoners but also of ensuring that a de facto situation was enshrined in law: conscientious objector status, awaiting the eradication of all armies, which was certainly not going to happen overnight . . .

The predicament faced by objectors was horrific for those who stood by their decision as they faced prison term after prison term; weaker ones, unable to stand their ground, left the prisons for the mental hospitals or the graveyards. And for the strongest among them, there was never any end to their years behind bars.

When Louis kicked off the campaign, there were ninety objectors behind bars. Edmond Schaguené* was the doyen, with nine years. Nevertheless, he relied upon his determination to live in the open air, but he gave priority to the voice of his conscience and answered "no" in court every time, no to the army, no to war . . .

If he was to carry out this campaign, Louis was going to need a newspaper. He cashed in his assets and handed some of the proceeds to his daughter. Then his friends raised a certain sum. Well-known painters like Bernard Buffet, Vlaminck, Kischka, Van Dongen, Atlan, Lorjou, Grau Sala, etc. . . . forwarded him paintings that were raffled off, raising three million francs.

Pooled together, these funds made it possible to put out the weekly newspaper *Liberté* on January 31, 1958. Premises were made available by Sébastien Faure's old friend, Alexandre.

A Prisoners Defense Committee was set up, and friends like Pierre Martin, Conem, and others joined the team.

The objectors included men of varying persuasions: Catholics, Protestants, anti-social types, drop-outs, Jehovah's Witnesses. They were not all pacifists and were prompted by differing motives.

In order to reach the target, he had given himself, Louis had to use all sorts of means, petitioning deputies and VIPs likely to lobby the authorities, leafleting, holding meetings and rallies: together with *Liberté*'s managing editor, Dufour,* he was jailed at the request of a Monsieur Legendre for inciting servicemen to disobey orders.

As he set out on this campaign, Louis knew the risks he was running: the gold tassels in the Rue Saint Dominique had their minds made up to defend their privileges. However, the court acquitted the accused pair, Lecoin and Dufour. This was a step in the right direction.

In the wake of the war in Algeria, the campaign lasted a lot longer than anticipated. It required overtures and interventions and articles in *Liberté* and, to finish, a twenty-four-day hunger strike mounted by our friend Louis in June 1962, despite his advanced years! The whole business took nearly five years.

In the interim, Schaguené had been freed, as had several of his comrades who had spent five, six, seven, and eight years behind bars. That was a success in itself. All of them were Jehovah's Witnesses. Later, it transpired that they were not all made of the same stuff and that once the status had been voted through they abided by orders coming from their leaders in America and declined the status so dearly won. On that day, I saw tears rolling down our friend's cheeks:

"The bastards," he said, "How could they do me this way?"

Luckily, he was able to count on the commitment of his friends who came forward in different manners: from newspaper articles (and let it be said that *Le Canard Enchaîné*[7] did not play down his efforts) to approaches to the prime minister and indeed the President of the Republic. It really needs to be said that it came as quite a surprise that it was a general who pushed the status through, despite the banana skins laid by military figures and certain deputies, including Monsieur Debré, who completely deformed it with his amendments, when no Socialist government had ever even broached the issue.

Hundreds of newspapers around the world carried protests by the thousands.

The courts had to step in and, on the instructions of an examining magistrate, Louis Lecoin was picked up and taken to hospital and several people from his entourage were charged failing to assist a person in danger. True, the doctors feared for his life and were afraid that he might slip into a coma at any moment.

There was some back and forth between the Elysée palace and the Bichat hospital, some promises made, but Louis held firm and wanted a communique signed by the prime minister himself. After some protracted tussling, this was done. It took the great little man's tenacity to break down an entire system.

What would Louis say these days, faced with the situation of objectors? Ever since the Bregançon decree, a gift from Pompidou and Debré, young folks who have been granted conscientious objector status have been refusing to report to the National Forestry Office, to which they have been assigned for the first year of their term of service. A number of them (about three hundred per year) are brought before a court martial and, depending on the mood of the judges and the length of their hair, have been variously sentenced to between one and six months of imprisonment or a suspended sentence.

I myself have made overtures to the Army minister and the Council of State. But to no avail. In the Chamber, not a single deputy has stepped up to raise the matter seriously. And this situation shows every sign of lasting for a long time to come.

In consequence, there are more and more draft dodgers who run the risk of two years behind bars rather than accept the hobbled version of conscientious objector status.

---

7 Founded in 1915, this irreverent French paper with its staunchly republican beliefs had always been close to the libertarian outlook holding to its own brand of pacifism, anti-clericalism, and anti-militarism. The paper supported the work of Louis Lecoin and Picqueray worked there for over thirty years as a proofreader.

After struggling for five years to arrive there, it is rather disheartening!

The Commission itself is hobbled, since it either accords or doesn't accord the individual status while collective demands, consequently drafted in the same fashion, are very often turned down. Without any great success, the young fight on with tenacity, and we will carry on offering them our support until the government eventually gets around to making a decision.

In the spring of 1971 Louis Lecoin entered a clinic for surgery, nothing particularly dangerous (said Louis) and one from which he hoped to make a full recovery.

He had begun a campaign to abolish war, thousands of pamphlets were sent out all over France and he was full of plans that he was looking forward to realizing. His big idea, his hobbyhorse some said, was French disarmament. Obviously, any such plan would require a Louis Lecoin:

"I'll tell them that France would be honoring itself if it was the first to disarm," he was forever saying.

Dear Louis, you dear Don Quixote, you set your sights too high . . . It would have taken so much for that dream to come true. And every day, when I used to drop in on you, there were fresh projects and new ideas . . . The latest: a hunger strike in concert with the abbe Pierre, a man whose humanitarian sentiments you appreciated.

His plan struck me, as it did some of his friends, as hard to pull off, given the forces he was intending to tackle and what was at stake; hard, though not impossible.

"So, you've lost confidence in me?"

"Yes, I know you, and I know what you are capable of, but do you appreciate just how strong the enemy is? Even if you were to conjure a huge mass movement, they will break you; your lives will not be a consideration as far as they are concerned ..."

But he was confident.

"If I can pull this off and countries disarm, that will mean the economy sorted out, war factories turned into peace factories, work for all, a reduction in hours, people happier. A resurgence of producer and consumer cooperatives and profiteers banished. There are so many beautiful things we will be able to do. Take it from me! I simply have to take this on no matter the size of it. I will succeed, or I will perish in the effort. What if I do not come out of this clinic alive? Well, not to be presumptuous, but my campaign will fizzle out, for who else do you see taking on the risks? Some organization? No, because it will all have to do not with paper-shuffling but with action, and I do not see them as capable of that!"

That was the sort of conversation that passed between us during his final days.

On the last evening, I left him quite late and he was no more tired than usual and was quite upbeat and optimistic . . .

Very early the following morning I had a phone call from the clinic: Louis had passed away at around one o'clock. He had been discovered sprawled on the ground near his bed. Nobody had heard a thing . . . That was the brutal reality of it.

I made for the clinic; his body was barely still warm, and he had been cleaned.

"Beloved comrade of so many years, up until your final hour you will have lived for your dream: the joy of men!"

Friends and family will file past his body. I gave him a final kiss and left, my heart aching with pain.

His body was to be shipped off in a refrigerator to Père-Lachaise for cremation.

It was necessary now to alert our comrades, his collaborators, his many friends. It was determined that there should be a final edition of *Liberté*. We had to buckle down to the task.

I was mulling over what he had recommended in the event of his departure!

"*Liberté* is my child; it is very egotistical of me but I would like it to die with me. You can come up with some other paper for the dissemination and defense of our ideas. Hey, you can call it *Le Réfractaire*, since you're such a Jules Vallès* fan! I am not leaving you any cash, but you have my books, several thousand of them, and that will help you get started. And don't forget the publication of my discs. You have got what you need and with a synopsis plus some clippings you can come up with a splendid double album, I trust you. For the financing? Well, you can hold a gala at the Mutualité, you're used to that sort of thing, you'll manage! . . . For assistance, look to Sadik who, when he wants, can be very efficient. And there's good Chalard too!

"As for my funeral arrangements, don't forget: no speeches! Which may wound a few friends, but I want no speeches. I'm relying on you!"

At the Columbarium, a large crowd of comrades and friends from every corner of France gathered for one final farewell to their comrade-in-struggle. To the fighter. Tears ran down the lined faces of the elders. The cremation ceremony is a gloomy one—no music, a heavy, oppressive silence. Each of us was leafing through our memories. Yves Montand and Simone Signoret left the room. "This is too sad. We cannot bear it," they told me as they passed.

Exiting was something of a rout. No condolences, no handshakes. Some were stunned and asked for more details about Louis's death and what was to follow. Others left saddened, distraught, some traveled in from far away. I arranged to meet up with them that afternoon at *Liberté*'s headquarters in Rue Alibert.

There we were startled to discover that Louis had not left behind a will, which was quite incomprehensible in a man as organized as Louis had been, but so it was nonetheless!

Moreover, Louis's final wishes, as articulated by him to several of us, did not fit in with the ones mentioned to us. True, the paper was to be wound up, but everything relating to the *Liberté* funds were to be remitted to an organization with which his relations had been rather chilly for a number of months. The person in charge was already on the scene to take possession, having been alerted by the family. I was distressed, and I was not the only one. I offered my version. But how could one not defer to the wishes of his nearest and dearest? Which is what I did.

And so, there we were, no premises, no materials to share. The campaign was to be picked up by the organization appointed, and we wished it luck. The books would be remitted, as would the list of subscribers. Goodbye to our plans for carrying on with *Liberté*.

Since Louis had already left a deposit with the Mutualité, they asked if I would kindly organize a celebration on behalf of the campaign. I agreed, but the profits, if any, were to be shared: half to the campaign, half to issuing the records. The thing was a success. The Mutualité was packed. Some profit was made, but I never saw any of it. On the other hand, I was offered a "payment" for my trouble, which I declined.

I did, though, get the discs released after taking out a loan.[8] Albeit sabotaged, the release of the discs was something of a success with

8 In 1972 the Association des Amis de Louis Lecoin released *Louis Lecoin, His Action and His Life* as a 2xLP taken from broadcasts by France Culture (part of Radio France) in November 1966.

Louis's friends and the faithful and his sympathizers. One of Louis's wishes was fulfilled, and that left the second one, rather more difficult given the lack of funds. We did try to gather some of his friends into the "Friends of Louis Lecoin Association" and, using the monies raised by membership fees, Le Réfractaire was launched.[9] It was to toe the Liberté line: its irreplaceable driving force was missing but we would do our best.

All but two of our collaborators, who defected to the beneficiary organization, afforded me their support, and it was thanks to them, their effectiveness, commitment, and expertise that, despite hell and high water, Le Réfractaire made it to its fifty-first edition. Naturally, a few young people turned up to join us older hands. I regret that there were not more, since the paper was being published for them.

One old female friend of Louis's, a landlady, was afforded us access to some quite tiny premises, a former lodge, in the heart of Paris. Thanks to Marie-Louise Richebourg, our worries about premises were over. We saw to it that the place was staffed and young conscientious objectors or others in need of advice were at all times to find a welcome there.

For some years, a female friend who had helped Louis free of charge showed up to support and lend me a hand—and how! in what was a rather onerous task for one in her eighties! I hope Margot Gieure* will accept these lines as my friendly acknowledgment. Having retired to the Midi, her place was taken by some young students and workers who spent much of their free time with me in welcoming folk who dropped by, young and old, and in dispatching the paper, etc. And all of it in a climate of joy and friendship.

At a time when the young are so often criticized, wasn't I fortunate to have the assistance of Françoise, Christèle, Anne, Elisabeth, Jean, Jean-François, as well as Jean-Pierre, Michel, and the Marcs? Such young people are heartening, refreshing, and effective. Without them, I would have been nothing and achieved nothing.

As for the editorial team, I mentioned it earlier, and it too deserves my warmest gratitude, because what would Le Réfractaire have been without them?

Without Jeanne Humbert,* erudite and pioneer of contraception who handled the literary criticism column with such clarity of

---

9 The paper (in English, The Refractory) ran from April 1974 to December 1983. Its name had been taken from a collection of reportage by the radical Communard Jules Vallès called Les Réfractaires, 1866.

judgment: or René Gieure,* cinema specialist and whose columns are greatly appreciated: or Marcel Body, whose articles dealt with international affairs and, more specifically, the situation inside Russia, which he knows top to bottom, having spent many a long year there and at a crucial time: or Jean Gauchon, well known to readers for his undiluted pacifism, regarding which he had published an interesting pamphlet, and for his knowledge of the armaments of France and others. Nicolas Faucier, Louis's old comrade, one hundred percent anarchist and anarcho-syndicalist and author of several works on working-class life and the press, subjects in which he has some expertise and about which he has written two books. Charles-Auguste Bontemps, another of Louis's old comrades, an individualist to his very soul, author of numerous publications about individualism and a gifted poet. Francis Agry,* fastened to current affairs and who misses nothing. Emile Véran, who spent years supporting the conscientious objectors and who specialized in war and its consequences. The convicted anti-militarist Marcel Pourrat, who was unsparing in his attacks on those responsible. Our friend J.V., whose news articles packed with precise facts and figures were high-minded and very rich in content. Saint Els scratched, pawed, and bit at our leaders with a highly personal and prized humor. Père Chat, the young teacher, who covered a range of always interesting topics. Cavannié, an old hand himself, from time to time sent us forceful articles from the provinces.

There were the contributions, few and far between but precious, from youngsters like J. Turiot, X. Pasq, Frank Neveu, our friend Claude and her "No Comments." Lime left us for naturism to which she committed herself whole-heartedly.

And then, and then, there were our poets . . . most loyal among them Eugène Bizeau, who published his first poems at the turn of the century or thereabouts and for whom, despite the passage of the years, the Muse still had a soft spot, tenderness for life's dispossessed and a harsh and lucid word for those responsible and guilty of all our afflictions.

And let me not forget our illustrators. Our friends from *Le Canard Enchaîné*, all of them full of talent: Moisan, who, for a long time, was our front-page illustrator; or Cardon, Vazquez de Sola, Leffel, Lap, Kerleroux, Honhuet, Liogier, Escarro, Pino Zac, Guiraud . . . . Later, Plantu and our youngsters Dominique, Didier Le Bornec, Ritche, Jean-Paul, etc. . . .

A touching recollection of our treasurer, Eugène Guillot (Jacques), a one-time conscientious objector who left us abruptly last year following a heart attack.

Thanks to all of them, thanks to our readers, may their numbers never stop growing . . . Thanks to the young people to whom we appeal to bring us their thoughts, their youthful talents, their presence, and also their criticisms. According to the letters we receive, our paper, of little means, is appreciated, not just in France and across Europe but also in the United States where it is a feature in several universities, in Mexico and Canada and New Zealand and New Caledonia, in Australia and Japan, and I forget where else. It proceeds on its merry way. Planting its seed . . .

For how much longer will it survive? I have no idea. I have done my best, with every ounce of energy I had. I hope it will be picked up by the youth who will improve it, respect its line, keep it alive, and love it as if it were their own child. That is my most cherished wish.

10

THE FIGHT GOES ON

I am no longer very young, but I am in no hurry to take my "retirement." My son Lucien "orders me" to "take it easy." I don't know how. And I am terribly disobedient.

In principle, the only thing I should be occupying myself with is the newspaper *Le Réfractaire*. In fact, even though it only comes out every month, it takes up quite a bit of my time. But it gives me great joy and satisfaction. In the little concierge's space, which serves as my office, I take my breath of hope from contact with the young people who drop by to visit. This restores to me the strength I need to keep fighting the good fight.

But it was a waste of time asking me to make do with such "sedentary" employment. I cannot sit still. I am well aware that it has nothing to do with my age, but I still have the itch to get directly in on the action.

The Morlaix objectors' group had asked me to come down and take part in a gathering of the region's objectors and anti-militarists. By the time I arrived on the scene, I could see that around six thousand people had shown up from Brest, Lannion, all the Breton departments, and from the West. The exhibition grounds had been placed at their disposal and the singing and discussions lasted three days.

The organizing group from Lannion has seen to it that the "enemy within" event was a success and in this it fully succeeded. There was not a single incident; instead, there was a warm sense of brotherhood. The lesson we may draw is that Europe has thousands of young people well able to mobilize themselves around the theme of anti-militarist struggle.

It all began with a few objectors in Finisterre whose solidarity and coming together over the months spread to other pacifist movements through a series of milestone events.

We know all about the objectors' refusal to perform service with the ONF (National Forestry Office) under military discipline during their first year. That "small blessing" had been bestowed upon them by Messrs. Pompidou and Debré during their vacations in Bregançon, hence the Bregançon decree. And we know what ensued: hunger strikes, court proceedings, prison sentences, and the list goes on . . . At the same time, messages of sympathy and support came flooding in.

So, as far as the Finisterre objectors were concerned, the purpose was to marry the anti-militarist struggle with the social struggle. Ultimately, the aim was to parade the stance of the conscientious objector clearly before the greatest possible number of people. (Yes, we know that the Law on Conscientious Objection, in its Article 50, prohibits, on pain of prosecution, publicization of the very existence of the law and its contents.) Absurd, no? And for this we are indebted to Monsieur Debré, who on that day was, along with others, quite inspired!

The exhibition grounds had been rented out to the Finisterre objectors by the socialist town council in Morlaix. Furthermore, that council had made a bit of a name for itself back in 1973 at the time of the hunger strike mounted by four objectors, when it passed a motion of support for them, a motion that had become famous in pacifist circles for the depth of its analysis.

Two hundred volunteers agreed to run the crè-che, the bars, the stands, the snack-bar, the first aid post, and so on . . . The organizers wanted to draw a distinction between activism and the event itself. On the one hand, there was the main hall where, over three days, singers such as Maxime Le Forestier and Graeme Allwright, among others, performed, and where the Breton *fest-noz* was held—and the other stands.

Side by side, there were ecology movements, non-violent movements, anarchists, conscript defense committees, high school committees, etc. As for the conscientious objectors, they had put up stands relating to Le Larzac, the Renseignements Généraux,[1] and the army. There was a mix of facts and figures, graphics, and professions of faith.

There was singing and movies and theater and fresh young talent exposed to the public.

But there were also a few interventions, scheduled or spontaneous. There was one by Rocard from the PSU, and by Daniel Guérin,* the well-known libertarian writer and public speaker, and one by "Louis Lecoin's widow," as they mistakenly announced me. There were great debates about the army, non-violence, a people's army. I was particularly struck by the young people's thoughts on the latter and for a long time, as far as I can recall, I made a point of bad-mouthing the people's army just as much as the national army. Being in the habit of discussing issues near to my heart with a certain vehemence (which comes from my heart and soul), the following morning I found myself in a hospital bed in Morlaix, transported there following a heart attack.

The same thing happened again in a lecture hall at the university in Jussieu in Paris, during a very heated debate about that thorniest of issues: the Baader-Meinhof Gang, because, while the aims and ideals of the young people involved in it were not my own, I refused to ally myself with a police force and a court system that had acted in a particularly odious fashion in dealing with them.

Each demonstration found me alongside the youth fighting to make possible a future where war will not seem an inevitability and where it will be possible to resolve inevitable human conflicts by other means.

As far as the objectors go, I will always support them with all my might, and as for the official status granted, with its shortcomings that ensure that the objector does not have the status in France that he deserves, even after the struggles waged over more than seven years by Louis Lecoin and his team, I actually hope that someday someone qualified and cognizant of the issue's importance can lead the government to take a more liberal and frank stance, so that we can ensure that prison is not the only acceptable argument of our day.

1 The Intelligence Service of the French police.

So, when are we going to get around to showing the young some respect, understanding their plans and their ideals? When are they going to get the status they deserve within society?

The youth of 1979, restless, lost, marginal, and marginalized, less afraid of dying than of misspending their lives, *enfants terribles*, pure products of the twentieth century!

Given the lack of understanding and bad faith they encounter from many adults, by my reckoning, I think that it will not come to pass without a few clashes, and the sooner the better.

During the summer of 1975, well-meaning folk mobilized on behalf of Le Larzac. Le Larzac is one hundred and three families that the army wishes to evict and drive off their land, so that friendly armies can come and play at war games where the sheep used to graze peaceably.[2]

The peasants rebelled and called for support to wider society.

"*Garderem lo Larzac*" was the rallying cry.

Thousands of voices reiterated that Occitan demand, whether on the pavements of Lille or through the drizzle in Brest. The major newspapers barely reported this. The defenders of Le Larzac need to know this: they should trust only themselves and close ranks, with women and men who are determined, come what may, to defend their limestone soil to the finish.

Le Réfractaire is united with them: "We mustn't let them be beaten!" When, over many long months and years, one has mustered, hour after hour, day after night, all one's strength, derisory by comparison with the huge machinery of army and civil service, then one is entitled to have one's doubts. Once more into the breach . . .

One factor stands. The appeal from a militant or the handshake of a friend, and one is back with fresh hope for the day ahead. The army's attempts at intimidation must not make us back down. If the hundred and three who have been in the forefront of the fight for the past four years need some time out, then we can find lots of volunteers among the hundreds of thousands of French people who, in one way or another, have expressed their solidarity with the peasants' battle, volunteers ready to invest

2 In the 1970s the French government decided to expand an army training camp in the Le Larzac area of the Massif Central from 3,000 to 17,000 hectares. Local farmers fought the plan and were aided in their fight by various radical and environmentalist groups. As a result of this agitation the plan to expand the army camp was defeated in 1978.

their energy and their time to afford these hundred and three peasants some respite during which to draw breath and replenish their fire. We will be stubborn, pig-headed.

Let's learn the lesson of a man who refused to surrender, Guiraud, who told the army "No" when all "reasonable" people were urging him to give in. We will fight on the limestone soil. We will fight in Millau. We will fight in Paris. We will fight throughout the length and breadth of France, but, friends of Le Larzac, we will never surrender.

The call is launched.

At the time, there was an outpouring of solidarity on every side to help the Guirauds rebuild the home blown up by the army's explosives. But, even then, there were warnings issued:

"It'll be blown up again once you've rebuilt it!" Isn't that lovely?

Watch out! Thus far the peasants have been nonviolent, but if the authorities deliberately, or out of interest, introduce their killers into the equation, that will have to change.

And then there are the tens upon tens of thousands of people who have poured in from all parts to lend a hand to peasants on their limestone soil. It is black with people. Black? No, multi-colored in the sunlight. The women's dresses lend the gathering a note of gaiety.

There are stands all around. We have ours. We set it upon on some bales of straw. Our banner, unfurled, spells out what is in all our minds: "Down with the army! Down with arms!" We bring our penny's-worth to this struggle between soil and sword, but, who knows? Let us be of good hope . . .

I have just returned from three days in Barcelona, attending the "*Jornadas Libertarias*" [Libertarian Festival] and I am filled with enthusiasm. I was invited by some friends from Toulouse. I'm going to stop over for a few hours and say hello to them.

In the home of those friends, I find three young teachers who have just been expelled from Morocco and who are on their way to Creys-Malville to join the peaceful demonstration against the building of a nuclear power station.

"We have two cars. Would you like to come along?"

I take them up on the offer, and there I go, off to the demo with them. The tent is put up, we have a snack, and go off on a tour of the "forum" where the arrangements for tomorrow morning (this was on July 30, 1977) are being thrashed out.[3]

The order is: "Get as close as we can to the site and, if possible, reach it. No violence."

The area is swamped with CRS barring the approaches and being belligerent and provocative. At six o'clock on the morning of July 31, they raid the site where several thousand of us are camped. They wake people, rifle the tents in search of weapons . . . which they do not find. It rained overnight and the campsite is a veritable marsh; we drink hot coffee while quacking like ducks and then head for the muster-point. My three companions slept in the tent and I in one of their cars, wrapped up in a beautiful Moroccan blanket. I slept soundly in the warmth to the song of the rain falling on the roof.

And now, off we go! With no raincoat and sandals on my feet, all I have is my corduroy jacket and a scarf on my head. In next to no time, I was drenched. No matter, my heart was in it. The three camps are due to meet up at a road junction, and about 60,000 people are now making for the agreed location.

At the head of the procession walk a few dozen young people, helmeted and carrying batons and banners. I ask: "Who are they?"

I am told: "That's the protection squad."

They don't look too scary, albeit that they are very young and full of spirit.

We skirt the fields of corn; the road narrows; then we come to a sort of a natural amphitheater, a muddy field into which we sink ankle-deep and deeper still. We are now in the area placed off limits by prefect Jeannin who, the previous evening, had had the Germans expelled from Morestel, terrifying the local populace, screaming from the rooftops that the town hall had been invaded and the archives set on fire. It was all nonsense. A tile had been broken accidentally, and that had been enough to unleash a climate of xenophobia. The prefect had issued the order to "mop up" that "Baader-Meinhof Gang."

In front of us, the village of Faverges was cordoned off by the CRS. They lined up facing us, clutching their shields and rifles. Without warning, grenades rained down on us. The smoke was dense and the air unbreathable. The youngsters from the protection squad surged through, clutching their batons, and tried to create a clear space.

3 On July 31, 1977 between 40–90,000 demonstrators protested against the proposed building of a nuclear reactor in Malville. The CRS reacted brutally as Picqueray outlines. In 1998 construction on the site was halted.

They were quickly swamped by the cops, who were firing in every direction. And then came reports of a death, a young physics teacher, and then of the wounded: one lost a leg, one a hand. The CRS were using assault grenades. One CRS man had a hand blown off . . . The youngsters retaliated by throwing stones and the odd Molotov cocktail. But that was nothing compared with the thousands of grenades (some of them chlorine-laden) the CRS were sending our way.

What were the leaders going to do? Press on and clear a space to let the youngsters withdraw. Some of us questioned this. For crying out loud, there were about 60,000 people there, and we could not stand by and let that handful of youngsters fight on alone and be slaughtered. Something had to be done.

And then the answer came, clear, neat, and shattering:

"We have reached our target [which was a lie, as we were supposed to have headed for the power station site itself] . . . Our demonstration has been a success. Let us head back to the camp-site. Those who want to fight can stay on, but we're off . . . "

We argued long and hard with the leaders. They were unbending. With a few comrades, we tried to circumvent the police and get back to the village. The CRS were already there, forcing their way into the farmhouses, climbing story by story, lashing out at the demonstrators who had sought refuge there. They smashed up everything in the apartment of one elderly woman who was protesting for all she was worth. (She was to die a few days later.) A grenade was tossed from a window into the farmyard where some children were playing.

For the remainder of the day and into that evening, there was an organized man-hunt, arrests on the spot, haphazardly, for assaulting the police and the forces of law and order, if you please! The many injured persons were ferried away by improvised ambulance drivers.

All of it—the repression, the assault grenades, the denials of justice—yes, all of it, was predictable, and yet the majority of the anti-nuclear activists had not been expecting it! The powers-that-be were out to make an example!

Was this the nonviolent activism we had heard so much about?

If it amounts to issuing watchwords and then not carrying them out and exposing tens of thousands of people to a hail of grenades, and then heading back to camp, happy to have "done our duty" and leaving young people who had been accepted as "protection" to be slaughtered without affording them any assistance and treating them, or allowing them then to be treated as mindless thugs and anarchists and so on, then count me out, count me out!

Two of my comrades, as disappointed and disheartened as I was, headed back to Toulouse. Jean-Charles took me to his brother's place near the Swiss border, where we were going to take a shower, dry ourselves off, and spend the night before setting off again for Paris.

Some days after that, I was to attend the Bourgoin trial, a sinister farce at which "judgment" was passed on the young people who had been arrested far from the scene of the "brawl" (twenty kilometers away) and eight hours later and who had played no part in it—seven of them German and three French and two Swiss, aged between twenty and thirty-two. The trial was to last for twenty-five hours. By the early hours of the morning, the prosecutor and one of the assessors had dozed off. It was held that the accused persons had been caught *in flagrante delicto* (!) and the *anti-casseur* law was invoked against them. The confiscated weapons were two pocket knives, some builder's hard hats, and a motorcycle helmet, two bolts, a bottle of beer, fourteen wooden stakes, an umbrella hilt . . . and a travel bag full of books.

Some CRS officers, invited to identify the accused, stated that they could not do so:

"It was dark, we had helmets on, there were the fumes . . ."

Some of the rank-and-file guards, however, did identify the accused and were absolutely all on the same page.

The accused were sentenced to between one and six months in prison, effective immediately or suspended. "Justice was done."

So, falling into line behind the bestial police crackdown, the judicial crackdown had cut down the "Malville defendants" to set a boundary for the anti-nuclear movement, nationally and internationally.

There is a storm brewing across the globe. Can you hear its howls? It is the sound of revolution on the move.

Take a good look around you. Fascism is a fact. It is spreading. To be sure, it is not a solution, and it will not be able to survive for long, but it carries revolution in its bosom. Bolshevism is a fact. It is spreading. To be sure, it is not a solution, it is not going to be able to survive for long, but it carries revolution in its bosom. War roams the world, roving here and there and is already a fact, spreading and carrying revolution in its bosom . . .

Do you think that certain countries will be able to stand outside these formidable convulsions—which draw nearer with utter inevitability? Or do you think that it is our "democracy" that will stop them and overpower them?

The future depends greatly upon the younger generation. Have you seen how it lives at present? Have you given any thought to what modern youth has in store for you? Utterly unbalanced, idle, inhaling from birth the poisonous air of this rotten society, caught up in the twentieth spring by the school of violence and murder, heart and head empty, they say. It is ready for anything, and it is tough. In this ferocious, despicable society, it has nothing to look up to, nothing to love, nothing to respect.

We think we can turn it all the more easily into a compliant, blindly committed instrument in the hands of those who run this world on paper and serve these young people their daily grass in the trough of the sacrificial lambs.

We are wrong: all these young people, the millions who today perform the "goose step" or the "Roman step" on the roads and squares of certain countries, those who are unemployed, bored, demoralized and driven to despair—all these young people carry revolution in their bosoms.

Sooner or later, they will understand. Sooner or later, the young will wake up to the crime committed against them. And then the response will be terrifying. The greater the crime, the greater the response. The young will have their revenge. And their vengeance will sound the death knell for this society.

There is a storm brewing across the globe. Sooner or later, it will drag everything into its vortex just as it did in 1914, just as it did in 1940. On those occasions, the vortex was war. This time, it will be revolution.

All we can hope for is that the spilling of human blood is spared ... insofar as that is possible and that the revolution will not fall into the clutches of some dictator of the right or of the left.

And because I am not prostrate blindly before dogma, you administer to me the word "anarchist," which, incidentally, will not displease me. No, I do not resent that description with the grotesque indignation of those who do not understand the meaning

of words, or of the supporters of the iron fist who, out of ignorance or hypocrisy, divorce the word from its meaning by invest-
ing it with the meaning of "disorder."

To my mind, anarchy signifies: no struggles of ambition, no
envy of one's neighbor, no murderous hatreds, since the term
"anarchist" rules out every leader, every master, all despotism
and all the domination spawned by wars and enslavement.

I admire and respect or venerate the person who can teach,
advise, and enhance his kind, especially when he serves as an
ideal example. As to the other masters, I can only compare those
to the most demented murderers.

In art as in life, you assert yourself and act as a disciplined
subject. Me? I declare myself an anarchist and strive, in a society
inimical to my ideas, to free myself as much as possible.

—P. N. Roinard

I hesitated for a long time before writing these lines without any pre-
tension. Reliving one's life is a hard, difficult task, and sometimes
there is a lump in one's throat, but this book may be of some use to
those who will read it. That is the reason why I have finally made up
my mind to allow its publication.

For me, I believe that running from demo to demo, hawking
the paper on the streets, impassioned arguments, that is all over.
Moreover, I have been forbidden . . . have "pushed my luck" and nearly died "on the job" on three separate occasions, which is a lot! But
how I regret not being able to travel back in time . . . to do again what
I have done.

So! Is it all wrapped up?

I believe to have, throughout many long years (though they
seemed so short to me), to have been faithful to my ideals, to my
friends, to Louis Lecoin.

Let the young (and I have in mind especially the many who have
shown me their sympathy, their friendship and their esteem) take up
the torch, let them learn and be unsparing in their efforts. Should
events evolve (and unfortunately in the wrong direction!), the anarchist philosophy is still relevant. It is achievable, and it is the most
beautiful thing, the thing that will bring man happiness through freedom and *joie de vivre*.

Long live Anarchy! Go for it, young people! Go for it! . . . for Love, Fraternity, and Liberty!

—MAY

APPENDIX

In the anarchist ranks there are no stars and no leaders. There are merely militants who do their jobs and seek no glory. I have mentioned many of them already. Here are some more. Since I have written this book, they deserve a place in it.

THE OLD WOMAN'S ELDERS

I wish I had been born ten to fifteen years earlier so that I might have experienced the turn of the century, a time of agitation and sacrifice. And known the first tranche of anarcho-syndicalists: James Guillaume, Fernand Pelloutier, Emile Pouget and his Le Père Peinard, Zo d'Axa, Elisée Reclus (I did meet his nephew, Paul), Francisco Ferrer (whose daughter Sol and granddaughter Lily were friends of mine). And I won't shun the likes of Ravachol, Vaillant, and Emile Henry who, by their very personal choice of method, sacrificed their lives for the ideal, albeit that these days that ideal is none too widely accepted! (I read in one anarchist newspaper that an analogy was drawn between Emile Cottin, the anarchist who shot at Clemenceau and missed, and Hitler and Stalin. That takes some doing!)

Militants such as Malatesta, Max Nettlau, Jules Vallès, Louise Michel, who was more of an activist than a theoretician . . . for whom I have great admiration.

On the other hand, I did have the good fortune to meet, among the Italians, Armando Borghi and his wife Andrea, a gifted poetess; our beloved Camillo Berneri, his wife Giovanna, and his daughter, Marie-Louise (all active militants), who died too young. And Giovanni Mariani, sentenced to life imprisonment for an attempt on the life of Mussolini and who, having been pardoned, welcomed me warmly to Sestri Levante.

Among the Germans, there were Rocker, Mühsam, Augustin Souchy. Among the Russians: besides the unforgettable Alexander Berkman, Emma Goldman, and Nestor Makhno, my friends Arshinoff, Schapiro, J. Doubinski, and the "Russian old guard." Among the Bulgarians: Bouhov, Itso, Miloch, and Balkanski. Among the Spaniards: Ascaso, Durruti, Jover, and thousands of other outstanding comrades.

Among the individualists: X. Y., Emile Armand (not that I agreed with all of his ideas), Charles-Auguste Bontemps, René Guillot, Stephen and Mary MacSay.

From the "Bonnot Gang": Victor Serge (whom I bumped into again in Moscow in 1923); the partner of Vallet (A. Dondon) who passed away recently at the age of ninety-six; Rodriguez, Dieudonné, on his return from penal servitude. Among the others who also returned were Jacob, J. Duval, and Rousset (Rousset returning from Biribi). From the "Gang," I have not forgotten Rirette Maitrejean, whom I met during my proofreading career and with whom I associated right up until her death.

Then there was the *Plus Loin* [*Further Along*] group, driven by Dr. Pierrot, Jean Grave and *Les Temps nouveaux*, [*New Times*] shunned over their stance at the time of the 1914–1918 war. They were part of the "16" who signed the declaration to the effect that "until such time as Prussian militarism has been defeated, there will be no chance of evolution." P. Kropotkin was another signatory to it.

Gaston Leval, a sound militant who, while in Moscow as a delegate in 1921, lobbied the authorities to let imprisoned comrades go free.

He brought into being the *Cahiers de l'Humanisme Libertaire* [*Notebooks of Libertarian Humanism*] and the *Cahiers du Socialisme Libertaire* [*Notebooks of Libertarian Socialism*].

His life as a militant was one long struggle, not merely in France, but also in Spain and in South America where he spread anarchist ideas. His review perished with him.

Aristide Lapeyre, a disciple of Sébastien Faure and gifted public speaker, he gave talks galore and specialized particularly in contraception and vasectomy.

Robert Proix, who was a contributor to the review *Témoins* [*Witnesses*] and who, like myself, spent many years putting together *Liberté*, which was also indebted to him for some very fine articles. He parted company from us when Louis Lecoin died. And then passed away of illness a few years later.

André Prudhommeaux, and his partner, Dora, anarchist militants. André is now dead. Together they wrote many social and anarchist books.

Aurele Patorni, husband of Régina Casadeus, he was an attorney and the author of numerous social and pacifist books.

Marcel Voisin, a one-time member of Sébastien Faure's "La Ruche" colony, he just edited his memoirs, entitled *C'était le temps de la Belle époque*; even at the age of eighty seven, he still drops in on *Le Réfractaire* for discussions with young objectors.

Louis Simon, son-in-law of Han Ryner, he showed the utmost devotion in spreading the philosophy of that author of multiple books, each one more intriguing that the rest. He published the revue *Les amis d'Han Ryner* [*The Friends of Han Ryner*]and gave lots of talks.

Louis Louvet, Simone Larcher—they both joined the movement sometime around 1926. In those days, young anarchists had just published a leaflet *"La crosse en l'air"* (Reverse Arms), meant for distribution in the barracks. Simone was arrested in the act and taken to Saint-Lazare, where she was given a six-month prison sentence. Her real name was Willisek: she was of petit-bourgeois background and, after leaving her parents, she had thrown herself into the anarchist struggle where she met Louis Louvet. They shared, then, their activities and their affections.

Initially, they produced *L'Eveil des jeunes libertaires* [*Young Libertarians Awake*] and *Controverse* [*Controversy*] which reprinted talks given under the auspices of the *"Causeries Populaires,"* in which Sébastien Faure, Han Ryner, and Georges Pioch took part, plus the newspaper *Ce qu'il faut dire* [*What Needs Saying*], taking up the baton from Sébastien Faure.

Both took up the trade of proofreading, and Louis served as secretary of the union from 1944 until 1960. Comrades found the warmest of welcomes from him.

Louis Louvet had embarked upon a *Histoire de l'anarchie* which was seen as a companion piece to the *Encyclopédie de l'anarchie* published by Sébastien Faure. But Louis's death on March 15, 1971, interrupted that grand undertaking.

Both of them played their parts in every fight against all manner of abuses and injustices.

PACIFIST MILITANTS

Among the militants with whom I was acquainted, I should mention:

Camille Drevet, who fought against war by giving talks and publishing pamphlets. From one of these I borrow the following: "Fretting about the times ahead, I should like to send out a supreme appeal to all pacifist forces. No more wars, no matter the cost. Not one man for war. No cannons, no munitions, no planes, and no explosives . . . "

Marcelle Capy, another pacifist: "Up with the living and down with arms! Let a general uprising of consciences insist upon disarmament, revision of the treaties, international monitoring of industries potentially of service to murder, and active collaboration between the peoples—bread and peace for each and every one of us."

Madeleine Vernet*: "The rifle too must be outlawed. We call for a massive campaign to be launched in France and brought to the government's attention, a campaign for the abolition of mandatory conscription and for the disarmament of our country."

She set up the Epone workers' orphanage.

Helene Brion: "I am the enemy of warfare, because I am a feminist; war is the triumph of brute force."

She was prosecuted for her defeatist remarks and hauled in front of a court martial in 1917.

Nelly Roussel: "No more children for capitalism, which turns them either into work-fodder or marks them down for exploitation! No more children for militarism, which turns them into cannon-fodder to be martyred! No more children for poverty, for disease, for servitude, for death!"

Madeleine Pelletier, doctor: "It is a vile aberration to contend that men have some entitlement to let themselves be killed just so that their group can enjoy ascendancy over another."

Dr. Pelletier always campaigned on behalf of contraception, family planning, and abortion rights. And against war.

Henri Jeanson. I visited Henri Jeanson with Louis Lecoin.

Since Louis Lecoin no longer saw well enough to read and write, I used to read out his post and the articles destined for the paper. I also translated the love letters he got from two little English women living in London who came to see him during their holidays. For us, they represented a few hours of relaxation and ribbing about Louis's sex appeal . . .

I also used to accompany him on his visits, as he was loath to use his white cane and preferred hanging onto my arm. He received an invitation from Jeanson, who was unwell, and so we set, the two of us, one summer's day, bound for Honfleur, to that adorable little spot where Henri and his wife Claude had settled.

We had an outstanding lunch, Claude being an exquisite cook, and our entire stay was a veritable firework display. Every anecdote was tastier than the one before it, as were the witticisms, as Henri was one of those rare individuals I have met who uttered them so naturally.

What do anti-militarists talk about when they get together if not prison and pigs!? And Henri, like Louis, was inexhaustible when it came to those subjects.

Among other things, I have held on to this letter dated August 17, 1939, which Henri published in *S.I.A.*, a paper run by Louis Lecoin, and it really please me, but its aftermath proved very nearly catastrophic:

> They have, of course, assigned my modest self to a posting and mean to stop me from subtracting my second-class silhouette from duty in the trenches or the whims of some duty adjutant. A thousand apologies, my dear Daladier.
>
> I cannot deliver up that part of the territory that is my imperfect body as you would like. My mother gave it to me to hold in trust. I will hold onto it for her to my final breath. My body is mine! Private property! Watch out, you curs!
>
> Eighteen months in prison or no eighteen months in prison, I am not about to have it murdered on the recommendations of your administration or the recommendations of your friends.
>
> . . . which is why, regardless of your eighteen months in prison, I refuse to die for the councils of civil service.
>
> Not a night passes but that the day carries off with the setting sun some freedom slain over the afternoon by one of your hunters, so that, by the time you get around to posting your mobilization orders, the men who are to leave will be leaving behind a graveyard of their hopes and the already cold corpse of democracy.
>
> Take this however you like, Daladier, but I will not be fighting on behalf of those corpses!

Because of that letter, which was written in peacetime, Daladier had him prosecuted during the war and jailed in La Santé as a common criminal, as well as the paper's managing editor. And government commissioner Rodet also did not spare them: *S.I.A.*, an unmistakably anarchist paper, had helped the Spaniards during the civil war with shipments of arms, etc. In 1938, under the aegis of that paper, a defense bureau had been set up . . . the fight against fascism, and so on.

"What is more, the managing editor was renowned for his anti-militarist and pro-contraception beliefs and was regarded as a dangerous individual . . . especially in time of war, etc."

On reading this text, which has a rare beauty to it, an army of anti-militarist feelings must have been galloping through Henri Jeanson's mind.

He had the pleasure of hearing his friends speak out on his behalf. Among them: Marcel Achard, Jeff Kessel, François Mauriac, Tristan Bernard, Louis Jouvet, José Germain and some military men like André Hunnebelle and Antoine de Saint-Exupéry.

And here goes with the verdict: "5th. Is he guilty of having made himself complicit in inciting servicemen to disobedience? 6th. Is he guilty of inciting men called to the colors to dodge the draft? Answer: Yes, by unanimous vote."

As a result, the court rendered its verdict:

"The aforementioned Jeanson, by a majority, to the penalty of five years of imprisonment and a 3,000-franc fine."

The same sentence was given to F., the managing editor of *S.I.A.*

Paris was about to fall and Jeanson remained one of our strategists' few prizes in the war. We had to get him out of there. César Campinchi, a prodigious attorney and a man of generosity, saved him. A few days before the Germans entered Paris, Henri was set free.

Jeanson was to be back in prison several more times, which some might see as to his credit. He was one of those who did not pull in his horns when the author of the leaflet "Peace Right Now," printed by Louis Lecoin and signed by about fifteen personalities, was prosecuted. This was not the case with some very highly regarded persons who, for fear of imprisonment, turned yellow . . .

Henri Jeanson was a fine journalist, he was an outstanding contributor to *Le Canard Enchaîné* and a first-class screen-writer, but he was also and primarily a comrade with a heart of gold, whose name one cannot mention without a tear welling in the corner of one's eye. I really loved you, Henri . . .

R. Treno. Not only was R. Treno the director of the very widely read *Le Canard Enchaîné*, but he was also a friend of Louis Lecoin and a friend to anarchists. He proved as much to us on many occasions. No one ever appealed to him in vain.

His death in January 1970 came as a great loss to us, one that just causes were to feel for a long time.

During the conscientious objectors' campaign and the status vote, he had been on our side, his help and the help from *Le Canard Enchaîné* were precious, and I am not sure that Louis would have won the match but for him.

At the time, I was on the team at *Le Canard [Enchaîné]*, and I remember that on the morning of the day he was due to undergo an operation, while in the print shop compiling the paper, I took a phone call from the hospital.

It was our friend Treno, asking me to "pull" his article from the type-setters and amend it in accordance with the instructions he started to dictate.

That day was the last time I ever heard his voice, and I never set eyes on him again. But I retain an indelible memory of him.

AND ALL THE OTHERS:

There is not one aspect of the social struggle where anarchists have not campaigned and set the pace.

Jeanne Humbert and Malthusianism. As a young girl and later as a young woman, on marrying Eugène Humbert, Jeanne grew up in the most interesting of settings populated with doctors, writers, artists, most of them anarchists, whose main campaigning issue was contraception.

At the prompting of this group, the neo-Malthusian movement in particular boomed. There was a plethora of lectures and local talks. To publicize and spread their ideas, they launched the newspaper *Régénération* in 1900, then *Génération consciente [Informed Breeding]* and, finally, *La Grande réforme*.

In 1920, the *lois scélérates* were passed, and Eugène Humbert was jailed several times (he was to meet his end in prison in Amiens following an air raid, just two days prior to his release date).

Jeanne did not escape the crackdown either and knew imprisonment in Saint-Lazare and Fresnes. On her release, she reverted to her
propaganda activity and gave talks all over France.

She published a number of works, including *En pleine Vie*, a pioneering novel, and *Le pourissoir* and *Sous la cagoule* in which she de-
scribes her stay in prison. Then came a magnificent book, *La vie et
l'oeuvre de Eugène Humbert, néo-malthusien*. And another, equally priceless, *Sébastien Faure, l'homme, l'apôtre, une époque* . . .

And pamphlets such as *Contre la guerre qui vient, Gabriel Giroud,
Jean Vigo, Une grande figure: Paul Robin* . . .

Now aged ninety and as lucid as ever, she is a contributor to *Le
Réfractaire* and to *La Rue*, as a literary critic. While her health forbids
her from giving talks these days, she carries on with reportage and
through her pen and with some talent brings back to life old militants who, but for her, would remain unknown to today's younger
generations.

Thanks to the battles fought by the pioneering Jeanne Humbert,
the young women of today, whether from *Planning Familial* or from
the MLAC, can broach the issue openly and march through the
streets.

Georges Cochon, first of the squatters. This anarchist comrade
was, from 1910 onwards, a very Parisian personality. He became the
subject of caricatures and they sang songs about him. He was wholly committed to the venture that he had launched. As the forefather
of the squatters, he gave a hard time to the landlords, whom he had
personified as "Monsieur Vautour" (Monsieur Vulture). Back in those
days, the landlord was free to set his own rent and, above all, was at
liberty to toss to the pavement those to whom he had taken a dislike
or who could not make their rent.

An upholstery worker, Georges Cochon, had come up with the
idea of banding the homeless and the under-housed together into a
trade union. He was the inventor of the "moonlight flit" and the con-
ductor of the notorious "*Raffut de la Saint Polycarpe*."

Poor folks who were unable to make their rent and who were in
danger of eviction were extricated—through the doors or windows.
Their comrades stacked up their furniture and effects on a handcart
to the strains of a motley fanfare, with a huge *cloche de bois* being waved
around as G. Cochon's commandos set off gaily to look for empty accommodation to break into.

On April 12, 1913, at the head of several thousand homeless people, Cochon stormed the Hôtel de Ville, to the utter fury of prefect Lépine. On the April 24, he stormed the Madeleine church and settled several homeless families inside. On another occasion, at the head of fifteen thousand members of the Tenants Federation, which he had founded, he set about storming the Château d'Eau barracks to find accommodation for fifty families with a total of two hundred children. On another, the target was the Hôtel de La Rochefoucauld, where he housed eight families and thirty-six children.

These incursions did not always go off without scuffles with the police, but Georges Cochon gave no ground, and the powers-that-be always had to come up with accommodation for those he had settled in buildings unsuited to family life.

ANDRÉ CHALARD, AND THE ANTI-SLAVERY CAMPAIGN

André Chalard, a young French high school teacher in Tindouf (on the Algerian-Moroccan border), found himself expelled from there along with his colleague Oliel for "anti-Algerian activities." What activities?

These:

Our two boys had discovered that, in the Tindouf region, slavery was still common practice, with abductions of child slaves that were sold on to Colomb-Béchar and other locations. Those slaves were the black Haratins whose owners, the Reguibat, are "blue" men. Chalard and Oliel protested against this state of affairs. Result, expulsion, by order of the prefect of the Sahara. All letters sent from France to Ben Bella went unanswered.

Our friend Jérôme Gauthier from *Le Canard Enchaîné* wrote a letter to President Ben Bella asking him to look into the matter personally. A. Chalard had raised specific facts, including the case of little Aouicha, a seven-year-old girl abducted from her father, the black slave Mouissa, by her father's owner, Hacine by name, from Tindouf. "President Ben Bella, abstractions, ideas, and principles have eternity ahead of them. Priority must go to action, to anything that may, immediately, ease suffering and preclude injustice. It lies within your authority. Will you do it?"

Lecoin took the matter in hand. He organized a meeting at the Mutualité with personalities such as Théodore Monod, Germaine Tillon, René Cassin, Robert Baron in attendance. He set up a committee made up of another fifteen equally celebrated personalities. Everything was set in motion: the highest authorities were contacted; our friend Chalard launched a little newspaper, *La Dépêche Vecteur*, which he distributed to the public; *Liberté* also campaigned against slavery; lots of articles appeared. Result, one year later, little Aouicha was released and returned to her family. The matter was raised with the UN, UNESCO, the World Federal Union, the Droits de l'Homme organization, so that the campaign would spread and assume fresh dimensions. All of this thanks to André Chalard and Oliel.

Of course, they both lost their jobs. André Chalard took up a job with the PTT in order to earn a living and became an active member of the *Liberté* team. No task was too small for him. He was often to be found clutching his pot of paste with a parcel of posters under one arm.

Louis had grown attached to this young lad, offering him guidance in his readings and instructing him in what anarchism really stands for. He had managed to turn him into a "subscriber."

And then André Chalard lost his mother, to whom he had been very attached.

A few months after that, Louis Lecoin died and left us all (I am talking about the team at *Liberté*) desolate with grief and conscious of the void he left behind.

André Chalard was particularly distraught. I did what I could to raise his morale, to distract him, and to keep him busy.

He went off on holiday to his father's place in the Creuse and popped over to say goodbye to me. In his words, in his gaze, there was no pleasure at the time of his departure. I never saw him again.

He had indeed gone to the little village where his father was living; he had rented a car en route and arrived to find the place deserted at that hour (three o'clock in the morning), doused himself with gasoline, and put a match to it. A young girl, who had risen early to tend to someone who was sick, spotted the unusual flames and heard the screams of pain coming from the poor soul. She raised the alarm. André was transported to the hospital and died there the next day in horrific pain.

I was alerted immediately by his father who was dumbfounded by what had occurred and regretted that he did not get to see his son before his fatal act. I can still remember the last words spoken by the young man who, at the age of twenty-five, had lost his appetite for life: "It's all rotten, May, even around and close to us. Louis had confided his last wishes to us and what became of them? What are those who are to stand in for him going to do? Louis was forever telling us: 'Bureaucrats, yes, militants, maybe, but anarchists? No.' What can one do? As for me, I have made my decision. And I wish you luck, May . . ." He was in the depths of despair. I cannot get his death out of my head.

GASTON ROLLAND

It is 1916, in the middle of the war, the filthy war!

In Marseilles, there lived a young artisan, an artist in his trade: he made settings for jewelry and was highly regarded by the grandest jewelers.

That October, on a stormy evening, someone knocked on Gaston's door. He opened it to find himself confronted by a poor, pitiful wretch in drenched and shabby clothing; he was quivering from the cold, from fever, and with fear. He stuttered something, terrified, and was restless like a hunted animal. He cried and said that he was hungry, that he was exhausted, penniless, homeless, and friendless and that the court martial was after him.

Gaston scarcely knew this lost soul, but, being moved, he ushered him inside, warmed him at his fireside, sat him down at his table, and gave him clean clothes. In short, made him feel safe. Bouchard was a poor wretch of a deserter, enough of a recommendation for Gaston Rolland, draft dodger on principle and a friend to anyone who shied away from the ugliness of killing. Gaston was happy every time he got the chance to ease some suffering, but he was doubly delighted to offer some ease to a "refractory."

A few days later, Bouchard left; he found some work and there was no further word of him; rumor had it he had crossed into Spain. Bouchard returned to France shortly after that, committing imprudence after imprudence, and got himself arrested in Evian. A medical report depicted him as a drug addict, compulsive liar, and unstable. Brought before the judge, he "talked"; giving up the names of those who had given him succor and compromising Gaston Rolland and several others.

On the advice of some friends, Gaston was about to leave Marseilles, but on his way home, he was grabbed by some policemen.

His partner was arrested also. He was taken to the Saint-Nicolas fort, where he endured a thousand deaths.

He was put on trial and displayed an attitude that earned him the respect of those who heard him, except for the judges of course, who sneered when he declared: "Yes, I harbored Bouchard, I hid him, and I fed him, and I've done the same for lots of others." With the war raging, and in the face of wretched machinery that substituted discipline for consistency, here was an accused person staking his claim and for all others the right of asylum. From Hugo's *Hernani* he quoted: "What does it matter who you may be, Hernani the rebel, Hernani the accursed, you are my guest and I have a duty to protect you."

And he went on to say: "When a poor devil knocked on my door, it scarcely occurred to me to ask to see his papers. I was softhearted and friendly when I ran into a man persecuted by the social authorities and hounded for his refusal to kill. If you would convict me for having committed the crimes of pity and humanity, too bad for you!"

They convicted him. Gaston Rolland then escaped from the hospital to which he had been sent. Then, when he was recaptured, he was due to be judged by No. 4 court martial in Paris on July 19, 1918. His statements irritated the judges; this was an enemy, and they were keen to lash out at him. They were about to crush a nobility so beautiful so as not to humiliate them. The sentence? Fifteen years' penal servitude, later commuted to fifteen years behind bars. Five years for having broken the law, plus another ten for having had a conscience.

Philosopher Han Ryner was to pen some magnificent pages on the Gaston Rolland affair.

I am proud of our longtime friendship. Gaston Rolland remained true to himself and carries his ninety-three years well. He is what I understand an anarchist to be, a faithful comrade, the friend whom I wish many more good years alongside Simone, his loyal partner. My dear old chum!

Jacques Guillot. Our excellent comrade Jacques Guillot deserves a place in these memoirs. He was one of ours in the Place du Combat. As a young militant, he was part of the gang between during 1924–1925.

On January 10, 1930, he was hauled up before the court martial in Paris for having staked his claim to conscientious objector status. That court sentenced him to a year in prison. At the trial, VIPs such as Pastor Roder, Félicien Challaye, the philosophy teacher, Jean Bernamont, the physics graduate, Han Ryner and Georges Pioch, writers, turned out to offer their moral support and their fraternal solidarity.

Jacques later popped up in Spain in 1936, where he made the acquaintance of Berthe Fabert* who had just lost her partner, Ascaso.

This couple is known to comrades of every nationality who find kindness and solidarity in their vicinity.

Jacques went on to become secretary of the "Friends of Sébastien Faure" and the "Friends of Louis Lecoin." His loyalty and assistance were effective . . .

Unfortunately, a heart attack claimed his life in November 1978. In him we lost a reliable friend, a tried and trusted friend.

SÉVERINE

Was it because among my favorite writers I had a soft spot for Jules Vallès whose *L'Enfant, Le Bachelier, L'Insurgé*, and *Les Réfractaires* I have read and reread, that I loved his spiritual daughter when first I heard her come to the defense of Germain Berton (who was brought up before the criminal court for the killing of the *Camelot du roi*, Marius Plateau) with Léon Daudet and his pals lining up against her? Her warm tones and the kindness that radiated from her had overwhelmed and captivated me! The adorable Séverine!

I heard her many times for a variety of reasons: in Belleville, speaking on behalf of the Black Sea sailors, speaking at the Winter Circus on behalf of Sacco and Vanzetti. A pacifist, she had assumed the defense of "defeatists" who had been charged, "defeatists" like Lucie Collard, Rappoport, or the Mayoux, the teachers charged because they had spoken out against the war.

In 1917 when the Ligue des Droits de l'Homme organized a demonstration in support of the Russian revolution, Séverine, thinking about an entire enslaved people freed from its chains, addressed and whipped up the crowd. Freedom in jeopardy found an everyday defender in her. She was everywhere. No one ever knocked on her door in vain, whether the issue was protesting on behalf of those shot in Vingré (shot as examples to the rest) or the rescuing of a young soldier from the disciplinary companies. Same thing with the affair of trooper Rousset, who had come to the defense of a young soldier by the name of Aernould who had been bullied and tortured to death by a *chaouch* and an NCO; Rousset, in turn, was bullied and convicted. The affair created a huge stink in Paris, and when he was released, we threw a party for him.

In 1925 at the Peace Congress in the Sorbonne, she stood up for conscientious objectors, hailed refractories, and called for support for the victims of court-martials.

She was last seen in 1928 at the Winter Circus, where she was acclaimed by the crowd for lobbying on behalf of Sacco and Vanzetti who were under sentence of death. There were ten thousand people at that venue. Another twenty thousand outside; loudspeakers had had to be set up. She looked so grand, such a long way off from mediocre concerns that it looked to us as if she was about to faint. She passed away in her home in Pierrefonds a few months after that.

EUGÈNE BIZEAU.

My friend Eugène Bizeau may be ninety-six years old, but his Muse is still young. Ever since the turn of the century, his poems have been featured in numerous literary magazines and in our avant-garde newspapers. They have been collected into a number of anthologies. These days, he lives alone in his adorable little flower-covered house in the Touraine, and it is always a delight to find him there. Here are two of his poems of which I am particularly fond:

"The Precursors"
Only a few outside of the docile flock
Who walk, heads bowed, towards the human abattoir,
And whom the hostility of the imbecilic mob
Might have strung up brazenly from roadside gallows.

Only a few, standing up to the thousands
So that, someday, no creature will have blood on his hands
So that the love that is killed and the peace that is banished
Might reign amidst the Gauls and Germans alike.

They battled long against Hell and high water
For the brotherhood of the slaughtered plebs.
For a humanity with neither vanquished nor victors.

A dream too far, alas! Their barque is shipwrecked . . .

But, admiring the nobility and proud courage in them,
We keep their memory in the golden book of the heart.

"Man, Free Thyself"

Man, free thyself from the yoke that bruises you
Shatter all stocks and all shackles,
Leaving it to those bereft of heart and spirit
The pride of shouting out loud to show that they are brave!
Shame on him who cravenly floats off like flotsam,
Surrendering his annihilated body to the waves,
And in the harsh battle between master and slave,
A curse upon the resigned who said nothing!

And if the storm should claim so many martyrs,
While tyranny, howling like an animal,
Pushes a somber summons to death towards their noble brows.

It is because, faced with the executioners, no people has risen up
To proclaim its rebellion and to break the sword
Who spread pure blood on the altar of the golden calf!

I Am an Anarchist

For four months, we saw naught but sky and sea, with the occasional ship's sail upon the horizon like a bird's wing. The impression of distance was gripping. There we had all the time to
think.

Well, by dint of comparing things, events, and men, having witnessed the work of our friends from the Commune, so
honest that, who in fearing being terrible, their energy showed
only in the throwing away of their lives, I came quickly to the
conviction that decent people in power will be as inept there as
the dishonest ones will be harmful, and that there is no way that
freedom can possibly be wedded to any authority.

I sensed that a revolution reaching for any government was
a mere trick of the light, capable only of marking time rather
than opening up all the gates to progress; that the institutions of
the past, which seemed to be fading away, were lingering under

a change of name, that everything was tethered to chains in the bygone world and is therefore all of a piece and fated to vanish in its entirety in order to make way for the new, happy, free world under the sky.

I saw that the laws of attraction that forever draw the numberless spheres towards new suns, between the two eternities of past and future, also must govern the destinies of beings in the eternal progress that draws them towards a genuine and ever expanding ideal.

So, I am an anarchist, because only anarchy will bring humanity happiness and because the loftiest idea that the human intellect can grasp is anarchy, until such time as something better appears on the horizon."

—Louise Michel

She wrote this on board the frigate Virginia, *which carried her off to penal servitude following the Bloody Week.*[1]

---

1 A reference to May 21-28, 1871, the last week of the Paris Commune when many of its supporters were slaughtered by government forces.

Appendices to the English-language edition

APPENDIX ONE:
BIOGRAPHIES OF INDIVIDUALS CITED
IN THE TEXT OF MAY PICQUERAY'S MEMOIRS

Francis AGRY (1908-1991)
Ex-fitter who was a regular contributor to the newspapers *Le Libertaire*, *Le Monde libertaire*, *Liberté*, and *Le Réfractaire*.

Luciano "Toto" ALLENDE (1898-1983)
Spanish anarchist who fled to France to escape the draft. In the 1920s he associated with Ascaso, Durruti, and French anarchists Gaston Rolland and Louis Anderson. During the civil war in Spain he served in the republican army. Thereafter, he was interned in the French concentration camps of Argelès (escaped) and St Cyprien before being drafted into a Foreign Labour Company (CTE). He joined the resistance in Savoie and was arrested by the Gestapo and sent to Neuengamme concentration camp in Germany. After the war, he remained active in the CNT in exile and in the FEDIP (Spanish Federation of Political Deportees and Internees).

Albert BAYET (1880-1961)
French Radical sociologist and ethicist, interested in the fate of the lower classes. After the French fascist riots in Paris in 1934 he joined the Antifascist Action and Vigilance Committee. He was chair of the Educational League in France (1945-1950).

Pierre-Valentin BERTHIER (1911–2012)
Anarchist journalist, proof-reader and conscientious objector.

Germaine BERTON (1902–1942)
Metalworker nick-named "the black virgin" by the employer who
sacked her. Member of the Anarchist Union (UA), before leaving to
pursue a more individualist path. In 1923, unable to gain access to
intended target Léon Daudet, she assassinated Marius Plateau, an
Action Française leader. This was hailed by *Le Libertaire*. She was acquitted on the basis that Jaurès's assassin Villain had been acquitted.
Some doubt surrounds her claims regarding Philippe Daudet. She
gave up political activity after attempting suicide in 1924. Died of an
overdose in 1942.

Pierre BESNARD (1886–1947)
Railway-worker and single-minded syndicalist. Initially a "pure" syndicalist and associate of Victor Griffuelhes. Opposed CGT affiliation
to the Profintern. He then helped form the CGTU. Tried to side-
line the communists after the Clos-Poncet murders in 1924. Helped
launch the CGT-SR on the basis of a "Lyon Charter," an updated version of the "Amiens Charter" underpinning the CGT. Prolific writer
exploring the syndicalist option for a future society. Elected general secretary of the IWA in 1935. Warned the Spanish CNT about its
"deviations." The CNT had him ousted at the 1937 IWA congress,
re-making the international in its own image. His flirtation with
a Vichyist body during the war damaged his standing but he took
charge of international relations for the French CNT when it was
launched in 1946.

BLACK SEA SAILORS
In early 1919 a mutiny erupted among the French fleet involved in intervention against the Russian revolution. The ring-leaders—André
Marty, Tillon and Badina—and their fellow-mutineers—were given
long sentences. There was also a mutiny on board the *France* with
its crew of 1,200; that had been followed by an ambush of NCOs in
the streets of Sevastopol, with dead and wounded. The mutineers'
cause became a rallying-point for all sympathetic to the revolution in
Russia and it catapulted André Marty into national and international

prominence. He rose through the ranks of the French Communist Party and was later in charge of the International Brigades in Spain during the civil war there.

Marcel BODY (1894–1984)

Present in Russia in 1917 as part of the French Military Mission, he witnessed the revolution and soon went over to the Bolsheviks, mixing with the upper echelons of the party. He was close to Alexandra Kollontai. He returned to France in 1927 and sided with the opposition against Stalin. He drifted slowly into a libertarian position, taking part in the cooperative movement and writing for the pacifist press.

The *Bonnet Rouge* Affair

Le Bonnet Rouge was a satirical, left-wing pacifist paper during the Great War. The patriotic right, especially Action Française, was outraged by its lack of patriotism and scandalized by the kid-glove treatment meted out by the government to these anti-patriots (who included the former anarchist Miguel Almereyda). There was talk of German funding, out-and-out treason, and a promise by the government that the Carnet B list of suspects to be jailed on the outbreak of war would not be enforced. The upshot was a sensational trial and political scandal.

Charles-Auguste BONTEMPS (1893–1981)

A voracious reader, he frequented anarchist circles in Paris after the Great War. He became a war objector and by 1939 was vice-president of the World League Against Anti-Semitism. He remained wedded to a federalist, decentralized anarchist organization and wrote for *Le Monde libertaire*, *Liberté*, *Le Réfractaire*, etc., and defined his outlook as one supportive of a "collectivism of things and an individualism of people."

Jean Sellenet BOUDOUX (1881–1941)

Working-class building worker (scaffolder), anarchist, and syndicalist. Helped launch the anti-reformist CGTU after the Great War and was the driving force behind the 'anarchist federalists' within the CGTU, in opposing the inroads made by Moscow-leaning communist syndicalists eager to advance the French CP and Profintern causes. Appears to have been the intended target of the communist gunmen who killed syndicalists Clos and Poncet at the trade union headquarters in

January 1924. Later helped launch the CGT-SR, speaking publicly on its behalf.

Robert BRASILLACH (1909–1945)

Highly regarded writer and critic associated with the *Action Française* newspaper. He became more outspokenly pro-fascist after 1934 and during the Second World War wrote favourably about Nazi Germany. Executed after the Liberation, although many intellectuals not of his own persuasion lobbied for clemency for him.

Gaetano BRESCI (1878–1901)

The working-class anarchist assassin in 1900 of King Umberto of Italy in retaliation for the bloody repression of striking workers. He had returned from the USA to carry out the assassination. He was "suicided" in prison the following year.

Benoit BROUTCHOUX (1879–1944)

Larger-than-life anarchist miner and syndicalist activist. He spoke against Malatesta's view of syndicalism at the Amsterdam International Anarchist Congress in 1907. Having joined the CGTU, he then transferred his loyalties to the UFSAF, a loose federation of unions unhappy with the pro-Moscow trends within the CGTU. He withdrew from trade union and revolutionary activity in the late 1920s to confront a lingering illness that claimed his life.

Sante CASERIO (1873–1894)

Italian anarchist who assassinated French president Sadi Carnot in Lyon in 1894.

Valentin CHARLOT (aka BOULANGER) 1888–?)

Anarchist contributor to *L'Anarchie* and *La Guerre sociale* prior to the Great War. In 1911 he was arrested as a draft-dodger but escaped, only to be pursued by the military authorities.

Jules CHAZOFF (real name CHAZANOFF) 1891–1946

Electrician turned proof-reader. Member of the pre-Great War Anarchist Youth. Fled to London to avoid being drafted for service in the Great War. Later, he worked with *Le Libertaire* and was one of the editors of a French language *Bulletin of the Committee for Defence of*

Revolutionaries Imprisoned in Russia (1925). In 1924 he had published *The Bolshevik Lie* after returning from a trip to Russia. He also wrote *The CGT, A Soviet Colony* (1939) and *People, Behold the Traitors* (1940). He had a fraught relationship with the anarchist organizations in France during the 1920s. Louis Lecoin commissioned him to procure weapons for the CNT militias in Spain and he was an *SIA* (International Antifascist Solidarity) correspondent reporting on the Spanish refugees arriving in the south of France in 1939, before falling out with the SIA and Lecoin over what he saw as the misuse of funds that should have been helping those refugees. During the Second World War, he helped significantly to resurrect trade union organization in the Lyon area. He was freed from the Drancy camp by Allied troops in August 1944 and died of TB.

Lucien CHEVALIER (1894–1975)
Metal-worker and anarcho-syndicalist. Supporter of Besnard in 1922. Attended the 2nd Profintern Congress in 1922. There, Chevalier opposed affiliation of the CGTU to the Profintern as a trespass against trade union independence. Fathered May Picqueray's daughter Sonia. He was present at the shooting in January 1924 of Clos and Poncet. After the Second World War, he drifted towards the Socialist Party.

René CLAIR (1898–1981)
Celebrated French screenwriter and film director admitted to the Académie française in 1960. His early association was with the Dadaists and Surrealists and his mockery of the production line in his 1931 film *À nous la liberté* is said to have influenced Chaplin's *Modern Times*. For a time, he lived in Saint Tropez. He was "godfather" to May's son.

CLARTÉ
This was a post-World War One left-wing movement headed by novelist Henri Barbusse and with a wide appeal, which set itself the task of reviving internationalist, anti-militarist sentiment. It welcomed the Russian revolution and as the years passed drifted increasingly into a communist orbit.

Nicolas CLOS (?–1924)
Machine-fitter and revolutionary syndicalist. With Poncet, he was shot dead by Communist Party stewards at a meeting at the union

headquarters in January 1924. His widow was prevailed upon to allow the party to pay for his funeral (which made it look as if the anarchists and communists had suffered one fatality each) but his associates argued that he was in no way a communist.

Emile COTTIN (1896–1936)

French anarchist whose attempt on the life of Clemenceau in 1919 led to his being sentenced to death, before this was commuted to a 10-year prison term. His treatment was in stark contrast to the indulgent treatment received by the right-wing assassin of socialist leader Jean Jaurès in 1914. He later fought in the libertarian militias in Spain and died in action in 1936.

Gaston COUTÉ (1880–1911)

Poet and song-writer whose targets were the clergy, elected representatives and the propertied classes. His works were collected and published as *The Song of a Lad Who Went to the Bad*. Since 1968, there has been a renewed interest in him and his work.

A. COUTURE

Anarchist construction worker who opposed CGTU affiliation to the Profintern. After the CGTU affiliated to it "provisionally," he and Lagache were sent as Construction Union delegates to the Second Profintern Congress in 1922 where they lobbied on behalf of imprisoned anarchists, returning very critical of the USSR, denouncing the Profintern as just a front for the Communist Party. He attended the foundation congress of the IWA in Berlin in 1922. In 1932 he was a delegate to the CGT-SR's fourth congress.

Édouard DALADIER (1884–1970)

French politician, one of the promoters of the Popular Front coalition. Signed the Munich agreement in September 1938, declared war on Germany in September 1939 and was arrested by the Vichy government in 1940 and deported to Germany. Returned to politics following the Liberation

Léon DAUDET (1867–1942)

Prominent member of Action Française. Reactionary, anti-republican, and of monarchist sympathies, he was Germaine Berton's intended target rather than Marius Plateau. He seems to have alienated the feelings of his son (below).

Philippe DAUDET (1909-1923)

Alienated son of Léon Daudet; his (aged 14) death from a (seemingly self-inflicted) gunshot in the back of a Paris cab triggered a scandal, given his parentage, his strained relations with his parents, his visit to the offices of *Le Libertaire*, speculation that he was planning an anarchist attentat, his parents' suspicion of the police investigation and the police's political affiliations and the role of the anarchist and police informer Le Flauoter in supplying the gun that was used. Public interest in this scandal prompted *Le Libertaire* to switch opportunistically from weekly to daily editions.

Charles D'AVRAY (1878-1960)

Anarchist *chansonnier* and propagandist. Cabaret star and co-founder of the "revolutionary propaganda through the arts group" La Muse Rouge in the early 1900s. Remained a life-long anarchist (and freemason) despite prosecution and inroads made into the arts sector by the Communist Party.

Léon DEGRELLE (1906-1994)

Originally active in Belgian Catholic Action, this Belgian politician became leader of the fascistic Rexist movement. Served during the Second World War in the Waffen SS's "Wallonia" Division serving on the eastern front. Hitler's admiration of him and his own unquestionable bravery made him a reference point for neo-Nazis while in exile (fleeing a death sentence back home in Belgium) in Spain after the war.

Francis DUFOUR or DUFFOUR

Carcassonne-based French anarchist connected with *Le Libertaire* and the French CNT. He was secretary of the Anarchist Federation (FA)-linked "Han Ryner" group and a contributor to *Le Libertaire* and to Louis Lecoin's newspaper, *Liberté*.

Berthe FABER (ASCASO) GUILLOT (1895-1983)

During the 1920s, she helped her then partner, French anarchist Séverin Férandel, run the International Anarchist Bookshop in Paris. After Férandel left for Mexico, she became the partner of Francisco

Ascaso. After Ascaso's death in Barcelona in July 1936, she became the partner of the French conscientious objector, Eugène Guillot aka Jacques Salles. She was one of the driving forces behind the 'Friends of Sébastien Faure' group.

Nicolas FAUCIER (1900–1992)
Archetypal labour activist and anarchist. Worked as a ship's mechanic, auto worker, and later, proofreader from 1935. In charge of *Le Libertaire's* labour affairs page in 1936, during the strike wave in France, when he called for a "workers' take-over of the factories." Helped refugees from Nazi Germany and later worked for the Committee for Free Spain, going on to become prominent in the French branch of the SIA (International Antifascist Solidarity). Prior to World War Two he co-signed a pacifist protest called "Peace Right Now" (September 1939) and was jailed as a result. After the war, his focus was mainly on labour affairs, but later he became active in campaigns against the 1989 crackdown in China and against the Gulf War in 1991. He was also a mainstay of the newspaper *La Révolution prolétarienne* under Pierre Monatte.

Sébastien FAURE (1858–1942)
A towering figure in French anarchist history, he was an internationally renowned lecturer on anarchism and educationist. Co-founder of *Le Libertaire* in 1895. Active Dreyfusard, birth controller, educationist and anti-militarist. In 1925 he embarked upon the compilation of an *Anarchist Encyclopedia*. Devised an *Anarchist Synthesis* as a counter to the Arshinov Platform.

Henri FERRÉ (1898–1953)
Navvy then scaffolder, secretary of the Syndicalist Youth in Paris in 1921. Anarchist and revolutionary syndicalist. Belonged to Pierre Besnard's faction of "pure" syndicalists within the CGTU. After the pro-communist faction gained the upper hand within the CGTU in 1922 he helped rally the so-called "anarcho-syndicalist" faction. He attended the foundation congress of the IWA in Berlin in December 1922–January 1923.

Francisco FERRER y GUARDIA (1859–1909)
Educationist whose radical republican and later anarchist associations and challenge to traditional Catholic education, in the form of

his Modern School, made him a target for revanchist establishment elements when he was rail-roaded as "leader" of the anti-clerical riots in Barcelona in 1909. His condemnation and execution created a scandal around the world.

Senya FLESHIN (1894–1980)

Born in Ukraine, he emigrated to the United States where he became an anarchist in 1913, working with the *Mother Earth* group. In 1917 he returned to Russia and worked with the *Golos Truda* team in Petrograd. He joined the Nabat anarchist federation in Ukraine and was arrested by the Cheka in 1918, 1920, and 1922 and eventually banished to Siberia. In 1923 he was finally expelled from Russia. The then moved to Berlin and on to Paris, escaping France during the Occupation, leaving for Mexico in 1941, where he earned a living as a photographer. Partner of Mollie Steimer.

Miguel GARCÍA VIVANCOS (1895–1972)

Active in the CNT from 1916; a member of the Los Solidarios group from its inception. Divisional commander during the Spanish Civil War. Ended that war as a lieutenant-colonel. Spent four years in French exile in concentration camps and jails before he was liberated by the *maquis*. Expelled from the Toulouse-based "orthodox" CNT for his support for the CNT within Spain. A "naïve" painter of some repute in his later years.

Jean GAUCHON (1911–1986)

Prominent French pacifist active in the Pacifist Union of France and author of *Integral Pacifism* (1975).

Armand (Harmant) GOHARY (?–1923)

One-time secretary of the Anarchist Youth and *Le Libertaire* associate, found dead (suicide?) in 1923. He had previously told André Colomer of *Le Libertaire* of his efforts to talk Germaine Berton out of mounting attentats and that Berton had fallen under the dubious sway of LE Flaouter.

Margot GIEURE (1906–1982)

Took part in the six-week March–April 1923 general strike by the Parisian *midinettes* backed by the CGTU. In the 1930s she was active with her parents who lived on a commune. There she met René Gieure and, like him, contributed to *L'Unique*, *Liberté*, and *Le Réfractaire*.

René GIEURE (1911–2011)

Won over to anarchism by Sébastien Faure's lectures in Bordeaux. Involved in youth hostelling and met his partner Margot (Marguerite) while on a cycling tour. When war was declared in 1940, he was sentenced to a three-year prison term for "defying the draft in wartime" and was held in Avignon until 1944. After the war he wrote for *L'Unique*, *Liberté*, and *Le Réfractaire*, writing regular movie reviews for the latter.

Daniel GUÉRIN (1904–1988)

Historian, anti-colonialist, libertarian communist, and gay rights activist. In the 1930s, he was associated with the revolutionary syndicalists around *La Révolution prolétarienne* and by the end of that decade he was in the leadership of the PSOP (Worker-Peasant Socialist Party). Following brief imprisonment in Germany, he returned to France in 1942 and was involved in underground activity on behalf of the (Trotskyist) Internationalist Communist Party. By the mid-1940s, there were inklings of his plan to "de-Jacobinize" Marxism and reconcile it with anarchism, to produce a new libertarian communist option for anarchists and non-stalinist Marxists. Opposition to the Algerian war brought him close to the Libertarian Communist Federation (FCL) and its trade union offshoot, the UTCL (Libertarian Communist Workers' Union). In 1965 he published his book, *Anarchism*, which took off after the May '68 events. In 1966 he produced the anthology of anarchist texts, *No Gods, No Masters*.

Albert GUIGUI (1903–1982)

Anarcho-syndicalist trained in Paris as a fitter before moving to Algiers where he was behind the metalworkers' strikes in 1921. He backed the anti-reformist wing of the CGT and followed when most of it set up the CGTU in 1921. On moving to Paris, he was frequently sacked for trade union militancy. Following the murders of Clos and Poncet in 1924, he quit the CGTU for the UFSAF but, believing that the time for a third CGT (i.e. what became the CGT-SR) was passed, his union rejoined the CGT. He switched to proof-reading later. He supported relief efforts in republican Spain and wound up joining the trade union resistance in France under the Occupation. He eventually worked for the ILO at its headquarters in Geneva.

Jacques GUILLOT (1905–1978)

Eugène Guillot aka Jacques Salles. French anarchist and conscientious objector jailed in the 1930s for refusing to serve in the military. In Spain in 1936, he met and set up home with Francisco Ascaso's widow, Berthe Fabert. Returned to France in 1939, living under the name Jacques Salles. In 1968 he was made treasurer of *La Ruche Culturelle et Libertaire* (an umbrella group for the friends of Sébastien Faure, libertarian artists, writers, and lecturers) founded by May Picqueray in 1958. In 1974 he was treasurer of the Friends of Louis Lecoin society, founded by May in 1971.

Marie GUILLOT (1880–1934)

French schoolteacher and revolutionary syndicalist campaigner. Resisted Communist Party encroachment into trade union affairs. She was a feminist and set up the CGT's Women's Commission. During the Great War, she was a pacifist, going on afterwards to head the Revolutionary Syndicalist Committees. She served as secretary of the CGTU in 1922–1923.

G. (Georges) HARDY (pen name of Gabriel GIROUD) (1870–1945)

Teacher and neo-Malthusian (birth control) advocate, associate of Eugène Humbert at *Géneration consciente* (1914). Author of *Ways of Avoiding Pregnancy and Over-Population and the Sex Question*. Contributed to the Humberts' newspaper *La Grande Réforme* and to Sébastien Faure's *Anarchist Encyclopedia*.

Louise HEUCHEL (1892–?)

Paris-born working woman; successively labourer, laundress, and munitions-worker. Joined the French Communist Party; belonged to the CGT and later to the CGTU, serving on the latter's executive in 1922 and 1923. In 1922 she was arrested during strikes in Le Havre and accused of threatening to kill General Duchêne and incitement to murder gendarmes. The court threw out these charges. In February 1922, she was on the PCF's Central Commission on Working Women. In 1923 she addressed a Parisian rally on the cost of living and the threat of war. In 1923, described as being "from Metalworkers, Paris," she addressed a rally dealing with "Abstinence or Sexual Mastery," "Pornography, Social Poison," and "Free Love and Motherhood."

Lucien HAUSSARD (1893-1969)

Spent the Great War as a German prisoner. In 1918 he helped re-launch the Anarchist Federation. In 1922 he attended the foundation congress of the revolutionary syndicalist international, the IWA. Having served on the board of *Le Libertaire* he then launched *L'Idée anarchiste* which attracted a wide range of international contributors. From 1931 to 1939, he ran Marc Pierrot's newspaper *Plus Loin*. He served on the Committee for Free Spain, which became the French chapter of the SIA. During the Second World War he was jailed for sabotage and resistance activity and ran an escape-line into Spain.

Émile HENRY (1872-1894)

Anarchist who threw a bomb into the Café Terminus in Paris in 1894, killing one person and injuring twenty. He expressed regret that he had wounded so many and killed so few, on the basis that there were no innocents among the bourgeoisie. He was sentenced to be guillotined. "We mete out death and we must be ready to suffer it."

Joe HILL (1879-1915)

Swedish-born IWW campaigner executed for murder in 1915 by the state of Utah.

Lucien HUART (died sometime during the occupation of France)

Anarchist and revolutionary shoemaker who belonged to the CGT, then to the CGTU and then to the UFSAF. In 1926, he helped launch *La Voix du travail*, meant as the mouthpiece of the Berlin-based IWA. He later joined the CGT-SR and was administrator for its mouthpiece *Le Combat syndicaliste*. In 1931, he led a CGT-SR delegation to newly republican Spain. By 1936 he was associated with the Committee for Free Spain, the Anarchist Union and the SIA.

Eugène HUMBERT (1870-1944)

Co-founder, with Jeanne Humbert and "G. Hardy" (see above) of *Génération consciente*, a birth control newspaper. Chief editor of *La*

Grande Réforme. Killed in an air raid whilst serving a jail sentence for "contraception propaganda." Was once accused of having "cost France entire battalions" through that propaganda.

Jeanne HUMBERT (1890–1986)
Life-long anarchist, birth control campaigner, and publisher. Partner of Eugène above.

Marius JACOB (1879–1954)
Anarchist who led a gang of daring expropriators ("The Night-Shift") burgling wealthy homes in France, Italy, Spain, and Switzerland. He confessed to 106 "operations," raking in 5 million gold francs. He donated a tenth of his takings to workers' organizations and anarchist papers for propaganda work. He was banished in 1905 but brought back to France in 1925, after which he kept a low profile.

Joseph KESSEL (1898–1979)
Journalist, novelist, and aviator, decorated in both world wars. Member of the Académie francaise.

G. LAGACHE
Construction worker sent to Russia on a fact-finding tour. Attended the 2nd Profintern Congress. The French National Archives hold a dossier confiscated from him by the Renseignements-Généraux "Minutes and hand-written notes from the 2nd 'Bolshevik' international congress of revolutionary trade unions, 1922."

Paul LANGEVIN (1872–1946)
Prominent French physicist of left-wing views. Antifascist since 1923 at least, he helped form the Antifascist Intellectuals' Vigilance Committee in 1934; that body later played midwife to the Popular Front. Removed from his post by Vichy.

LANZA DEL VASTO (1901–1981)
French Catholic disciple of Gandhi who repudiated violence and appealed to shared ethical values. He set up a colony in the south of France where these values were acted upon.

Nicolas LAZARÉVITCH (1895–1975)

Belgian-born son of Russian Narodnaya Volya (People's Will) refugees, his sympathies were libertarian. After the February 1917 revolution, he formed a soviet with Russian POW escapees in Germany. He then went to Russia and served in the Red Army, directing propaganda at French interventionist forces in Odessa. Lazarévitch also worked in the rail workshops, steelworks, and mines there. He refused a full-time position with the Comintern and chose to return to the factory floor. In 1924, he was arrested as one of a group of unionists bent on restoring the unions' class war character. He served two years in a concentration camp and was allowed to leave the USSR in 1926. He wrote for *La Révolution prolétarienne* from newly republican Spain (1931). Later became a proof-reader. Interned in Le Vernet camp for a time during the Second World War.

Louis LECOIN (1888–1971)

French anarchist, anarcho-syndicalist, and anti-militarist. Gardener-turned building worker, he led the charge against the reformist leaders of the CGT and their policy of Sacred Union. He was the spokesman for the "federalist syndicalists" and helped form the CGTU in 1921. In 1928 he became a proofreader, helped set up the Free Spain Committee in 1936, and founded the SIA in 1938. In September 1939, he promoted a "Peace Right Now" manifesto. Spent the WWII behind bars for his anti-militarism. After the war his focus shifted to championing recognition of conscientious objector status and in 1962 his hunger strike extracted just such recognition from the government. He was nominated for the Nobel Peace Prize in 1964 and 1966.

Raymond LEFÈBVRE (1891–1920)

Socialist (SFIO member) who volunteered for army service in the Great War, out of which experience came his book *The Sacrifice of Abraham*. He was attracted by the Russian Revolution, joined the Committee for the Third International and travelled to Russia on a fact-finding mission, from which he never returned as he was "lost at sea" off Murmansk with Lepetit, Toubine and Vergeat in 1920.

Pierre Marie LE FLAOUTER (1884–1981)

Co-founder of the Syndicalist Youth in France. Later he became a red-hot labour agitator and was included in the Carnet B list of agitators to be arrested in the event of war. He sometimes wrote for *Le Libertaire* as "Flotter." In the 1920s he became a book-seller and was a paid informant for the Sûreté. He played some unsavoury but murky part in the death of Philippe Daudet in 1923. In 1925 he was convicted of stocking pornography and later left Paris for Nantes. In 1935 he was still on record with the police as an anarchist.

Albert (1876–1927) and Claudine LEMOINE

Albert was a revolutionary syndicalist radical within the National Rail Union and one of the leaders of the general rail strike in 1910. He was later forced out of that industry and became a metalworker and anti-war activist. In 1922, he visited Russia with his wife, Claudine, as a delegate to the 1st Profintern Congress and was critical of the repression of Russian strikers, Kronstadt, and the Workers' Opposition by the Bolshevik Party. In 1922, he was a delegate to the foundation congress of the IWA in Berlin. After the murders of Clos and Poncet in 1924, he led a Metalworkers' Union that broke away from the (communist-dominated) CGTU and in 1926, he helped launch a revolutionary syndicalist CGT (the CGT-SR).

LEPETIT (real name Louis BERTHO) (1889–1920)

Anarcho-syndicalist delegated to go to Soviet Russia on a fact-finding tour with Marcel Vergeat. Marcel Body hints that he was less than impressed with the system in place there. Throughout his time touring southern Russia he was in communication with Victor Serge. On his return to Petrograd he was less than impressed by a visit to the Putilov works. Body states that Vergeat and he "could not hide their hostility to a social system dominated by a single party, whose sovereign contempt for man was only too visible right across Russia." His being "lost at sea" was a better solution for the Bolsheviks than his delivering a damning report that might have turned French organized labour against the Third International.

Jean Jacques LIABEUF (1886–1910)

In an act of police harassment directed at his partner, Liabeuf, a twenty-three-year old unemployed shoe-maker, was charged with "living off immoral earnings" i.e. pimping. After serving three months in jail, he went in search of revenge, killing a policeman and wounding seven other people. Despite a campaign mounted on his behalf by the radical left, he was sentenced to death and sentence was carried out on July 1, 1910, in spite of a 5,000-signature petition, triggering riots across Paris and 30,000 protesters fighting the police.

Ramón LIARTE (1918–2004)

Durruti Column veteran, joined the FIJL Peninsular Committee in 1938 and may have served also on the Peninsular Committee of the FAI; he served time in a number of French and Nort African concentration camps, escaping from the one in Djelfa (1942) and thereafter joined the French resistance.

Louis LORÉAL (real name Louis RAFFIN) (1894–1956)

Revolutionary syndicalist who was on the pacifist wing of the trade union movement during the Great War. Thereafter, he wrote for the anarchist press and became a singer-songwriter associated with La Muse Rouge, the propaganda-through-the-arts group. He was jailed a number of times for anti-militarist articles in *Le Libertaire*, serving on its editorial board in the 1920s. After joining the proof-readers' union, he took to drinking and was expelled from the Revolutionary Anarchist-Communist Union (UACR). During the second world war, he was linked to the trade unionist wing of the Vichy regime. After the Liberation, he was barred from his union and briefly jailed.

Robert LOUZON (1882–1976)

Engineer and revolutionary syndicalist. Briefly a member of the Communist Party of France before joining Pierre Monatte in 1924 to launch the revolutionary *syndicalist La Révolution prolétarienne*. He had a strong interest in anti-colonial movements in French North Africa and French Indochina. Signatory to Louis Lecoin's 1939 declaration, "Peace Right Now." Interned by the French authorities during the WWII.

Alexander (sometimes Solomon) LOZOVSKY (real name DRIDZO) (1878–1952)

Russian who lived in exile in France 1901–1917 and was familiar with the French trade union scene, returning to Russia after the revolution to head the Profintern and serve on the Communist Party's Central Committee. He later became deputy commissar for Foreign Affairs, but fell into disfavour with Stalin and was executed in 1952. He was posthumously rehabilitated readmitted to party membership in 1954 (after Stalin's death).

Thomas MALTHUS (1766-1834)

This lecturer in political economy popularized the idea that the human population grew faster than the food supply and that birth control measures were necessary if this imbalance was not otherwise to be restored by means of famine and warfare. In France, birth controllers were often referred to as neo-Malthusians.

Georges MALKINE (1898-1970)

French surrealist painter and writer who married May's daughter, Sonia, and relocated to the United States.

Jean MARESTAN, real name Gaston HAVARD (1874-1951)

Belgian-born anarchist and freemason particularly active in the cause of birth control. One of the very earliest contributors to *Le Libertaire* and to *L'Anarchie* and wrote on birth control issues in Eugene Humbert's *Génération consciente*. Also wrote for *La Voix libertaire* and the *Anarchist Encyclopedia*. During the Second World War, he set aside his uncompromising pacifist beliefs and got involved in the resistance and was arrested and jailed as suspect. After the war, he resumed his collaboration with Jeanne Humbert on *La Grande Réforme*.

Victor MARGUERITTE (1866-1942)

Gave up a military career for literature of the realist school. His book, *The Tom-Boy* (1922) was a *succès de scandale*. In 1925 he issued "An Appeal to Conscience," calling for a review of the Versailles Treaty and the repeal of its sanctions and victimization of Germany. He wrote a number of books dealing with conscientious objection and peace maintenance. He also had an interest in rapprochement between peoples and wrote *The Human Homeland* (1931). He was a contributor to *SIA*, the weekly paper of International Antifascist Solidarity (SIA) and a signatory to Louis Lecoin's 1939 declaration, "Peace Right Now" (*Paix Immédiate*).

Charles MAURRAS (1868-1952)

French writer and politician who founded the Action Française movement, advocating a blend of traditionalism and nationalism. Successively supported Mussolini, Hitler, and Petain.

Alberto MESCHI (1879–1958)

Anarcho-syndicalist organizer. Having moved to Argentina, he served on the Executive Commission of the FORA. On returning to Italy in 1909, he started up the Camera del Lavoro in Carrara from nothing, making it one of the most combative in Italy. He was one of the first people forced out of the country after the fascist take-over. One of the first Italian volunteers with the Ascaso Column's Italian Section in Spain in 1936. Captured and interned upon returning to France. After the Liberation he was the first secretary of Carrara's resurrected Camera del Lavoro.

Gaston MONMOUSSEAU (1883–1960)

An anarchist-turned-revolutionary syndicalist-turned-communist who served as general secretary of the CGTU in 1922–1932. An anti-war, strike-provoking activist, he was Besnard's main rival within the CGTU and after 1922, worked to align the CGTU with the Communist Party, joining that party in 1925 and going on to serve on its Politburo in 1926.

Jeanne MORAND (1887–1969)

Maid, then seamstress, associated with individualist anarchism. She was the last partner of individualist firebrand Albert Libertad prior to his death and was involved with his paper, *L'anarchie*. She was especially committed to anti-militarist campaigns, fleeing to Spain with her partner, the deserter Jacques Long aka *Jakon* on the outbreak of the Great War. They were tried in absentia by a court martial for collusion with the enemy. Expelled from Spain in 1919 for anarchist propaganda activity, she fled to Holland, then Belgium. In 1921, she attended the foundation congress in The Hague of the International Anti-Militarist Bureau. After *Jakon*'s suicide in 1921, she returned to France and received a five-year jail term for her wartime "connivance with the enemy" i.e. opposition to the war effort. She was freed in 1924. She wrote for *La Revue anarchiste* and *Le Libertaire* newspapers. By 1932, Morand was exhibiting the signs of mental illness and was committed to a hospital in Paris in 1937.

Erich MÜHSAM (1878–1934)

German poet, dramatist, and anti-militarist who co-founded the Socialist League with Gustav Landauer. He supported the Bavarian

Socialist Republic in 1919 and flirted briefly with the Communist Party of Germany. Arrested and beaten to death (his hanging was faked) in Oranienburg concentration camp following the Nazi takeover in Germany.

"Nonore" (Eléonore) TEISSIER (1886?-1969)

In the 1930s, Nonore (or Eléonore) belonged to the Social Studies Group in Nice. After 1936 she became the partner of Robert Louzon. In 1937 she was a street-seller for *Le Libertaire* in the town. In 1938 she joined the SIA. Her home was a staging-post and letter drop for many anarchists travelling through the area.

Sakae ŌSUGI (1885-1923)

Japanese socialist writer turned anarchist in 1904, whose politics and personal life scandalized imperial Japan. In 1920 he travelled to Shanghai to attend a Comintern-sponsored Conference of Far Eastern Socialists. In 1922, he left for France via Shanghai and was arrested following an inflammatory May Day speech in Paris. He was then deported back to Japan where he (and his nephew) were murdered by the Japanese military police.

Philogone PÉSCASTAING aka TRECASTEL (1893-1971)

Garment trade syndicalist and member of the Anarchist Union. Secretary of the CGTU in the Bouches-du-Rhône area in 1922. He was wounded in the January 1924 shooting that claimed the lives of Clos and Poncet. Later, he left the CGTU for the UFSAF and then for the CGT-SR, becoming joint secretary of the latter's Paris organization. He was particularly active in the strike wave in the summer of 1936.

Rose PESOTTA (1895-1965)

Ukrainian-born anarchist who moved to the USA in 1913, rising to prominence in the ILGWU (International Ladies Garment-Workers' Union) opposing communist inroads into that organization, of which she became vice-president in 1934. Active in campaign on behalf of Sacco and Vanzetti.

Symon PETLIURA (1879-1926)

Ukrainian nationalist leader in the years of the Russian revolution. He and his supporters were accused of pogroms against the Jewish population. Assassinated in Paris for that very reason by Ukrainian Jewish anarchist Sholem Schwarzbard.

Sacha PIOTR (aka Sacha PIETRA or SCHAPIRO or Alexandre TARANOFF) (1890–1942)

Ukrainian-born Jewish anarchist who was involved, aged 14, in the 1905 revolution. Despite the loss of an arm, he served in the Makhnovist army before fleeing to Paris. In 1926 he was frequenting the anarchist circles in Berlin close to Alexander Berkman. In 1933 he left Germany for France. By March 1937 he was in Spain as a militiaman. On returning to France, he used the name Alexander Taranoff, under which he was interned in Le Vernet d'Ariège, before being moved to the Noé camp. From there he was taken to Drancy and thence to his death in Auschwitz.

Marius PLATEAU (1886–1923)

Royalist engineer who served in the Great War as a sergeant and helped organize the "Camelots du Roi" brawlers of the Action Française movement. Assassinated by Germaine Berton instead of her intended targets, Léon Daudet or Charles Maurras.

Louise POHU(T) (1899–1932)

Partner of exiled Spanish anarchist Luciano "Toto" Allende, helped run the Soliès naturist camp. Anarchist propagandist.

Raymond POINCARÉ (1860–1934)

French politician and lawyer. His reassurances to the Russian tsar prior to the outbreak of the Great War allegedly triggered bold action by the latter, accelerating the outbreak of the war. He supported the French law of 1913 making three years of military service obligatory and after the war broke out he championed the "Sacred Union," the patriotic submergence of all class and political differences.

Adrien PONCET (?–1924)

Plumber and member of the Anarchist Union's Paris organizing committee who attended a syndicalist protest against Communist Party use of trade union premises in Paris in January 1924. The communist stewards opened fire on the opposition hecklers and Poncet was killed along with Clos, with others wounded. The gunman was later identified as the communist Gabriel Ducoeur.

Pierre PUCHEU (1899–1944)
French industrialist and fascist who served in the Vichy government as secretary of state for the Interior. He later resigned and volunteered to serve as a captain in the French army but was arrested on arrival in French North Africa and sentenced to death and executed in 1944 for forwarding hostages (communists especially) to the Germans.

Rumanian writer called Rainier BIEMEL (1910–1987)
Rumanian (Brasov)-born author and translator who also used the name Jean Rounault. As a member of the German minority in Rumania, he was deported to the Donetz area to the gulags. As Jean Rounault, he wrote *Mon Ami Vassia* (1949) to expose the lives and struggles of the workers who had befriended him and stated in a complimentary copy of the book sent to Pierre Monatte that he and "Vassia" identified with the viewpoint articulated by *La Révolution prolétarienne*.

RAVACHOL (real name François KOENINGSTEIN) (1859–1892)
The greatest of the "propagandists by deed" in late 19th century France, leaving a trail of murder and mayhem in his wake through the use of bomb, bullet, and dagger. He positively sought martyrdom, saying: "If I carry on with the struggle, it is for the anarchist idea. It matters little whether I am sentenced; I know that I will be avenged."

Jehan RICTUS (real name Gabriel RANDON) (1867–1933)
The alias used by a poet acclaimed for his use of the common parlance and slang (*argot*) of ordinary people. Like lots of bohemians in the late 1890s, he flirted with anarchism. His master-work anthology, *The Poor Man's Soliloquies*, gave voice to a homeless person, prostitutes, battered children, ordinary working folk and house-breakers, etc. During the Great War, he became a die-hard patriot and was later drawn into the Catholic orbit, ending his days as a member of Action Française.

Rudolf ROCKER (1873–1958)
German anarchist expelled from the German Social Democratic Party. Settling in the East End of London, he became spokesman

for the East End Jewish colony and edited its Yiddish language paper, the *Arbeter Fraint*. He was interned as an enemy alien during the Great War. Helped launch and lead the IWA after the war before fleeing Germany in 1933. He later moved to the United States where he published the classics, *Nationalism and Culture* (1937) and *Anarcho-Syndicalism* (1938).

Gaston ROLLAND (1887–1982)

Individualist anarchist and pacifist. In 1914 he defied the draft, living in Paris under an alias and harbored another draft-dodger who, upon being arrested, turned him in. After sentencing, Rolland escaped from custody, receiving a 15-year term when recaptured. A public campaign spared him from being sent to French Guyana. His sentence was then commuted and he was freed in 1924. In 1931, he became secretary of the League of War Resisters. A public subscription was opened for him 35 years later in Louis Lecoin's paper, *Liberté*.

Ricardo SANS (properly SANZ GARCIA) (1898–1986)

Joined the CNT in 1916 and was member of Los Solidarios. He took command of the Durruti Column after Durruti's death. He was held in Le Vernet concentration/internment camp from 1939 until 1942.

Paulino SCARFÓ (?–1931)

Italo-Argentinean anarchist, an anarchist expropriator, associated and executed along with Severino Di Giovanni by the Argentinean military dictatorship in 1931.

SÉVERINE (real name Caroline Remy de Guebhard) (1855–1929)

Pioneering and crusading female journalist and public speaker. Of middle class extraction, she was introduced to socialism and journalism by the Communard Jules Vallès and, with him, revived *Le Cri du people* newspaper. She was an ardent Dreyfusard and one of the earliest members of the League of the Rights of Man. She campaigned on behalf of Clément Duval and, later, Sacco and Vanzetti.

Edmond SCHAGUENÉ (dates unknown)

Pardoned by De Gaulle and released from a ten-year prison sentence after lobbying by the National Committee for Recognition of Conscientious Objection.

Michele SCHIRRU (1899–1931)
Italian anarchist, naturalized American citizen, who returned to Italy to assassinate Mussolini and trigger an uprising against fascism. His plan was never implemented, but the plan to kill Mussolini was construed as an attack upon Italy and he was sentenced to death, a sentence carried out within hours of the verdict.

Sholem (Samuel) SCHWARTZBARD (1886–1938)
Ukrainian-born Jewish anarchist. After resisting pogroms in his homeland, he shuttled around eastern Europe before coming to Paris. During the Great War he adopted Kropotkin's pro-Entente stance and joined the French Foreign Legion. After being demobbed, he returned to Russia and Ukraine, serving as a Red Guard. Fifteen of his family members were killed during pogroms in Ukraine. By 1920 he was back in France. Although Makhno tried to talk him out of it, he was determined to strike back at the pogromists and he assassinated Petliura, the Ukrainian nationalist leader, in 1926. He was eventually acquitted due to public and political sympathy with his motives. Unable to secure a visa for Palestine he moved to South Africa, where he died of a heart attack. His remains were reinterred in Israel in the early 1960s.

SELLIER, Henri (1883–1943)
French municipal socialist, mayor of Suresnes 1919–1941. A member of the SFIO, he was interested in urban planning and helped create fifteen garden cities between 1920 and 1945, providing good quality housing for the working class. He served as Health minister in Leon Blum's Popular Front government before he was dismissed by the Vichy regime and placed in a camp for a month.

Victor SERGE, real name KIBALTCHITCH (1890–1947)
Journalist, translator, novelist; individualist anarchist-turned-Bolshevik supporter-turned-oppositionist. Born in Belgium to Russian political refugee parents and moved to Paris in 1909. Associated with the individualist *L'Anarchie* newspaper and was equivocal about "illegalism." Lived in Barcelona in 1917 and was returned to Russia (as part of a prisoner exchange) enthused by the revolution. Assigned the task of winning the French anarchists over to the Third International, in which he failed. Thrown out of the CPSU

in 1928. Was allowed to leave the Soviet Union in 1936. Fell out with Trotsky over the Spanish revolution. Settled in France before fleeing the Nazis and moving to Mexico. Retained his aspiration to see a libertarian socialism with a human face.

SOCIAL DEFENCE COMMITTEE (Comite de Défense Social)
Body launched around 1903 (and re-launched in 1908) to raise funds, drive publicity and arrange legal defences for working-class victims of the state and their survivors, mistreated conscripts and other "social" victims. It drew support from a wide range of trade union, political, and artistic factions and spectacularly exposed the abuses of authoritarian government and military figures in France. It was based in the headquarters of the CGT union confederation.

Augustin SOUCHY (1892–1984)
German anarchist and anarcho-syndicalist. Member of Gustav Landauer's Socialist League at the age of thirteen. Fled to Sweden in 1914 to dodge conscription and developed links with Scandinavian revolutionary-syndicalists. In 1919, he was one of the founders of the FAUD anarcho-syndicalist federation in Germany and in the 1920s visited Russia to attend the 2nd Comintern Congress. One of the first leftists to write critically of the Bolshevik regime, he went on to co-found the Berlin-based IWA or revolutionary syndicalist international. Served as an advisor to the CNT in Spain during the Spanish Civil War. Souchy was an on-the-spot witness to the outworkings of the Russian, Spanish, and Cuban revolutions and in the 1960s worked for the ILO helping set up trade unions in the Third World.

Mollie STEIMER (real name Martha Alperin) (1897–1980)
Ukrainian-born anarchist active in the Yiddish-language anarchist and labour movement in the USA prior to the First World War. Left for Russia in 1921 and was expelled in 1923. In France, she was arrested and interned during the Occupation but escaped to Mexico with her partner Senya Fleshin.

Léon TAUPIN (dates unknown)
In 1916 he attended meetings of the "Friends of *Par delà de la Mêlée*" ("Above the Fray") an anti-war faction—representing the individualist anarchist newspaper of Émile Armand. In 1924 he stood in

the parliamentary elections as an abstentionist candidate for the Anarchist Union.

(Lucien) Jean TEMERSON (aka TEMERSOHN) (1898–1956)
French movie and stage actor, of whom little detail is known beyond his acting career. His extensive filmography covers the period between the 1930s and the 1950s.

Alexander "Sasha" TOUBIN (?–1920)
French-Russian who served as the translator/interpreter for anarcho-syndicalist delegates Vergeat and Lepetit and the socialist Raymond Lefèbvre and perished with them in the Barents Sea in 1920 in controversial circumstances.

Albert TREINT (1889–1971)
French schoolteacher who reached the rank of captain in the French army in the Great War. A member of the socialist SFIO party, he belonged to the Committee for the Third International and joined the Communist Party of France in which he was Zinoviev's protégé. Uncompromising in his attacks on the communists' rivals. He carried out the "bolshevization" of the PCF and briefly belonged to the Communist Opposition after he was excluded. He rejoined the Socialist Party (SFIO) in 1934.

Auguste VAILLANT (1861–1894)
Anarchist who threw a bomb into the French Chamber of Deputies in 1893. Although no one was killed, he was sent to the guillotine. There are strong suspicions that his action suited a political class which was at the time under a serious cloud following the Panama scandal. His bomb led to the rushing through of the anti-anarchist laws in France.

Jules VALLÈS (1832–1885)
A radical journalist and author who issued his articles in an anthology called Les Réfractaires (1866). He was involved in the Paris Commune and sentenced to death when it fell, fleeing to London. Vallès's fiction was marked by outrage at the injustice of bourgeois society, sympathy with the common people, and an undertow of violence.

Émile VÉRAN (1905-1988)

Anarchist pacifist hairdresser, poet, and violinist who founded the League for Recognition of Conscientious Objection in France in 1932 and wrote for a number of libertarian and/or pacifist publications including *Union Pacifiste*, Louis Lecoin's *Liberté*, and May Picqueray's *Le Réfractaire*. In 1936, he was local secretary of the Conscientious Objectors' League and wrote for *Cahiers du Pacifisme* (1946-1963).

Marcel VERGEAT (1891-1920)

Anarchist metal-worker, delegated to go to Russia on a fact-finding tour, attending the 2nd Congress of the Comintern. Marcel Body stated that Vergeat was looking for reasons to recommend that the CGT support the Russian revolution but his diligent attendance at the proceedings and his experiences there made him more sceptical. He was invited to go on a study tour of southern Russia. For some reason the Bolsheviks organized his return and those of Lepetit, Raymond Lefebvre and their translator, Toubine, via the northern sea route. It was anticipated that their reports on Russia after her revolution would not be rose-tinted. A Norwegian vessel due to ferry them away failed to show up. Vergeat realized that their Bolshevik hosts were stalling to delay their return to ensure that they missed the CGT congress. Allegedly having set out on a soviet fishing smack, they were "lost at sea." Body makes it clear that, in his view, Zinoviev had some hand in their fate.

Madeleine VERNET (real name Madeleine Cavelier) (1878-1949)

The daughter of republicans and ardent free-thinkers, she was an anarchist writer, teacher, and pacifist, with a lively interest in providing for the needs of orphaned children. She founded the Society of the Future orphanage, delivering education based on the theories of Paul Robin and Francisco Ferrer. With no state subsidies, she drew her funding from public donations, largely from the libertarian and socialist left. She wrote for a number of anarchist publications at the time. In 1917 she co-founded the Womens' Anti-War League. In 1922, by which time the communists had captured control of the orphanage's board, she stepped down. In 1927 she launched the paper *La Volonté de Paix* (The Will for Peace); it was closed in 1936 when her husband was put on trial for his anti-militarist activities. During the Second World War, she managed to reconcile her Tolstoyan beliefs with resistance activities.

Georges VIDAL (1903–1964)

Expelled from school for his defence of Cottin, he was (1922) found guilty by a court of insulting the army and its officers by means of a poem he had published about Cottin. He then moved to Paris where he joined the team around *Le Libertaire*. It was there that he met Philippe DAUDET, whose subsequent death earned Vidal attacks from Action Française. He served on the Makhno Defence Committee. During 1926–1929, he wrote regularly for *L'Anarchie*. In 1927, he left for Costa Rica to join the nascent anarchist colony in Mastatal, writing home to France to describe the tough living conditions there. By 1929 he was back in France, publishing an account of the Costa Rican colony before withdrawing from activism to devote himself to literary pursuits and the writing of detective novels. He was in the proof-readers' union. Louis Lecoin delivered his funeral oration.

Violette (CHAPELLAUBEAU) (1917–2003).

May mentions her (by first name only) as associated with Edgar MORIN. Sociology student and resistance fighter (agent P1 and P2). In 1945, she married Edgar Morin, now a giant of French sociology and cultural studies. They divorced in 1970, after which she married Pierre Naville.

Charles WOLF (1905–1944)

Alsace-born journalist, musicographer, translator, and antifascist. Amassed a collection of 18,000 record discs. In 1932, he joined the French Language Proletarian Writers' Group. Visited Spain in the late 1930s to lobby on behalf of the POUM, which was being persecuted. During the Nazi Occupation of France, he worked with the escape network set up by American Varian Fry to help intellectuals, artists, and activists under threat from the Nazis. He became sector chief of the MUR resistance group but was arrested by the Vichyist Milice and tortured before being stomped to death in Toulouse.

Maurice WULLENS (1894–1945)

Spared by a German soldier in 1914, while serving unwillingly in the French army, the teacher Wullens published (1919) an anthology of German pacifist poets and writers that had been banned by the military authorities. He joined the CGT-affiliated Teachers' Federation.

He wrote for *Le Libertaire* and for *Revue anarchiste* and *L'En Dehors*. On a visit to the USSR in 1925 he lobbied on behalf of Nicolas Lazarévitch, but later turned on him. His uncompromisingly pacifist views on war led to inclusion of "questionable" articles in his magazine *Les Humbles* that appeared too indulgent towards Nazi Germany to friends like Victor Serge. During the Occupation, he had articles of his own published in collaborationist newspapers. Only his broken health spared him retribution after the Liberation.

Grigory (real name APFELBAUM) ZINOVIEV (1883–1936)
Old Bolshevik leader. He became chair of the Petrograd Soviet and served on the central committee of the Bolshevik Party, chairing the Executive Committee of the Comintern (Third International). He was Victor Serge's patron in soviet Russia. Having helped oust Trotsky from the leadership, he himself was thrown out of the party in 1934, charged with complicity in the Kirov murder and sentenced to death as an opponent of the regime.

APPENDIX TWO:
SOME DOCUMENTATION SUGGESTIVE OF THE
WORK THAT MAY CARRIED OUT DURING THE NAZI
OCCUPATION OF FRANCE

DOCUMENT 1

I, the undersigned Suzanne Charise, *née* Marenghem, residing at 5 Langham Court, West Wimbledon, SW20, England, do hereby certify that in February or March 1942, Madame May Picqueray showed up to look after me very devotedly when I was taken ill following what I had undergone in prison. At the time, I was an escapee from Castres prison and being sought very actively by the Gestapo, so anybody coming to my aid ran the risk of concentration camp and, most likely, death. Not that that stopped Madame Picqueray, who courageously did everything in her power to help me.

West Wimbledon, 26 August 1964
Signature: Suzanne Charise
Combatant Card No.: 176515
Interned Resister Card No.: 220111496
Volunteer Resistance Fighter Card No.: 090908

DOCUMENT 2

NATIONAL CATHOLIC COMMITTEE
For Aid to Refugees and Evacuees
102, Rue de l'Université, Paris
Paris, May 23, 1940

I hereby certify that Madame May PICQUERAY works in conjunction with our Committee and helps with the organization of the La Piscine and Les Tourelles barracks welcome centres for refugees and evacuees.

I would be obliged to the civil and military authorities if they would be willing to afford her access to the afore-mentioned centres and facilitate her efforts on behalf of refugees.

Delegate-General
Philippe Gaussot

DOCUMENT 3

NATIONAL FEDERATION OF PATRIOT DEPORTEES AND INTERNEES
10 Rue Leroux, Paris (16e)
July 2, 1946

The under-signed persons hereby certify that Madame May Picqueray, residing at 68 Rue Danton, Le Pré-Saint-Gervais, rescued them from the Nazi organization, whether by harboring them and supplying them with false identities or smuggling them over the demarcation line, in short, by making it possible for their lives to be saved from the clutches of the enemy. May she receive our whole-hearted thanks.

Mme Karmjian, 10 Rue Brissard, Clamart

M. A. Bojadjian, 28 Rue de Seine, Paris

M. Georges Valfis and wife, in Coulédoux

M. Statera, 19 Rue du Renard, Paris

M. De Lataille, in Poilly (Loiret) and 3 Rue Jadin, Paris 16e

M. Le Querrec, Pen ar Mardy, Ploubeyre par Lannion

M. Moreau, 2 Impasse Alexandre, Vanves

Major Pouliquen

M. Dutemple

M. J. Quinet, decorator, 72 Ave. des Champs Elysées, Paris

M. de Schryver, printer, Rue Potain, Paris 19e

Mmes Zerline

M. Yves Merlat, 6 Rue du Pont des Loges, Paris

Mme Eva Schwartz, Rue Jean Jaurès, Le Pré-Saint-Gervais

M. Pons, 81 Rue du Faubourg St. Martin

CIRA Bulletin (Marseille) No. 23/25, November 1985.

In December 1983, a month after her death, Issue No. 83 of May's paper *Le Réfractaire* published a special commemorative edition in her honor. These are some of the tribute articles it carried.

Apropos of the film *Ecoutez May Picqueray* (Listen to May Picqueray)

A testimonial by Bernard Baissat

I am currently finishing off the film about May and every day as I go through the dialogue, May speaks to me still.[1] Today, now that she has left us, I regret that I was never in a position to show her the finished article.

I should say that making a film about May Picqueray was no easy thing to do. Not that she refused to cooperate with the production of it; quite the opposite. She was very quick to grasp what was wanted of her and was very good at using the camera to get her messages across. No, it was because her generosity and her preoccupation with having all her friends appear in the film dragged us down a lot of byways. Thus, at first, she was keen that the "old hands," her fellow campaigners should appear, and then it was turn of the youngsters, the objectors and draft-dodgers to have her worry about them. She also wanted to talk about her mentors: Sébastien Faure, Louis Lecoin, and the team around *Le Réfractaire*. Had I not, from time to time, steered things back to herself, viewers might not have learnt much about her battles and her life as an activist.

---

1 *Ecoutez May Picqueray* premiered in Paris at the Studio Saint Séverin cinema on December 17, 1983. [The film is available on YouTube.]

It was my pleasure to have her follow with great interest the compilation and distribution of my previous films about André Claudot, Jeanne Humbert, Eugène Bizeau, and the Paris Bourse du Travail. She showed the same sort of interest in following every stage of the film about her struggles. She was forever looking for and finding rare documents to show and was forever concerned to educate and set an example for the younger generation and encourage it to carry on with the struggle under way. To the very end, she worked with me on splicing and selecting the footage. Of course, there was material galore and choices had to be made. Whenever I spoke to her about cutting something, she always used to say to me: "It would be better if I were cut out and the *copains* left in." So all the *copains* were left in. Even though they may be only a fleeting appearance, they are all there. The ones we managed to film at any rate. Albeit that May was always sorry that she could not be flanked by them all!

I hope that I have remained true to May.

A big-hearted militant, she was an inspiration to the men and women who were fortunate enough to have been her fellow-travellers for a stretch.

I hope that all who love her will find her just as they knew her.

—Bernard Baissat

A Beautiful and A Noble Life

Always the rebel, May was no more resigned to the absurdity of our mortal condition than to the social injustices that she always kicked against. She had such an appetite for life! She clung to life so tightly that those around her almost finished up believing in the unlikely prospect ... Life, which is just a freak of the universe, struck her as all the more precious because of its very rarity. But the merciless laws of nature, whilst it may grant reprieves, spare no one; and inevitably the die was cast; in May's case, in the early hours of the morning of November 3rd.

I was late in making her acquaintance, only to be expected given that I was living in the provinces for a long time. So, in the expectation that others will speak of her good works and merits, her proclivity for embracing just and humane causes, defending the weak, the poor and the oppressed, all I shall offer here are a few lines in remembrance.

I missed out on very few of the gatherings of friends that May used to organize at the turn of each year in the function hall of the Pré-Saint-Gervais town hall as a means of raising some money for propaganda. They were always great fun. Léo Campion was there, with his funny stories; Charles Bernard would regale us with his dry humour; René-Louis Lafforgue, who was to perish in a car crash south of the capital, would be there, singing *"Julie la Rousse"* as ever; Léo Noel—another untimely death—would be grinding out his *"Piano du pauvre"* (arm in sling); and May would to the bill with a cordial, informative and long-winded address applauded by one and all. Come the interval, Louis Louvet or somebody else would distribute the pocket surprises won in the draw, amid a cheerful band in which we could pick out the familiar faces that she was there to see again: Clément Fournier, Lauron-Néjean, Louis Simon, pushing his *Cahiers des Amis de Han Ryner* on all and sundry.

Meanwhile, Louis Lecoin had launched *Liberté* and May regularly helped out with that. She would drop by the printer's to correct the proofs and copy; she kept that up until that old anti-militarist, libertarian campaigner passed away and his fiery review *Liberté* petered out, at which point she launched her own *Le Réfractaire*, brazenly borrowing the singular rather than the plural form from an anthology of reportage by Jules Vallès. Fitful (on my side) correspondence kept us in touch. I saw her again, always active, always enthusiastic, in spite of the doldrum days imposed by the first indications of her illness, once at *Le Canard enchaîné* offices where I was dropping off some books. And then her illness got worse. She called me on the phone one day when she was out of sorts, to ask me to go to the Gare du Nord to pick up the proofs of her flagship, which had been set in Saint-Quentin in the workshops of *L'Aisne Nouvelle*. From season to season, her illnesses and indispositions grew worse. By the spring of 1983 she had to call a halt to the publication of *Le Réfractaire*.

Our last meeting was by her bedside in the Cochin hospital. Remember that following all the preliminary tests, she deliberately postponed her operation just so that she could go and wish a happy birthday to Eugène Bizeau, who had just turned a hundred. Rising above the pain and debilitation, she had made a priority of that act of friendship above all else.

If it be true that "it is the battlers who live," then May Picqueray lived a beautiful and noble life to the full. The book in which she retraces it affords us a thrilling insight and is an inspiration to all who encourage revolt or are on the look-out for enlightenment.

—P-V Berthier

The Last Article

Trying to address a comrade who has left us for her final journey is going way out on a limb. Since you left, I have had a stack of things to say to you and I find it impossible to believe that you are gone from Le Pré-Saint-Gervais. However, there are issues that need debating, upheavals in this derailed world bound, in its madness, for a solid conflict that will end in utter silence. Just think, May dear, that you set off on your journey at a time when there were worldwide muddles galore. It may not be in fames yet, but we can hear the crackle of far too many sparks not to feel somewhat uneasy.

You, who shunned the smoky ideologies of religions and political clans, which talk more than they act, you are the true embodiment of the anarchist ethic. Ever since the launch of our *Réfractaire*, you have been a living example of what a strong-willed individual can accomplish. Those unfamiliar with what it takes to put the paper together need to understand that the sum of work involved for every edition was the handiwork of one woman, pig-headed and determined to succeed. The gathering-together of articles, letters, phone calls, the topic for the edition and the trips out to the printer's in L'Aisne. Then back to Paris, sometimes during the night; then collecting the printed matter from the Gare du Nord, transporting it, folding it, with an ever-shrinking team and finally dispatching it; this whole ballet of demanding exertions has been pulled off since 1974, thanks to you.

And as if this whole display of courage was not enough to ask of your capacity for work, your home had turned into a talking-shop for draft-dodgers and objectors dropping in on the "charitable mother" in search of advice and sound assistance. As for myself, you were my moral physician, and the same goes for many others. Do you remember your determination and how you gave me a shake in Brittany that summer when we were arguing about the possible date for the forthcoming edition, in October, say? I forgive you. You know, your staunch belief, despite all set-backs, in the same idea—that's what kept you forever young. You, the unbeliever, were always, right to the very end, a believer in the perfectibility of the disconcerting beast that we call man. Here's to you, our own Mother Courage.

—Francis Agry

Carnet B—A government list of potential "enemies within" (radicals, etc.) and subversives to be interned in the event of the outbreak of war.

CGT—General Confederation of Labor. The main French union central.

CGTU—Unified General Confederation of Labor, formed after anarchists and other (communist) revolutionaries broke away from the reformism of the post-1914 CGT.

CGT-SR—General Confederation of Labor—Revolutionary Syndicalist. Formed by revolutionary syndicalists and anarcho-syndicalists as an alternative to the reformist CGT and (by then, communist-dominated) CGTU.

CIO—Congress of Industrial Organizations. USA union central based on industrial rather than craft unions.

CNT—National Confederation of Labor. Spanish anarcho-syndicalist union confederation.

CRS—Republican Security Companies. French riot police, with a reputation for brutality.

CTE—Foreign Labor Company. In the late '30s and 1940s, conscript labor teams made up of immigrants.

FAI—Iberian Anarchist Federation, launched in 1927.

FAUD—Free German Workers' Union. Post-WWI anarcho-syndicalist union confederation in Germany.

FCL—(French) Libertarian Communist Federation, platformist.

FEDIP—Spanish Political Deportees and Internees Federation.

FFI—French Forces of the Interior. Gaullist resistance organization.

FIJL—Iberian Libertarian Youth Federation.

FORA—Argentinean Regional Workers' Federation, anarcho-syndicalist.

ILGWU—International Ladies Garment-Workers' Union. US trade union known at one time for its libertarian, anti-communist outlook.

ILO—International Labor Organization, the UN's labor wing.

IWW—Industrial Workers of the World, "The Wobblies." American revolutionary syndicalist organization.

MLAC—Movement for Free Access to Abortion and Contraception (in France). A campaigning group which existed between 1973 and 1975, after which it was disbanded since the government had legislated for abortion rights.

MUR—Unified Resistance Movements, umbrella for a range of pro-De Gaulle resistance movements in WWII.

ONF—National Forestry Office, to which French conscientious objectors were deployed on non-military service.

PCF—Communist Party of France.

POUM—Workers' Marxist Unification Party. Anti-stalinist communists (Spain).

PSOP—Worker-Peasant Socialist Party. Anti-stalinist communist party in France led by Marceau Pivert in the 1930s.

PSU—Unified Social Party (France). A loose amalgam of socialist groups that broke away from the official French Socialist Party in 1960 over the latter's support for France's war in Algeria.

PTT—French Posts & Telegraphs Service.

SFIC—French Section of the Communist International, another name for the early Communist Party in France.

SFIO—French Section of the Workers' International, the French socialist party, from which the PCF emerged.

STO—Obligatory Labor Service, the conscription of French labor for service in the labor-short, wartime German economy. Its introduction fueled the emergence of the *maquis*.

SUB—Amalgamated Construction Union, a stronghold of anarcho- and revolutionary syndicalism and opposition to Communist Party intrusions into labor affairs.

UACR—Revolutionary Anarchist Communist Union, a platformist avatar of the Anarchist-Communist Union; lasted from 1928 until 1934.

UFSAF—Federative Union of Autonomous Unions of France. A loose association of unions which had withdrawn from the CGTU due to communist dominance there. Many, but not all, of these unions went on to form the CGT-SR.

UTCL—Libertarian Communist Workers' Union, the trade union offshoot of the FCL.

AK Press is small, in terms of staff and resources, but we also manage to be one of the world's most productive anarchist publishing houses. We publish close to twenty books every year, and distribute thousands of other titles published by like-minded independent presses and projects from around the globe. We're entirely worker-run and democratically managed. We operate without a corporate structure— no boss, no managers, no bullshit.

The Friends of AK program is a way you can directly contribute to the continued existence of AK Press, and ensure that we're able to keep publishing books like this one! Friends pay $25 a month directly into our publishing account ($30 for Canada, $35 for international), and receive a copy of every book AK Press publishes for the duration of their membership! Friends also receive a discount on anything they order from our website or buy at a table: 50% on AK titles, and 20% on everything else. We have a Friends of AK ebook program as well: $15 a month gets you an electronic copy of every book we publish for the duration of your membership. You can even sponsor a very discounted membership for someone in prison.

Email FRIENDSOFAK@AKPRESS.ORG for more info, or visit the Friends of AK Press website: HTTPS://WWW.AKPRESS.ORG/FRIENDS.HTML.

There are always great book projects in the works—so sign up now to become a Friend of AK Press, and let the presses roll!

What is the Kate Sharpley Library?

The Kate Sharpley Library is a library, archive, publishing outfit and affinity group. We preserve and promote anarchist history.

What we've got

Our collection includes anarchist books, pamphlets, newspapers and leaflets from the nineteenth century to the present in over twenty languages. The collection includes manuscripts, badges, audio and video recordings, and photographs, as well as the work of historians and other writers who have documented the anarchist movement.

What we do

We promote the history of anarchism by reprinting original documents from our collection, and translating or publishing new works on anarchism and its history. These appear in our quarterly bulletin or regularly published pamphlets. We have also provided manuscripts to other anarchist publishers. People come and research in the library, or we can send out a limited amount of photocopies.

Why we do it

We don't say one strand of class-struggle anarchism has all the answers. We don't think anarchism can be understood by looking at 'thinkers' in isolation. We do think that what previous generations thought and did, what they wanted and how they tried to get it, is relevant today. We encourage the anarchist movement to think about its own history—not to live on past glories but to get an extra perspective on current and future dangers and opportunities.

How we do it

Everything at the Kate Sharpley Library—acquisitions, cataloguing, preservation work, publishing, answering inquiries is done by volunteers. All our running costs are met by donations (from members of the collective or our subscribers and supporters) or by the small income we make through publishing.

How you can help

Please subscribe to our bulletin to keep up with what we're doing. There are four issues of the Bulletin a year. Or become a Friend, a KSL Friend subscription gets you the Bulletin and all our publications as they come out.

You can send us anarchist material that you don't need any more (from books to badges)—we can pay postage for large loads, but it doesn't have to be large. A couple of pamphlets will be as gratefully received as anything. Even if you send us duplicates we can trade with other archives for material we do not have. If you publish anarchist material, please add us to your mailing list!

You can send us money too. Details are on our website at: http://www.katesharpleylibrary.net/doc/donations

Keep in touch!
www.katesharpleylibrary.net

www.facebook.com/KateSharpleyLibrary

Postal address:
KATE SHARPLEY LIBRARY
BM HURRICANE
LONDON, WC1N 3XX